AF100161

OUT OF THE DARK

A Memoir
by Marian Elliott

Cirque Press

Copyright © 2024 Marian Elliott

All rights reserved. No part of this publication may be reproduced, distributed or transmitted in any form or by any means, including photocopying, recording, or other electronic or mechanical methods, without the prior written permission of the publisher and author, except in the case of brief quotations embodied in critical reviews and certain other noncommercial uses permitted by copyright law.

Published by
Cirque Press

Sandra Kleven — Michael Burwell
Editors and Publishers
3157 Bettles Bay Loop
Anchorage, AK 99515

Print ISBN: 979-8-89443-599-2

cirquejournal@gmail.com
www.cirquejournal.com

Cover art and design Mary Salvante
Author photo Will Elliott
Graphic design Dale Champlin

OUT OF THE DARK

DEDICATION

For Dan, My Light
For Mary, Margie and William, My Joy
For Joey, Forever in my Heart

ALASKA
YUKON
CANADA
FAIRBANKS
DELTA JUNCTION
TALKEETNA
ANCHORAGE
TOKSOOK BAY
WHITEHORSE
LIARD HOT SPRINGS
ALBERTA
DAWSON CREEK
JASPER
BANFF
BRITISH COLUMBIA
Pacific Ocean

SASKATCHEWAN
MANITOBA
ONTARIO
QUEBEC
NEW BRUNSWICK
NOVA SCOTIA

MOOSE JAW
KENORA
SILVER ISLET
SMOOTH ROCK FALLS
RIVIERE-DU-LOUP
MONTREAL
GASPÉ
WOOD ISLANDS PEI
MURPHY COVE
SCHOODIC POINT
NORTHPORT

Atlantic Ocean

Author's Note

Except for some names of people and places that have been changed, everything written is true to old memories I still recall and the long-saved letters, photographs, and detailed journals of that time.

Part One

Yet why not say what happened?
Pray for the grace of accuracy
Vermeer gave to the sun's illumination
Stealing like the tide across a map...

Robert Lowell

Snow fell lightly in the night dusting the ground with a fresh white blanket. Jeanne woke to a world transformed. She took the dog for his morning romp and came to a raised walkway that appeared to float like a magic carpet hovering above the surface of the snow-covered marsh. At the end of the pathway, snow-brushed birch branches formed a frilly arch over the gap in the trees leading into the woods. The portal beckoned her to follow. She hesitated. She wasn't sure why the scene brought Mirkwood to mind. It wasn't particularly gloomy. But something about it spoke of the Hobbit standing before the great forest dreading the dark unknown. She had an uncanny notion of elves in the trees. Putting aside her reservations, she stepped forward, the untrodden snow crunching beneath her boots. With the dog padding behind her, she headed across the marsh and entered a snowy white fairyland shrouded in mist. The subtle scent of sulfur filled the air. Vapor rising from the warm green water of the rock-bound pond had crystallized in the frigid night coating everything it touched with hoarfrost, every needle of the spindly evergreens, every branch and twig and curling tendril of aspen and birch, and every stem and sprig of high bush cranberry. She brushed the frost from the bench and took off her clothes and piled them there, then tiptoed over the frosty ground to sink into the lovely warmth. The dog lay watching her swim a gentle breaststroke sending quiet ripples across the water. She rolled onto her back and let her limbs float freely. The warm water caressed her skin. She looked up into feathery snowflakes twirling out of the sky and watched them melt away in the warm air rising from the pond. In her peaceful levitation, the last residue of long-buried dread and inner turmoil drifted away.

Chapter 1

Jeanne was barreling along the Trans-Canada Highway, with Joey's German shepherd-collie, Gulliver, curled up on his blanket beside her, when once again her vision blurred in tears. Even now, two years later, she crumpled in grief remembering Joey turning away and climbing the garden steps, while she fixed her eyes on his thick wavy hair brushing the collar of his brown leather jacket. He paused at the door to look back her way, and their eyes met sharing a brief pause. She was sure he had something he wanted to say from the way he looked at her with hesitation, but he said nothing, merely smiled and waved goodbye.

She had started that morning on a positive note, the Rockies only a day away. Big tractor-trailers hustled alongside her, dwarfing her '78 F 250. She drummed her fingers on the steering wheel while Willie Nelson's *On the Road Again* pumped up her mood.

Captivated by the golden prairie gleaming in the morning sun, she momentarily tuned out the music until the punchy notes of the harmonica and Willie's iconic guitar strums brought her back to the tape, reminding her to hit the eject button as soon as the song ended. She was wary of Willie's sad laments in the song coming up.

But her attention wandered in awe of the landscape stretching before her and she missed her chance. Willie was well into *Angels Flying Too Close to the Ground* when, mid-song, the familiar refrain caught her unaware.

I knew someday you would fly away.

It was too late to hit the eject button. Joey was already there, walking away, climbing the stairs.

She steered the pickup to the side of the highway trying to swallow the sobs. Gulliver tilted his head with a questioning look and gently grabbed her arm with his paw. Patting his blanket on the seat, Jeanne told him to lie down. "It's okay, boy. It's okay." The old dog settled alongside her laying his chin on her lap. She stroked his warm brow, as she quietly cried.

In the two years since Joey died, she thought she had learned to handle her grief, yet here she was once more, back to the beginning, the pain in her throat, the ache in her empty arms. She kept returning to Joey's last goodbye. Would she ever put it to rest? Would it always be this way, some moment she didn't see coming, bringing him back, making her wonder what he wanted to say?

She let the tears come, let Joey come with them, allowed herself his company, gave him her time.

Chapter 2

As Jeanne sat in the truck on the side of the highway, her thoughts kept returning to that final day. She wondered what her memories would be if that day had been different. Had fate not intervened, and she not been delayed, would she even have had that last goodbye?

She had been looking forward to the weekend for days, excited to finally take the long drive to the family cabin in the Catskills, excited to see the fall colors on display. She'd have the rare luxury of the whole cabin to herself. Her husband, Gary, would be on Naval Reserve duty, and her daughters tied up with school plans—Katy with her project at the School of Visual Arts, and Peggy rehearsing for the high school play. And there was no need to worry about Joey. His life was his own these days. She could use her time however she pleased, make that long hike up the mountain she always wanted, or sit on the deck and read, uninterrupted by someone's need for attention.

Her plan was a quick getaway from school as soon as all her students were dismissed and then a straight run to the highway, but the small matter of the cabin key left behind at home required a detour. When she arrived at the house, Joey's car in the driveway surprised her. She hadn't expected to find him home. She could hear him up in his room on the phone and, not wanting to delay any longer, called to him to say she was leaving.

She had just put the key in the ignition when he came rushing out the back door waving his arms, calling for her to wait. He bounded down the garden steps with Gulliver close behind, wagging his happy tail. The dog had his father's short hair and shepherd colors, but his collie mother prevailed in his sweet, loyal nature. He rarely left Joey's side.

She watched her son come her way, feeling the usual pleasure whenever she laid eyes on him. Brushing back the errant curl from his brow, he leaned forward, resting his arms on the open window frame of the truck door. He looked at her with his familiar teasing grin, the usual trace of mischief in his eyes. Unlike Gary who was always searching the room, afraid he might miss something, Joey's gaze reached out and grabbed hold. He had his grandfather's black Irish warmth, always fully engaged with whom he spoke. "What are you doing home, Ma? I thought you wanted an early start."

"Forgot the key. There's always something." They gave each other matching sighs. "So what are you doing this weekend?" she asked.

"My friends are having a barbecue. Everyone will be there."

"Well, don't get up to any mischief, you hear?"

"What?"

"You know what I mean."

He grinned at her for a moment before saying, "You better get going, Ma. Friday night traffic. And it's the thirteenth, so you don't want to tempt fate."

Jeanne called after him as he headed for the steps. "Don't forget to feed Gulliver," and then added out of habit, "And no drinking and driving, right?"

"You don't have to keep telling me that, Ma." Behind him, the sun was arcing west, his face backlit, lost for a moment in the glare.

Jeanne eyed his back as he climbed the stairs, his thick wavy brown hair brushing the collar of his leather bomber jacket. She hadn't noticed before how he had filled out, his shoulders wider, his broad back more like her father's build than Gary's narrow frame. He stopped at the door and looked her way again. Jeanne waited for him to say something, but he merely gazed at her for a moment before he waved goodbye and disappeared into the house.

Finally on the highway in the last shreds of daylight, Jeanne gave up on her plan to see the fall colors. Darkness was already creeping in on her.

She reached the Cross Island Parkway, heading for the Throgs

Neck Bridge about the same time as all the other weekenders trying to escape the city on a Friday evening. A river of hoods and bumpers barely crawled before her as she slid the pickup in and out of second gear. It was well past ten when she exited the highway and headed up the mountain road.

One last turn, and the familiar crunch of gravel as she eased the truck down the narrow drive and pulled up to the back door. With the engine stopped, she paused a moment in the dashboard's amber hint of light, savoring the silence, the stillness of a sleeping world she wanted to linger in a while longer, to draw about her shoulders like a quilt. Then with a sigh, she pulled the keys from the ignition, opened the door, and stepped into the dark.

Chapter 3

In the morning, Jeanne carried her breakfast out onto the roomy deck. Wispy clouds scattered across the violet sky, warming to orange above the hillside's eastern rim. The earthy scent of fresh country air filled the early hour.

From atop the long grassy slope where the cabin sat, she looked across the open field to the edge of the state forest where trees stretched before her in all their autumn glory: the fiery crimson of the red maples, the vibrant orange of the sugar maples, the brilliant yellows of the poplars, all flashing against the rich emerald green of fragrant pine.

However engaging the beauty of the morning, it wasn't long before its chill chased her inside. She was sitting at the wobbly kitchen table finishing another cup of coffee when she heard gravel rattling in the driveway. Through the kitchen window she saw her Northport neighbors, Anna and Tony, pulling up to the back porch. She wondered what brought them to the cabin. She couldn't recall telling them she would be there. When she glanced out the window again, they were still talking in the car.

Puzzled by the looks on their faces, she opened the door and waved to them to come. The cooling motor quietly ticked. Sun glinted on the polished hood and scattered through the swaying leaves: a scene laid out as if from someone's life, there at hand, and everything awaiting.

As they came up the steps, Jeanne sensed something amiss. Her friends weren't their usual jovial selves, no wisecracks from Tony, no sassy banter from Anna. They kept looking at each other, something passing between them. Backing away from the door to make room for them, she tried to sort out what might be wrong. "What?" she said, "What?"

Tony took her hands in his. "There's been an accident," he said, choking on his words.

She pulled away from his grip, stumbled to the back of the room, paused a moment looking at the wall. Somehow she ended up in the bedroom stuffing things into her bag, looking about for anything she had missed. She left the bag, went to the kitchen, ran water in the sink.

Tony came beside her and turned off the tap. "We should go. I'll drive the truck." His voice had a hollow tone. "Anna can drive our car."

She nodded and left the dishes in the sink, the food on the table, the unmade bed. A fleeting thought about the checklist for closing up the cabin tried to take hold, but Jeanne was too distracted to decide what to do about it. She grabbed her purse digging out the keys.

On the way to the highway, they drove in and out of sunlight streaming through the trees. Jeanne wavered between telling herself it wasn't Joey, then asking herself: *if it isn't Joey, why didn't Tony say so?* "There's been an accident," was all he had said, and Jeanne, fearful of what she would hear, couldn't bring herself to ask for details. Everything about Tony's mood—the sound of his voice, the words he didn't say—suggested the worst.

For a moment, she let herself think maybe it's Gary, not Joey, but that didn't last. Tony would have told her that. He only said there's been an accident. Then nothing. *If it weren't Joey, he would have told me.*

As Tony's words worried her mind, she searched for a grand bargain. *Please, God. Please, God. Don't let him be dead. He can't be dead. Please, God.* But, she couldn't come up with anything to offer other than to go to Mass every day, which she knew in her heart was an empty promise. Besides, she was certain her mother was on her knees storming heaven with her prayers, her grand bargain already made.

In the end she stopped trying. She turned instead to the Rosary, using her fingers to count off Hail Marys. If she just kept repeating the Hail Mary, she might keep the tortured thinking out of her head. Tony's words kept getting in the way. She kept losing count, her mind returning to thoughts she didn't want. *Please God.*

They had reached Route 17, where she remembered the rest stop up ahead had a payphone. "Tony, I need to call Gary."

Tony hesitated. "It might be better to keep going so we don't get caught in traffic."

"I need to call, Tony. Please."

Tony pulled up to the public phone as Jeanne scrounged in her purse for a quarter.

Peggy answered, her voice so strange Jeanne wasn't sure who it was. For a moment, she couldn't speak. She hadn't expected her daughter to be home. Peggy was supposed to be staying with a friend. She couldn't bring herself to ask her about her brother. Suppose it was the worst. How could she put that in words? Instead she asked Peggy to put her father on the phone.

"He isn't here right now, Mom."

"Where is he? Is he at the hospital?"

Peggy didn't answer her question. "Just come home," she said.

"We're waiting for you to come home."

"When will he be there? I'll call back."

More urgently now, "Mommy, come home. Please, please, just come home."

Back on the road, she kept replaying the phone call in her mind. If Joey's in the hospital, why didn't she say so? Say he has a concussion. He broke his neck; he's in a coma. She could even settle for that. *Please dear God.*

She considered stopping at the next rest stop, but cars had slowed to stop-and-go as they neared the bridge, and she kept hearing Peggy's sad voice. *Just come home, Mommy, come home.*

A white Mustang crept along in the lane beside them full of young people, heads bobbing to the loud music blaring through the open windows. Something familiar in the way the driver leaned over the wheel. His wavy brown hair touched the collar of his jacket. As the truck pulled alongside, Jeanne turned in her seat to look at his face. He met her gaze with raised brows, a question in his eyes. She couldn't turn away.

Hours later, in the gathering dark, Tony drove down her quiet suburban neighborhood. Cars lined the road in front of her house and her mother's house directly across the street. Tony turned into her driveway and stopped beside Joey's white Mustang parked in its place behind the sailboat, as if a memory, right where it was when she had left. The light was on in the garage, and through the open door, she saw his blue Kawasaki leaning on its kickstand, ready and waiting to go for a ride. She sighed with relief. *Thank God. He didn't drive.*

A desperate ray of hope took hold as she rushed up the front steps, only to have all hope disappear in the contorted anguish of Gary's face when he came through the door. He reached out to hold her, but she pushed him away and stumbled across the porch, knocking over the geraniums, banging into the wicker chair. At the end of the porch, she grabbed hold of the railing, gasping for breath. Then she leaned her back against the wall and crumpled slowly to the floor. From somewhere above her came a disembodied cry—"Joey's dead. Joey's dead."

Chapter 4

Slumped on the porch, Jeanne wrapped her arms around her knees pulling them tight against her body. She sensed Gary was near, but couldn't see him. The scroll of the wrought-iron railing filled her view, the black metal gleaming in reflected light. She kept wondering where the strange light came from until an unfamiliar voice, clear and insistent, intruded in her head. *You can't just sit there. Get up.*

The sharp bang of the front screen door startled her out of her daze. Unaccustomed to the excessive loudness, it took a moment for her to understand what it was. She turned her head to see Peggy and Katy standing side by side, their faces projecting as strange masks searched out by a beacon, their wide eyes filled with worry. Or fear. The voice in her head chastised again. *You're scaring them. What will they think?*

Jeanne echoed the voice murmuring to herself, "I can't just sit here. I need to get up." Somehow she stumbled to her daughters and tried to speak, but words wouldn't come. The girls wrapped their arms around her and led her to the den, where she heard sounds and sensed that the room was full of people, but only her mother's face came into focus. Jeanne flinched when she saw her tears.

She backed away, retracing her steps through the kitchen and the hall into the living room where she stood for a moment, looking out the window until she saw the Mustang.

Repulsed by the image, she withdrew to the couch where she sensed a presence beside her that she couldn't see. It followed her as she headed for the stairs, Gary's voice throbbing in her head. *Joey's dead. Joey's dead.*

In her room, she fell on the bed and pulled the pillow over her head. She heard the soft panting of the dog as he pawed for attention, but she didn't respond. A tortured litany played in her mind. *How can this be? He can't be dead. He didn't drive. He can't be dead.*

A sudden shiver caused her to get under her quilt where she

buried her head beneath the pillow again, disbelief continuing to haunt her until the slam of a car door brought her from the bed. "Joey!" She rushed to the window, but all she saw were the headlights of Tony's car backing down the driveway. Then her eyes fell on the Mustang. It brought to mind the motorcycle in the garage, Gary coming through the door, his face a wound. *Oh God.*

Sometime in the night, she woke to a strange sound from somewhere below in the house. "Joey!" She jumped out of bed trying to shut out the intruding voice insisting: *it's not him.* She had to see for herself. As she descended the stairs, she realized the sound was coming from the basement, and when she opened the door to the basement stairs, she recognized what it was. Someone was sobbing, a raw and rasping wail.

The light on the basement floor came through the open door from the garage. That's where she found him, sitting astride the motorcycle, bent over in grief. The need to comfort him overcame her. She walked over and put her arms around him, but he stiffened and pulled away. "What are you doing here? Go back to bed."

"Come with me, Gary. You can't sit here all night. It must be late."

"No!" His loud and angry retort left her confused. Too overwhelmed to think, she managed an "okay," and turned to leave. She was heading for the door when he called after her. "You should have been here."

Not sure what she heard, she stopped and looked back.

"He would have called you. You should have been here." This time he loudly emphasized each word.

"I don't understand? What are you saying?"

"Joey would have called you for a ride. He wouldn't have gotten in the car with a drunk driver. He knew better than that. He would have called."

"But he never calls anymore. If he doesn't use his own car he counts on his friends."

"He would have called. I'm sure of it. Why couldn't you stay home?"

She wasn't able to argue. An ache in her throat made it difficult to talk.

Back under her quilt, she kept hearing Gary's words, trying to understand. Joey wouldn't have called her. That she knew. Throughout the night she woke, again and again, thinking she was having a nightmare, thinking to check if Joey was home yet, followed the next moment with the cruel reality, reliving Gary's words on the porch, *Joey's dead, Joey's dead.*

In the early hours of the morning, she woke to the nightmare once again, Gary's words refusing to go away. She gave up her restless sleep and got out of bed, careful not to wake Gary, who had joined her in the night.

In the kitchen, the dog waited by the sliding glass door and she let him out to run into the woods behind the house to check for what may have come in the night. She put on a sweater and took her coffee onto the back deck to watch the light come into the sky. A soft early morning pink tinted the horizon, the sun coming up at the break of day the same as always, with no acknowledgement that the world as it once was had ended.

Gulliver came and sat by her side pressing his chin in her lap, signaling with tiny nudges his want of a pet. She looked at him with pity. His favorite person was gone, and he would never understand why he wasn't here. Joey would just be gone. Here one day and gone.

From her place on the deck, she could see the kitchen table through the sliding glass doors and imagined Joey sitting in his chair, up early enough to have breakfast with her before she left for school. They'd laugh together and have discussions without the teenage angst. He had argued his reasons for putting college on hold with not a tinge of defensiveness in his voice. "I don't want to be an engineer. That's Dad's thing, not mine. I want to live my own life. It doesn't make sense spending money on tuition until I figure it out."

At the time, she sat back and looked at him full of delight to have him home. Now, as she looked at his empty chair, she was overcome with regret. *I should have made him go back to school. He might still be alive. What have I done?* Her anguish brought back the ache in her throat. It spread into her arms and down into her chest. She hugged herself tightly, squeezing her arms to bring relief.

The longer she looked at the empty chair, the more she felt compelled to move it away. The girls would be awake soon. She didn't want them to see it. She carried it down the basement stairs and left it in the garage, hoping it might blend in with all the other discards.

Gary was pouring coffee when she returned. He didn't seem to notice what she had done. They sat together at the table, eyes averted, voices subdued. "I spoke to the undertaker yesterday," Gary said, eyeing his coffee as he stirred in the sugar. Then he looked directly at her, his face full of fury. "My brother came with me so I wouldn't have to go alone. You weren't here."

There it was again, the accusatory words. He continued with his grievance. "I had to go to the morgue by myself. Do you have any idea what that was like? You should have been here."

"I'm so sorry," Jeanne said, as she reached out and touched his arm, thinking how hard it must have been for him. She wanted to hold him and comfort him, but she remembered his reaction the night before and hesitated. He didn't look open to an embrace.

Her apology brought a deep sigh from Gary. After a pause, he spoke in a more measured voice. "We need to be at Nolan's at 11:00. They want us to pick out a remembrance card, other stuff for the wake." He paused before choking as he added, "And we have to bring his suit."

"He doesn't have a suit. I gave it to the thrift store when he left for college. It didn't fit him anymore. He still hasn't bought a new one. I mean..." She realized how wrong that sounded.

They were talking when Katy and Peggy joined them in the kitchen, their sad eyes showing signs of recent tears. Out of habit, Jeanne proposed breakfast, but the girls weren't hungry. When she suggested they go together to buy Joey a suit, first Peggy and then Katy collapsed in loud sobs. Gary and Jeanne rushed to comfort them. They stood in the kitchen holding on to each other, a sorry tableau, wrapped in grief.

Chapter 5

The minute they walked into Modell's, Jeanne felt oppressed by the loud music from the store speakers. People bustled about, oblivious to her family's catastrophe. Gary was searching through the rack of suits when a chipper salesman arrived at his side.

"These don't look like your size. My guess is you need a Long."

"It's not for me, it's for my son," and grief took charge of his face, trembling his lips and watering his eyes.

The clerk tried to act as if he didn't notice. He spoke in a less chipper tone. "Why don't you send him in to try it on?"

Katy answered for her father. "It's for his funeral."

The salesman hesitated as he began to comprehend, looking from face to face, with his confident smile fading. His "I am so sorry. I am so sorry," gripped everyone in an awkward pause.

They bought the first suit the store clerk showed them in the right size and were at the cash register paying for it when the background music became louder as though someone had turned up the volume.

Goodbye, Papa, it's hard to die when all the birds are singing in the sky.

Jeanne gasped. Her heart pounded. A chill rushed through her, weakening her knees. She looked at Gary in a panic, wanting to shield him, but he didn't appear to have noticed the music. A quick glance at her daughters told her they had. Their worried eyes were searching her face.

Blind to the people around her, Jeanne bolted for the rectangle of light framed in the front door, her hand over her mouth, trying to swallow the flood threatening to engulf her, praying to God to let her get out of the store. As she ran, the music pounded in her ears.

We had joy, we had fun, we had seasons in the sun, but the wine and the song like the seasons are all gone.

In the parking lot, the sobs escaped her control. Until then, too numb to cry, she now cried uncontrollably. She stumbled toward the car at the end of the row, pulled desperately on the door handle, and finding the car locked, slid to the ground with the refrain still playing in her head.

Goodbye, Papa, it's hard to die.

By the time Gary and the girls arrived, Jeanne was numb once more. Gary asked, "Are you okay?" as he helped her into the car. In a voice full of sympathy, he proposed he bring her home.

"No, I should go with you."

"You don't look like you can handle it right now."

"It doesn't matter. I need to see him."

At Nolan's, Jeanne stood beside Gary and looked upon her dead son. Katy and Peggy stood weeping beside them. The undertaker stayed close at hand for whatever comfort he might offer, but he needn't have concerned himself. Jeanne, once again, was numb to the core. Joey seemed to be only sleeping in peace until she leaned over to kiss him and was startled by the scent of death, the coldness of his face.

After some time, Gary whispered they should leave. They followed the undertaker to his office, where he reviewed the details of the days ahead, the words going by Jeanne in a blur. She kept nodding, relieved that she wouldn't have to figure it all out herself, but she worried there must be other things she had to do. If she could focus long enough, she was sure she could figure out what they were.

She kept thinking about it all the way home. They hadn't eaten. She had to remember to feed everyone. She had to make sure everyone had something to wear. *Something black.* And she needed to call her mother. She still hadn't talked to her mother. She wondered if she needed to contact the church. There must be a reason to call the church, she was sure. *I'll call Aunt Elizabeth when we get home. She'll know.* She worried they hadn't talked. She and Gary. The girls. She was sure it was something they should do.

When Gary pulled into the driveway, Jeanne didn't remember what she wanted to do. She walked into the house and took herself upstairs to fall on her bed and once again, pull the pillow over her head.

Exhausted with grief, she fell into a troubled sleep.

She dreamt she had boarded a train at the last minute before it pulled away from the station. Looking for an empty seat, she moved down the aisle of the hot, stuffy car, filled with commuters heading home from work. Her fellow travelers sat buried behind their evening newspapers. Thick smoke from their cigarettes circled upward, swirling around the bare light bulb blurred in a sickly yellow haze.

Midway through the car, Jeanne found an empty seat and had barely settled when the door between cars opened at the far end. A man came through attired in the uniform of a city commuter: gray rumpled suit, tie askew, holding a briefcase. He stopped for a moment, holding the door until a woman followed in her version of rumpled gray.

Together they walked forward, one after the other, swaying side to side to the rock of the train. As the man passed by, he gazed at Jeanne with something familiar in his eyes. Jeanne wondered what he wanted to say. She turned to watch the pair as they moved up the aisle.

When she turned back in her seat, the door opened again and then hung, slightly ajar, for more than a moment before another passenger entered the car. He walked straight toward Jeanne with a teasing grin, up-to-something written all over his face. "Hi, Mom, fancy meeting you here."

"What are you doing here, Joey? I don't understand."

He laughed, his expression full of his usual mischief.

"But you're not supposed to be here." She shook her head sadly.

"I wanted to surprise you."

"But you can't be here, Joey. It's not right."

"Why not? Aren't you happy to see me?"

"But, you're dead, Joey. Don't you understand? You're dead."

His grin disappeared in sudden surprise as he stepped back, brows knit in confusion. For a long moment, he looked down the length of the car. When he looked at her again, his eyes bewildered, all his features had filled with disappointment. He turned back the way he had come and left without saying another word.

At once, Jeanne knew she had made a terrible mistake. She ran after him, calling, "Wait! Wait!" but he never looked back. She heard her name called and tried to ignore it as the brown jacket in front of her disappeared in the yellow haze. "Wait!"

Chapter 6

"Jeanne. Jeanne. Are you dreaming?" Jeanne's mother spoke in a whisper. "People are downstairs. Do you want me to tell them you're resting? To come back tomorrow?"

Jeanne wanted her to go away. She needed to stay asleep so she could find Joey. Visit with him. Hold on to him. Fill the unfamiliar ache in her arms that wouldn't leave. "Not now, Mom. Not now. I need to sleep."

"Joey's girlfriend Tricia is here with his friends. I thought you might want to thank them for coming."

Awake now, Jeanne reluctantly dragged herself out of bed.

Joey's friends filling the kitchen seemed like empty containers of their former selves. The room felt eerily vacant, all their spirit gone, their brashness and youthful energy spent. All eyes were on Vinnie who sat bent over, his elbows resting on his knees, his chair pushed back from the table. He held his head in his hands, fingers entwined in his dark, thick curly hair. "Why did it have to be Joey? He was the good one."

Sitting beside him, Jeanne gasped, breathing deeply to stifle the tears, Vinnie's words, "the good one" sounding in her head.

Vinnie looked at Alan, standing along the wall, and raised his voice. "Isn't that right?"

Alan nodded, shock in his eyes, his mouth agape. Vinnie bent his head again, speaking so softly that Jeanne couldn't hear. "I'm sorry, Vinnie, what did you say?"

He bolted straight up from his chair. "I said it should have been me."

He headed for the door, repeating over and over, "It should have been me."

After he left, Alan tried to explain, fighting the choking in his throat. "Vinnie tried to wake him. He knows CPR, but he couldn't wake him. He kept trying but he couldn't. He feels awful. He keeps blaming himself." His tears came openly now. "Ronnie was driving crazy. We should have told him to slow down, we should have, but we were all laughing. Then the jeep rolled over and Joey was thrown out. He must have hit his head. Vinnie kept trying to wake him. He did. He kept trying." Across the table from her, Tricia shook in muffled sobs.

The urge to back away took hold. Until then no one had told Jeanne what had happened. She had guessed, but now she wasn't sure she wanted to hear the details. She was trying to decide how to gracefully leave when her mother, Mary, leaned over to say she had to go home to feed her cats.

As Jeanne walked her to the front door, Mary reported on all she had been doing while Jeanne slept. "Anna and Tony came by with baked ziti, but Anna didn't stay. She didn't want me to wake you. Tony stayed. He's in the den with Gary. Oh, and your neighbor, Eileen, sent some of her homemade chicken soup. I put it in the fridge with the ziti and all the other food people brought by. Can't remember it all now. Mostly casseroles. Oh, and lots of phone calls. Your school called. They don't want you to worry about your class. Melanie will sub on Monday and for as long as you need her."

Jeanne asked about Katy and Peggy.

"They're down in the street with Ronnie, trying to get him to come into the house." She shook her head and sighed, putting everything left unsaid in her gesture. Then the tears overcame her. "Oh, Jeanne, I am so sorry."

Jeanne held her mother, trying to comfort her, feeling her tiny frame tremble in her arms. After some moments Mary brushed away the tears. "Call me if you need me. I'll come right over."

When Mary left, Jeanne considered joining Gary and Tony in the den, but instead climbed the stairs to her bed, driven by the need to return to her dream. She hoped to find Joey. If she could get him to come back, she could fix her mistake. But it wasn't to be. He didn't return.

The following evening, with Mary beside them, the family went together to the wake. Watching for them at the front door, Mr. Nolan beckoned with a certain in-charge air in his professional attire and his well-combed hair. He led them down the side aisle, opening a passage through the crowd of young people who gathered in little knots along the walls. They stepped aside, their eyes averted.

Beside the casket, Jeanne knelt on the red-cushioned kneeler next to her mother and gazed on her dead son, such a beautiful man in his new suit and tie, oddly out of place, in a bed lined with white satin, a white satin pillow to match, white roses splayed like a blanket. Unable to pray, she rested her hand on his cold, lifeless arm.

After a while, Mary quietly whispered that they should let others say a prayer. Jeanne sat with her mother in the seats reserved for them, the girls off somewhere with friends, and Gary lost among the mourners. A lengthy line of visitors offered condolences, and Jeanne heard herself seemingly far off, repeating the same words:

"Yes, I have been getting some sleep. Thank you."

"Yes, I have been eating. Thank you. So many friends have stopped by with food. Everyone has been so kind."

"Thank you for coming."

"How good to see you."

"We must get together; it's been so long."

The inner voice reprimanded. *Do you hear yourself? You keep saying the same thing.* But what should she say? She didn't know how else to do it. How could she tell them her heart was broken? That would be unseemly. She didn't want to embarrass people. They could hardly look her in the face as it was.

Late in the evening, Jeanne was surprised to see Bill O'Keefe and his wife, Linda. She and Gary only knew them from brief encounters at the yacht club or at Sunday Mass. Yet here they were, not just mumbling "so sorry" and walking away.

Bill pulled up a chair facing Jeanne and her mother and gently took Jeanne's hands in his. He had a distinctive presence in his tailored suit, the gold cufflinks in his expensive shirt. His stylish wife Linda sat in the seat beside Jeanne and put a comforting arm around Jeanne's shoulder. With her long loose curly hair and her Irish face, she and Jeanne could easily be mistaken for sisters.

Bill spoke with a softened tone in his raspy voice. "Let me tell you, Jeanne, Joey was a fine young man. Everyone will miss him very much." Until then Bill was the only one to mention Joey by name. He paused for a moment, searching Jeanne's eyes. She nodded her head, urging him to continue.

"I know there is nothing we can do to change this terrible accident. And that's what it was, a terrible accident. Just a terrible accident. God didn't do it. Don't let anyone tell you that. And He doesn't need more angels. Don't let anyone tell you that." Jeanne looked around for Gary. She wished he could hear what Bill had to say.

Bill hadn't finished when Father Mahoney came and stood beside him nodding his head as though Bill's words were his own little homily. He offered to meet with her in the rectory if she wanted to talk. He wondered if there was any special prayer she wanted to include in the funeral liturgy, but nothing occurred to her. She had never had reason to give it any thought. "Whatever you think best." She saw the disappointment on his face.

"How about hymns, are there any special hymns?" Joey's eighth-grade graduation came to mind, the folded mimeographed program with the picture someone had drawn of the rising sun. She remembered Joey's delight with the graduation song the class picked, and how surprised she had been to learn how much he liked Cat Stevens. "Joey liked "Morning Has Broken." Can the choir sing that?"

"That would be perfect." He was more animated with something he could do, that small thing to comfort the family. He told Jeanne he planned to take some time to talk to all the young people before leading everyone in prayer. Jeanne hoped he wouldn't take long. People wouldn't leave until they said the Rosary, and she wanted Father to get it done so they all could go home and give her some time alone with her son.

Chapter 7

The limo turned the corner onto the quiet neighborhood street. Trees lined the road like an honor guard standing sentinel, oblivious to funeral conventions in their sunny display. Jeanne sat between Gary and her mother with Katy and Peggy in the extra seats, all of them avoiding any sustained glance. Occasionally, Mary wiped her eyes.

In the side-view mirror, Jeanne watched the train of cars coming around the corner behind her, the same train that had slowly followed her from Nolan's Funeral Home to the Church, the hearse behind the patrol car with its flashing lights clearing the way. Then again after the Mass, as the steeple bells tolled, they followed her down Main Street, through the middle of the village, past strollers on the sidewalk who stopped to gawk, past the waitresses who came out of the ice cream parlor, and the chef who stood watching in his apron outside his diner.

The long train continued, following the limo past the high school, past the faces in the classroom windows. They slowly circled the football field only picking up speed when they reached the highway. They followed her through the cemetery gates and filled all the spaces on both sides of the lane near the gravesite and the next lane and the lane after that. Now, Jeanne watched them all following her home as though pulled along, each tethered to the one in front.

For the last few days, in the back of her mind, she knew the family would come back to the house. She kept thinking she needed to get ready, but something always stood in her way, someone on the phone, or at the door, or sitting in the kitchen trying to be kind while Jeanne made an effort to be polite, all the time wishing her visitors would go home and let her do whatever she needed to do, even if she couldn't think what that might be or muster the energy it would take to do it. She never stayed with anything long enough before feeling the need to escape to her bed.

Her sister, Ginger, had once mentioned the after-party, but she never broached the subject again. Jeanne hoped to grab her as soon as they got home and send her to the deli for cold cuts and potato salad. It was so unlike her not to have the perfect lunch for her guests.

The limo pulled to the top of the driveway while down in the road, cars parked in front of the house or made u-turns to line up on the other side of the street, all of them discharging their passengers in twos and threes and more, the steady rhythmic whump of closing car doors resounding in the air. They stood in the road sharing quiet greetings before heading for the house, flowing together from the right and left, the quiet procession merging in the driveway where the subdued parade suddenly came to a halt.

Jeanne had stopped abruptly on her way up the stairs to scan the gathered crowd for Gary. She needed him to get the coffee urn from the basement, but he was down on the street on some mission of his own. She searched instead for her sister and waved to get her attention when she spotted her with Mary across the street. Ginger never looked her way.

As Jeanne stood holding on to the railing, trying to decide what to do, her uncle Buddy came up beside her, his courtly manners common to her father's family not allowing him to let her walk alone. He gently eased his hand beneath her elbow and escorted her the rest of the way up the stairs. The waiting entourage began again to follow, moving up the driveway, looking at each other with apology in their eyes.

Jeanne yielded to her uncle's lead and let him walk her into the house. From the front hall, she had an unimpeded view of the dining room where Anna and her next-door neighbor, Eileen, stood by the table with aprons over their funeral clothes. She didn't understand how they got there before everyone else until the full picture came through her fog.

Her crocheted Irish linen cloth covered the table, just as if she had put it out herself. Casserole dishes and bowls of salad sat at one end of the table while the other end held roast beef and baked ham dressed in pineapple rings. An ample array of yellow mums arranged in her

Waterford vase served as a centerpiece. Cookies and cakes sat on the server in front of the window and on the buffet, with her best cups and saucers, her best plates and silver all neatly arranged, the coffee urn sat perking away, filling the air with its welcoming aroma.

Overcome with relief, Jeanne turned to her uncle "Oh look, Uncle Buddy, how nice it all is. They've taken care of everything." Her stoic, quiet uncle lost his composure. His face collapsed in grief, as he quickly turned and took himself away.

Jeanne's Aunt Elizabeth, Buddy's sister, stepped into his place and took her arm, leading Jeanne into the sunny living room and sitting beside her on the blue brocade couch. Someone had moved the dining chairs into the room and set them around the perimeter wherever there was a space.

Across the room, Katy and Peggy sat squeezed together in the wingback chair engaged in conversation until they looked her way and abruptly stood and left the room. Jeanne wanted to go after them, but her aunt was chatting about something Jeanne wasn't following until she heard her father's name. "Albert gave this to me for my birthday when I was twelve. I think today is the right time to pass it on to you."

She handed Jeanne a present she had taken out of her purse. In her knack for doing everything with style, she had wrapped the gift with an elegant bow. Jeanne sat holding it, not sure what her aunt expected until her aunt took it back and said, "Let me open it for you."

She unwrapped an elegant antique lavaliere of silver filigree with a purple amethyst set in the oval pendant. The clasp on the silver chain looked old in the delicately etched lacy design. "I think this is the perfect way to have your father here with us. Just think how happy he must be up in heaven with Joey by his side."

Jeanne was stunned. She knew her aunt meant only to be kind, but she couldn't imagine her father happy that Joey died so young. Knowing how much he cared for his grandson, she imagined him as devastated as she was. Her aunt looked at her expectantly and Jeanne knew she should thank her for the gift but she couldn't speak.

"I'll get us some coffee," her aunt said, brushing away tears as she left the room.

Hours later, as people slowly began to trickle away, Gary and Jeanne with Mary alongside them, stood at the front door, thanking everyone for coming. Long heartfelt hugs followed condolences, many wiping away tears.

When their final guest had said good night, they gathered with the girls in the den. The lamp in the corner filled the room with a soft yellow glow. Peggy sat beside Gulliver on the carpet in front of the fireplace, rubbing his ears. Katy came in from the kitchen carrying a pot of coffee and some mugs on a tray with a plate of cookies someone had brought for the buffet.

Now and then, someone made a quiet comment. Mary mentioned all the cars in the funeral procession. She wondered how Father Mahoney knew Joey so well to tell all those stories at the funeral about how wonderful he was.

"He didn't know him that well, Grandma," Katy explained. "Father picked up those stories at the wake. That's why he talked to all the kids."

"We should have had Uncle Nick play his bagpipes. I know Joey would have liked that," Mary said.

"No!" Jeanne startled her mother with her loud retort. "No! Joey would not have liked that. He wouldn't have liked anything else I've heard today, how this would make him happy and that would make him happy. Someone said he must be happy to see so many people. No. It wouldn't make him happy to see so many people."

Mary squeezed next to her on the couch, putting her arm around Jeanne's shoulder trying to comfort her. "There, there, I know, I know."

After some time, Peggy retrieved her guitar from the corner and started to sing.

Morning has broken like the first morning.

Blackbird has spoken like the first bird.

Peggy sang softly, her voice full of pathos. As Jeanne listened, Gary reached over and pulled her close. She leaned against him, felt his warmth. The brief, quiet moment softened Jeanne's pain.

Part Two

Grief fills the room up of my absent child,
Lies in his bed, walks up and down with me,
Remembers me of all his gracious parts.

William Shakespeare

Chapter 8

Watching the traffic speeding by on the highway, Jeanne became anxious to get back on the road. But, whenever she turned the key in the ignition, intrusive memories brought her to tears. She couldn't escape Joey's expression when he waved goodbye, or Anna's and Tony's faces in the driveway, or Gary's anguish when he came through the door. The wake and the funeral were more of a blur, but she remembered the evening in the den, listening to Peggy's soft voice, feeling Gary's warm embrace. How desperately she wanted to continue that moment of comfort. But in the days that followed, it proved a delusion.

She often found Gary sitting on the deck, oblivious to the frosty air, an ashtray filled with cigarette butts hinting at a night of chain-smoking. He'd barely acknowledge her "Good morning" as he sat staring into space. When he came in from the deck, he'd head through the kitchen, eyes blank, as though he were somewhere else. Later she'd hear him upstairs in Joey's bedroom, his deep agonizing wail bringing her flying up the stairs. She'd find him holding onto Joey's football trophy or some other leftover piece of Joey's life. He'd push the door closed, his "Leave me alone," bringing tears of her own.

She looked for a way to comfort the girls. Although they no longer cried around her, she saw their swollen eyes. Most of the time, they stayed in their separate rooms. Or they'd disappear from the house, Peggy with her boyfriend, John, and Katy into cars of friends who whisked her away Jeanne knew not where.

While the girls worked hard to hide their tears, Gary remained torn with anger and grief. She worried constantly that they were missing something important. They hadn't talked. Whenever she brought up the accident, it became awkward when he changed the subject, and although she saw his sadness, she still didn't know how to help. But how could she? She didn't know how to help herself. They mostly coped alone in their separate worlds.

Thinking over those early days, she wondered if the family might have fared better if she had known how to help them console each other in their grief. She never found a way to make it work.

Chapter 9

Only a week had passed since the funeral when Katy and Peggy returned to their classes and Gary went back to work. With everyone gone, Gulliver was Jeanne's only company. He laid his chin on her lap while she sat at the dining room table tackling thank-you notes for all the flowers, sympathy cards and Mass cards waiting to be acknowledged, as well as the many acts of kindness in the days after Joey died.

Reading the condolences, her reluctance slowly mounted, until she was too overcome to put thoughtful words on paper. The suggestion that she now was rich, with treasures of gold locked in her memories, left her both angry and sad. How does one respond to that? Sentiments of roses growing on the other side of the garden wall, or angels trying out their new wings, brought back the now-familiar ache in her throat. It moved into her chest and down her arms. She hugged herself, pulling her arms tight, trying to relieve the pain.

Gulliver, sitting beside her, pulled on her arm with his paw, his brown eyes searching her face. When condolences meant to console only brought more tears, she pushed away from the table, climbed the stairs, the dog padding behind, and once again crawled into bed. From under the covers, she heard his sad whines.

The phone often interrupted her sleep. Her mother called every day and made a habit of coming for coffee, cooking something for her to eat, or keeping busy with dishes and such, trying to ease Jeanne's burden and fix things that couldn't be fixed even as she did her best to cope with her own grandmotherly grief. They didn't mention Joey unless they forgot, and one or the other realized what she had said and suddenly had something to do in the other room.

The weekend arrived, and for the first time in days, the four of them would be together for dinner. Jeanne hoped the quiet comfort the night of the funeral would return. Perhaps they'd have the conversation she thought they should have, even as she feared the conversation. She hugged herself, pulling her arms tight, trying to relieve the pain.

Somehow she found the energy to make lasagna, their favorite meal. The girls sat subdued at the table, trying, out of politeness, to show enthusiasm for her effort. They had finished dinner when Gary announced he had something to say. Brows knit with hesitation, he told them, "Sperry is moving my project to Florida." He looked around the table and paused before adding, "I told them I'd go."

Jeanne sat speechless until she found her voice. "You're leaving? Now?"

Her reaction had him defending his decision. "They offered to send someone else under the circumstances, Joey and all, but I explained it wasn't a problem. It's my project. I won't let them turn it over to another project manager. That's what will happen if I don't go."

"Shouldn't you have at least mentioned it to me first?"

"Well, they needed an answer right away. You know how important this project is to me. Right?"

What could she say to that? "When are you going?"

"The sooner, the better. I'll go in tomorrow to tie everything up here so I can be there Monday morning."

"Monday morning! But the monument company is expecting us Monday morning."

"You can do that, can't you?"

"Without you, Gary? No, I can't. I mean, not without you. I just know you. Whatever gravestone I pick, you won't like it. But that's not even the point. We need to do this together. He's not just my son; he's yours too."

"Was."

"What?"

He glared at her. "Was my son! Was!"

After a moment of quiet, Gary spoke in a softer voice. "It shouldn't take that long. Maybe two or three months. I'll be coming up most weekends. We can make another appointment. As far as I know, they can't put a gravestone in place before the spring, so there's no hurry."

Jeanne wanted to object, but to what end? She didn't expect him to change his mind. Still, it gnawed at her. How would they ever confront this new tension hovering around them, with him 1,000 miles away?

With the girls back in school and Gary gone to Florida, Jeanne returned to her students, urged on by her mother, who kept telling her school would do her good. Get her mind off things.

When she walked in the classroom, her students gathered about her and took turns giving her hugs. Jeanne was happy to see them until little Sarah wrapped her arms around Jeanne's waist and said, "I'm sorry about your little boy. Are you sad? Don't be sad." It took every bit of Jeanne's effort to keep her composure as she signaled to Melanie to take over the class and got out of the room.

The following week Jeanne tried again hoping to keep the tears at bay. But she couldn't teach. All her energy went into trying to smile. More and more she relied on Melanie, while Jeanne sat by in the role of teacher's aide.

Gary hadn't come home the first weekend after he left, as he had promised, nor the weekend after that. Then, on the phone, he said he might as well wait for Thanksgiving. That didn't happen either. Then instead of coming home for Christmas, he talked her into bringing the girls to Florida, arguing it might be easier for them to be away from too many reminders.

They got through their first Christmas without Joey by going through the motions of preparing for the holiday, buying presents and searching for the perfect tree. Jeanne guessed Joey was on everyone's mind, but it seemed they all feared to mention his name. She was sure they were doing it all wrong. They should do something special to remember him. Talk about him. She lay awake at night, looking for a solution, but nothing presented itself. It always seemed better to leave it alone.

Most of the time, she sat on the beach thinking about Joey, wondering if life would always be what it had become. Constant dread. The fear every night going to bed knowing she'd wake in the morning and face the trauma of his loss again. The fear of going through the day knowing at some point some unexpected reminder would cause her to lose her composure and hoping no one would be there when she did. Afraid to see people. Afraid of what they might say.

She didn't mention the gravestone. They'd take care of it when he came home in January. Gary was more relaxed than he had been, not losing his temper or finding fault as much, and she wanted to keep it that way.

Once back on Long Island, she resented Gary for not being there with them. He was often hard to reach, and on the rare occasion when she got him on the phone, his hello was "I only have a few minutes." He didn't know when he'd be home. "At the end of the month, if all goes well."

January came and left without him, his assignment extended, his project the only thing on his mind. More and more depressed, Jeanne wandered from room to room or sat on Joey's bed wrapped in his quilt, holding it close, breathing the scent of him until the tears abated or she fell asleep.

Often the urge to go to the cemetery got her out of the house. She'd climb into the truck with Gulliver, while fighting the fear of the familiar pain of seeing his grave. An old maple stood like a beacon at the end of the row where Joey was buried, a peaceful place to be close, as though they were in the same room. She'd think of him with nothing distracting or interrupting until the urgent need to get him his blanket took hold. She'd tell herself what a silly idea it was, but she couldn't suppress the compulsion. It began the day she watched them put him in the ground and thought he must be cold. Despite her effort to ignore it, the need still haunted her. She'd leave as devastated as she had come.

She became more and more reluctant to go to school, worried about trying to teach on the verge of tears. Her neighbor Anna came by one day with one of the ziti casseroles that she had a habit of bringing and asked Jeanne what she was doing at home. "I keep seeing the truck in the driveway. I thought you went back to work."

When Jeanne merely shrugged her shoulders, Anna gently brought up counseling. She insisted that's what people do. They get help. They don't just keep crawling into bed. She gave Jeanne a brochure for Compassionate Friends, a group of parents helping each other through their grief. "I'll go with you if you want."

Jeanne knew she couldn't just keep stumbling along unable to function, but she wasn't sure she wanted to join a counseling group. She couldn't understand how dwelling on the sorry details got anyone past the sorrow. How could she talk about Joey with strangers without falling apart?

She started going to movies to fill the day, but she often left before the show was over, when some too familiar detail started her tears. Other days she drove to the Mall, hoping a little shopping might distract her, but it only deepened her gloom. She'd wander from store to store, hoping she wouldn't run into people she knew. It was always awkward watching them try to avoid her, but she was thankful when they did.

Strolling listlessly along one day, Jeanne saw a man in a brown leather jacket walking in front of her. His thick wavy hair brushed his jacket collar. Gripped with a compelling need to see his face, she hurried to catch up to him, following him to Macy's, into the store, and up the escalator. The voice in her head was back. *It's not Joey*. But she ignored it. She knew it wasn't Joey; she still needed to see his face.

When he finally turned her way, he was not what she wanted. She couldn't imagine him breaking into a mischievous grin. Devastated, she held on to her tears until she got to the truck.

At the pharmacy one day she stood behind a man leaning with his forearms resting on the high counter. He wore a brown leather jacket, his brown hair thick and wavy. She froze in her spot, looking at his back, waiting for him to turn around, only to have the same crushing disappointment when he did.

She began to avoid public places, anywhere that brief half second of Joey would grab her, bringing unwanted tears when she saw the truth.

One afternoon, driving home from the cemetery, she fretted over her new inclination to look for him in strangers. It wasn't just the weirdness of it; it was the grief that overcame her, the tears when it turned out to be someone else, even though she knew it would be someone else.

Deep in thought as she drove along, she came to a stop sign at a T in the road and realized she didn't recognize the street. For the second time in a week, she didn't know where she was. When she finally found her way home, she searched through the desk drawer for the flyer Anna had given her for Compassionate Friends and called to ask when they were meeting.

People, scattered around the auditorium, listened to the moderator welcome them in a comforting voice. In her blue blazer, and her neatly finished hair, she looked like an executive's efficient assistant, someone who invited trust.

She told them they would find it difficult to get through the days ahead and explained the impact on everyday life when one's child dies. "You wake in the morning and find it hard to get out of bed, much less attend to all the normal requirements of life. You wonder if you will ever feel normal again."

That was Jeanne's fear. Would she ever feel normal?

"You'll be driving down the road and not know where you are."

So I'm not alone, Jeanne thought.

"You'll find a videotape is constantly playing an endless loop in your mind, running through what happened."

There were two videos for Jeanne: the last time she saw Joey walking away up the garden steps and the moment in her dream when he came through the door of the train, and everything went wrong.

The moderator never mentioned an inner voice like the one in Jeanne's head chastising her or a fixation on following strangers, but when she said, "You fear you are losing your mental stability,"

Jeanne nodded her head.

Then she startled Jeanne with a statistic: "And sadly, as much as eighty percent of your marriages will have problems. Many will end in divorce."

That can't be right, thought Jeanne raising her hand. "I don't think I heard you correctly. Did you say eighty percent?"

"Yes, I did. I know it may sound unbelievable, and while some studies suggest a smaller percentage, there's plenty of evidence for eighty percent."

"But why? That doesn't make sense?"

"When two people are so devastated, they can't be there for each other because they can hardly take care of themselves. Sometimes it is misplaced anger, one of the typical characteristics of grief. Sometimes, they might even be angry with their child for leaving them, but they can't acknowledge that, so they project their anger on the person closest to them, their spouse."

Jeanne couldn't concentrate on what the moderator was saying. Her thoughts were all about Gary. Was it his grief that had him snapping at her all the time? Something nagged her about that, but she let it go. All she could think of was the "eighty percent." If this was happening to them, she needed to do something about it. She fretted all the way home, the thought of this threat to her marriage adding to her angst.

Chapter 10

Jeanne hadn't seen Gary since Christmas, which only added to her inner turmoil with "eighty percent" continually weighing on her mind. Although she understood that was the extreme, it ate at her anyway. How would she fix things with him so far away?

Gary's temporary assignment had been extended, then extended again, and when he implied in their latest conversation that he wouldn't be back for Easter either, Jeanne insisted he come home. "You need to be here, Gary. We have things to do."

"You mean the gravestone, I suppose."

"You promised we would have it for Spring."

"I still don't understand why you don't get it yourself. I'm not there, and you are."

To keep the peace, Jeanne let it go and brought up the girls.

"They miss you, Gary. They need to see you. We all miss you. We haven't seen you since Christmas."

He sighed, saying he'd do his best. "And tell the girls I miss them too."

His best was to arrive the day before Easter with plans to return to Florida Easter night. Jeanne kept her disappointment to herself, hoping to persuade him to stay longer. The four of them with her mother and Peggy's boyfriend, John, filled an entire row at Easter Mass; then they went to the cemetery with a cross of white lilies. Jeanne tried to ignore the missing gravestone. Maybe Gary would notice it missing on his own. It might prod him to do something about it.

Her mother mentioned it instead. "Shouldn't the gravestone be here by now?"

"We're working on it," Jeanne said as she glared at Gary.

Back at the house, she brought up her mother's remarks. "I'll bet my mother isn't the only one who's noticed. We can't keep ignoring it."

"Oh, God, don't start that again."

"What is the problem? It can't take more than an hour."

"How can you act like it's not a problem, as though it's just another errand, like going to the store? It may not be painful for you, but it's painful for me." The shock on her face drew a more apologetic tone. "I'm sorry, Jeanne, I didn't mean that. I'm sure it's just as hard for you. But I just don't have the time right now. Can't this wait until my vacation?"

"But you said this Spring. Remember?"

He was back to the sharp retort. "Did you hear anything I said? I can't do this now."

"And that's another thing. Why are you in such a hurry to get back to Florida? Couldn't you stay a few extra days for Joey's birthday? This will be our first birthday without him. It didn't occur to me you would skip that."

He stared at her, his brows knit. "His birthday? Damn, Jeanne, I'm sorry. I can't believe I forgot. My project has me going in circles. I wish you would try to understand."

Jeanne wanted to be supportive, but coping with Gary's going off to Florida when they had so much to deal with was hard enough without the missing gravestone nagging her day and night. Then on top of everything he'd forgotten Joey's birthday. What had him so distracted he'd forget Joey's birthday?

Their goodbyes at the airport were frostier than ever. Jeanne thought about it all the way home. She had to find a way to diffuse the tension between them. It didn't bode well for their future together. As she searched for some solution, a whisper of something familiar in his behavior nagged her. She felt strongly she had seen this Gary before. But she couldn't quite get hold of it. It was easier to believe it was his grief.

When they next spoke on the phone, she avoided mentioning the gravestone. She would wait like he said until he came home. She turned her attention to planning their summer vacation, hoping a sail on the Sound or time in the Catskills might bring them together like the night of the funeral.

Gary arrived in June, in an upbeat mood that surprised her. She hadn't seen that Gary in a long time. "You look like the cat that ate the canary."

"That's because I've got great news." He beamed.

Jeanne couldn't hide her excitement. "You're coming home!"

Gary's glee disappeared in his knitted brow. "Uh, no. Tell you what, let's wait for dinner when we're all together."

At dinner, full of delight, he made his announcement. "Sperry is promoting me."

So that's it, Jeanne thought. "Oh, congratulations, Gary, that's so great." She walked around the table and hugged him.

"The best part is my new position is in Florida. It's a permanent transfer, so that means we'll have to move."

Everyone stared, trying to digest what he had said. Peggy spoke first. "I'm not moving to Florida, not me!"

Katy was right behind her. "Well, I won't be going, that's for sure. I was hoping to move into the city to be near school." She looked at Jeanne defensively. "Sorry, Mom. I didn't talk to you about it yet because I didn't want to upset you, but if we're moving anyway, I might as well move into the city. I can find a place near my college to share with friends that won't cost any more a month than commuting on the train."

Jeanne didn't respond to her daughter. She was fixed on the words he used: permanent transfer. "How permanent is it?" she asked Gary.

"Permanent means permanent. I'm moving to Florida. I expected everyone would want to come with me."

"No way!" The words were out of Peggy's mouth before Jeanne could respond. "All my friends are here. It's my senior year." She repeated it with outrage in her voice. "My senior year!"

"Well, it won't happen right away. It will take time to get things organized. Mom can stay here with you until you graduate if that's what you want."

Jeanne didn't like Gary's assumption she would stay in Northport without him. Peggy wouldn't graduate for another year. "Or you can move across the street with Grandma," she said, looking at him to make her point.

"Look, I guess I hit you all with this too quickly. Can we let it go for now? We don't want to spoil our vacation. There'll be plenty of time to figure out what's best for everyone. I really want everyone to be happy."

The next day they packed up the truck with the food they needed to stay the week at the cabin. With Gulliver in the back under the cap and the four of them squeezed in the cab seat, they headed out early to drive up the thruway. Approaching the Throgs Neck Bridge, Jeanne began to have reservations. The last time she crossed this bridge was when Joey died. She worried the bridge might bring sad reminders and hoped she hadn't made a mistake, but when no one made any notice of the bridge, she realized the memory was hers alone. Better to keep it to herself.

Shortly past noon, they pulled up to the cabin and, out of habit, quietly went about the routine of unloading the truck and getting everything in place for their visit. They opened all the windows to let in the fresh mountain air as they dusted and swept and made up the beds.

In the following days, they searched out their old haunts. Jeanne saw Joey in all his favorite places, splashing in the creek or challenging them to catch him as he ran ahead up the trail. The girls often shared memories of him with an ease that had been missing. Each in their own way, they were growing more comfortable talking about him without anything she did or didn't do to make a difference. Listening to her daughters quietly reminisce without tears, Jeanne lost her trepidations that their trip might not go well. She was glad she planned this time together. They needed to talk about him. They couldn't just let him fade away.

On their last night at the cabin, with the dishes done and most everything packed up to leave early the next morning, they sat quietly conversing on the porch, watching the day fade away. Gulliver slept at Jeanne's feet, occasionally thumping his tail when she gave him a pet. Gary promised the girls the decision about where to live would be theirs. There'd be a place for them in Florida if they wanted it. Peggy said she wished they didn't have to go home.

"How about we do this again next summer," Gary said. "We can come after you graduate, or even better, go up to Maine and camp. What do you think?"

"You mean camp, like in a tent?" said Katy, a hint of sarcasm in her remark. "That sounds real cozy."

"You know what would be great?" said Gary, "if we had a camper on the back of the truck. They have some that sleep four. We could go to Bangor and see the old family homestead, or Corea where the family summer camp used to be."

Jeanne latched onto Gary's idea, *Travels with Charlie* coming to mind. Ever since she read Steinbeck's book, she harbored a secret wish to make a road trip. Hoping she wasn't getting ahead of things, she said, "I love that idea. When it's time to go to Florida, Gulliver and I could go together in the truck. With a camper on the back, I could take my time and sightsee along the way."

"Sounds like John Steinbeck," Gary said with a laugh.

Jeanne wondered how he knew.

They were only back from the cabin a day when Gary hung up from one of his many phone calls and announced he had to get back to Florida.

"What about the *Quest*?" asked Jeanne. You said you'd take us for a sail."

"I can't do that now. No time. I'll be taking the motorcycle, so I'll need a few days to get there.

"The motorcycle? All the way to Florida?"

"It's no good to me here."

"Okay, but we still need to talk about your promotion. I know how much it matters to you, but what about us? If I stay here with Peggy until she graduates, we'll spend the entire year separated. I don't think that's smart unless you plan to come home more often than you have."

"Look, we can work something out to make the best of it, but I don't have time to talk about it now."

"Fine, but what about the gravestone? You plan to go with me, right?" Until then, Jeanne hadn't mentioned the gravestone. Immediately, she was sorry she did. The new warmth between them from their days at the cabin disappeared with Gary's angry response.

"Oh God. That again. Can't you ever quit? And how am I supposed to do that and get the motorcycle ready to leave? It takes time to tune it. I can't just hop on it and ride to Florida without giving it a test drive."

With knots in her stomach, she let it go again. She didn't want another chilly departure like the last time.

He wasn't back in a week or two or the rest of the summer. October arrived with Joey's anniversary looming and Jeanne dreading the upcoming weeks. Jeanne's mother sensed her distress and stayed close, going with Jeanne to the Mass of Remembrance and then to the cemetery with a bucket of mums.

As Jeanne drove through the gate, she saw the maple waiting, brilliant in its autumn color. She parked beneath it and reached behind the seat for the pitcher she kept handy for water, then filled it from the spigot attached to a post by the tree. Mary took special care arranging the flowers as if the bouquet would sit in the center of the dining room table when the aunts came for tea.

She knew how much her mother cared about such things: all the flowers, the visits, the Hail Mary's, the Christmas wreaths, the Easter crosses. To Jeanne, it was never more than a useless effort. Joey was still dead and cold in the ground, and she still felt the need to get him his blanket.

Chapter 11

The autumn leaves turned brown on the ground as Fall moved toward winter and Jeanne continued to struggle. She wished she could find a way to escape the constant fear of living with never-ending grief. Now she had the added complication of worry over her marriage. Joey had departed, and if she didn't figure something out, she might lose Gary as well.

She was raking leaves in the front yard, trying to rally her spirit when her father-in-law, Lou, pulled into the driveway. With his secretary, Susan, sitting beside him, Jeanne sensed they had come for more than a friendly visit.

Susan worked with Lou at Sperry Corporation where he ran the control tower. The jeans and sweaters she liked to wear gave her a youthful appearance despite her gray hair. She lived in the apartment over Lou's garage, but she spent more time in the house with Gary's family often playing hostess at family affairs while Gary's mother, Phyllis, stayed in the kitchen with dishes and such. Susan never hesitated to weigh in on family discussions with her opinion. Gary's brothers and their wives often welcomed her suggestions, unlike Gary, who didn't care for her unsolicited advice.

Over coffee, the three of them exchanged small talk until Susan asked "So when are you going to Florida? You should be down there, don't you think?"

So that's what this is about, Jeanne thought.

"I think that son of mine has been footloose and fancy-free too long," said Lou. "Peggy can stay with us until she graduates. You need to go to Florida. I bet he hasn't been here in weeks, has he?"

Susan leaned forward in her seat to make her point. "The way I see it, Jeanne, you two have been apart way too long. It's not good. I know Peggy won't mind. She'd love to stay with Pop and her grandmother."

"Well, if I weren't here, she could always stay with my mother.

It's closer to her school. But Gary thinks it better if I wait until she graduates. I argued at first, but I came to see that it's best for Peggy if I stay. There's so much to deal with for graduation and college applications and the prom. I can't just abandon her."

Lou and Susan shared a glance Jeanne wished she could read.

"I won't be ready to move before then, anyway. With all I have to do to get packed and organized, it's probably the best plan."

Susan told her not to worry about getting things done. "We can always help with that. Pop and I can deal with the house. I bet your Mom would help too. And your sisters."

"It's just that whenever we discuss it, Gary always ends up saying he won't be ready for me to move down now. He needs time to get things worked out."

"What things?" Susan used her fingers for imaginary quotes to emphasize "things." "We all know what he's like Jeanne. Believe me we hear all the rumors at work every time he has a new fling. I know you'd prefer if nobody talked about it, but let's be honest. We know, when he got involved a few years ago, you and Gary almost broke up. None of us want that to happen."

And just like that Jeanne knew what was bugging her about his behavior. His short temper, snapping at her all the time was just like the last time he got involved. This was Gary's personality whenever he had someone on the side. "You're not telling me he's involved with someone are you?"

"No. No. We haven't heard anything like that. We just think it's prudent not to leave him on his own like he is now."

"I just don't believe he would do that. He couldn't. Not now."

Lou looked at the table, then out the door, then at Susan, everywhere but at Jeanne. She sensed something left unspoken but thought it better not to ask. Little was said after that. When they stood to leave, Susan told her they had stopped at the cemetery. She asked about the gravestone. "We thought it would be there by now."

Jeanne explained that Gary always seemed to run out of time

when he's home to arrange for it to be installed, and she didn't think she should do it by herself. It didn't sit well with Lou. "I'll talk to him about it. He really needs to take care of this."

When she walked them to the door, Jeanne could see they were disappointed. She worried they might be right about the two of them being separated, but she couldn't believe he would get involved again. Not after the last time. Not after all the remorse, his tears, his promises. She believed him when he said he didn't want to lose her. And she was sure he knew she meant it when she told him the next time she would leave.

Jeanne was mulling over her conversation with Lou and Susan, fretting about what to do, when loud barking at the ringing doorbell interrupted her thoughts. Through the front door window, Jeanne saw Joey's friends, Vinnie and Alan, looking at each other, it seemed to her, for moral support. She thought they seemed older. Their hair was longer than she remembered, and they both wore red Converse sneakers, Joey's favorite. Jeanne feasted her eyes on them. "Come in, come in. I'm so glad to see you." She led them through the kitchen to the back deck and offered them a beer. "I have some nice cold ones in the fridge."

Vinnie declined. "That's okay. We just wanted to say hello and see how you're doing."

They sat on the deck, enjoying the warmth of the Indian summerday with Gulliver trotting from one to the other, wagging his tail, as happy to see them as Jeanne was. Alan, the quiet one, was rubbing Gulliver's ears when he pulled himself up straight and blurted out, "We visited the cemetery for the anniversary, I hope it's okay to say."

"Oh, thank you for that, yes, how thoughtful of you."

"But we didn't see Joey's gravestone," said Vinnie. "We were surprised because it's been a year and we've been watching for it."

Oh no, Jeanne thought, that's why they're here.

"We talked to the people in the office thinking it must be their fault, but they said they didn't have an order for it."

They looked at each other, both hesitating, then Alan cleared his throat. "We were going to take up a collection, all us guys." He cleared his throat again. "But my Mom said we had to ask you first."

Both embarrassed and fuming with Gary, Jeanne tried to stay calm. "Oh, Alan, no, you don't have to do that, no. But I'm touched, I am."

"But we really would like to help. All the guys feel the same way."

"The problem is Gary is working in Florida and keeps trying to find time for us to arrange it. I'm just as upset about it as you are. But really we don't need help. As much as I truly appreciate your offer we really need to do this ourselves."

"We didn't want to bring it up, you know, talk about Joey, and make you feel bad."

"Oh please, don't ever feel you can't talk to me about Joey because you think it will make me feel bad. I'm always happy to talk to his friends."

She turned the conversation to what they were doing lately, but they didn't seem to want to talk. When she said goodbye to them at the door, she promised to call them as soon as the stone was installed.

The minute they were gone, she picked up the phone. To Jeanne's "hello," Gary said, "You're calling me at the office? Can't this wait until tonight?"

"No! It cannot!" She told him the story, how the kids offered to take up a collection. "They think we can't afford it. For God's sake, Gary, it's been over a year."

As usual, he exploded. "Whose fault is that? Don't I have enough problems without you constantly reminding me my son is dead? Do you constantly have to harass me? Is that it? Refuse to do it yourself so you can have a reason to harass me? If you can't do it yourself, you'll have to wait. Stop calling me about it." He slammed down the phone.

Jeanne sat stunned, ignoring the dial tone buzzing on the phone, while she replayed the conversation in her mind, hearing his harsh words to stop reminding him his son is dead.

Like last year, Gary didn't come home for Thanksgiving. "I can stay longer for Christmas," he said. He never mentioned the gravestone, and since she had determined not to let the impasse ruin their Christmas, she didn't mention it either. If she concentrated on planning for things they enjoyed as a family, they might get back some of the warmth they had at the cabin and find some Christmas cheer. Perhaps they could go to the Messiah Sing-in at Lincoln Center again or to the Nutcracker like they did last year.

Determined to make the house festive for the holidays, Jeanne searched out the Christmas decorations in the piles of boxes stored in the basement. She had a string of lights spread across the floor and was changing bulbs repeatedly, trying to get the lights to work when the television evening news was interrupted with a commercial. A beautiful trotting horse pulled a sleigh through a Currier and Ives winter scene. The music played:

I'll be home for Christmas. You can count on me.

Sitting on the floor she tried to see through the tears, overwhelmed once more with grief, aching for her son. She wondered how many others watching the commercial were having their hearts broken over loved ones who would never be coming home.

Despite her hopes, Christmas was a dismal affair. No one was interested in going to the shows. Most of the time Peggy was out with John. Katy went back to the city after only four days. Jeanne and Gary worked at staying out of each other's way until he left early to get back to Florida, not even waiting for New Year's Eve. She tried to bury the nagging thought about why he was in such a hurry to leave.

The dreary winter days of January sapped any effort she made to lighten her mood. More and more she'd call Melanie to take over the class. She'd get in the truck with Gulliver, the one place she didn't fear the tears, and drive aimlessly.

She had been driving for hours one night, not conscious of where she was, until she realized she was heading for the outer islands on the south shore. Silver rays of moon glow lay a gleaming pathway across the Great South Bay. Enthralled with the beauty of the night, she kept driving ahead to Ocean Parkway. When she came to a sign for Gilgo Beach, on impulse she pulled into the parking lot.

Undeterred by the chilly night, she and Gulliver followed the walkway under the highway down to the beach. Along the moonlit shore a few hardy anglers cast their lines in the surf. Except for those fishing, she and the dog had the whole beach to themselves. She walked with Gulliver along the water's edge breathing the salty scent of sea air. Ocean dew caressed her face. The crash of winter waves quickened her pulse. She could feel the tension lighten, her anguish drain away.

More and more, in the days and weeks to come, she headed to the ocean to seek relief. Bundled against the cold, with Gulliver faithfully trotting beside her, she walked the beach, watching the ebb and flow of the surf, invigorated by the crashing waves. She saw Joey everywhere, charging into the water, kicking knees high as he was wont to do, riding the waves back to shore. Instead of tears, the memories brought smiles and filled her with warmth.

As weather warmed to Spring, she drove to the ocean almost every day. She'd imagine Joey beside her, sharing her awe of the setting sun painting the sky. When night fell, she'd help Gulliver into the back of the truck and crawl in with him under the cap. Snuggled in her sleeping bag, she let the night embrace her. The crashing waves lulled her to sleep.

The call of the gulls would wake her early and she'd head for the concession stand at Captree for morning coffee and a fried egg on a roll, one for her and one for the dog. She'd find a spot on the pier to sit and watch the charter boats moored side by side, the busy fishermen gearing up for a day at sea. Longing to climb aboard, she'd watch them sail away until the last boat disappeared around the point.

Chapter 12

Two weeks before Easter, Gary called to say he wouldn't be home until Peggy's graduation, but he had good news. Before Jeanne could get excited about what that could be, he told her he bought a camper for the truck and that he had arranged to pick it up at a dealership when he got back in June. "We can take that camping trip I promised the girls."

Jeanne was tempted to ask how he managed that when it seemed impossible for him to get a gravestone, but she restrained herself. Nothing would be gained. She would only be raining on his parade.

When Gary got home, they drove straight to the dealer. Excited about bringing the camper to Peggy's graduation party, he couldn't wait to get it.

Jeanne's sister, Ginger, had volunteered to have a barbecue for Peggy, and Jeanne was happy to accept. Parked in Ginger's driveway, shiny and new, the camper was the center of attention. The model was called Skamper, which Jeanne thought the perfect name. With the top raised and the window covers rolled up, the small camper cabin felt open and airy. The wide-open view of the trees surrounding Ginger's yard gave the impression they were deep in the woods.

Dozens of aunts, uncles, and cousins took turns climbing in and out, sitting at the dinette table, opening the cabinets, the refrigerator, looking under the bench to check out the water tank. Jeanne's brother, Kenneth, took his turn with a dreamy-eyed look. He stretched out on the loft bed, his hands folded under his head. "One of these days I'm going to get me one of these."

Like hosts of the mansion, Gary and Jeanne stood together at the camper door telling everyone how Jeanne planned to play Travels--with-Charley when she drove down to Florida with the dog. Gary highlighted the many side trips Jeanne could make on the way: the

Blue Ridge Mountains, The Outer Banks. "She might even spend a few weeks in the Keys."

Key West wondered Jeanne. Where did that come from?

When it was his turn for a tour, Ginger's brother-in-law, Paul, dubbed it the perfect vehicle to drive to Alaska. Paul and his wife Barbara were VISTA workers home on vacation from the small Yup'ik village where Paul was the school principal and Barbara his secretary.

"Why don't you come visit us in Toksook Bay?" Paul said. "It sounds as though you have time. Believe me, driving to Alaska is far superior to driving down the East Coast. And you'll save money if you drive across Canada. The public campgrounds are essentially free. No, it's true they're free. And they have lots of them. Just pull in at night and park."

"Well, some of them are free," said Barbara, "but he's right. It's not as expensive as you would think."

"It sounds like a wonderful trip, but all I really want is to get to Florida and start living a normal life." She looked at Gary. "We've been apart too long." In her mind, the whole idea was only party small talk, but Gary seemed to take it seriously. She saw the knitted brow, that look he gets when the wheels are turning in his head.

"How long does it take?" he asked Paul.

"A few weeks if all you did was drive, but you don't want to do that. You want to stop and see things. A better plan would be a month or two."

"Whoa, wait a minute. I am not driving to Alaska. I don't want to spend months on the road when it only takes a few days to get to Florida."

The "you should" chorus surprised her. Even her usually cautious sister Ginger was all for it. "You know, Jeanne, you could one-up old Steinbeck with a trip like that."

The next day Gary's parents, Lou and Phyllis, held another graduation celebration, this one for Peggy and Gary's nephew Freddy. Jeanne and Gary went alone in the truck, the girls coming in John's car because they planned to leave early.

On the way, Gary tried to sell her on his new plan. "If you leave for Alaska in late August and drop Peggy off at Fredonia on the way, you can cross the border into Canada by Niagara Falls. If you take your time and enjoy the trip, you would get to Florida in October. The best thing about that is you'll avoid the summer heat. You know you don't like it when it's too hot."

"Gary, stop. I'm not going to Alaska, period. I'm heading for Florida. We need to get our life back."

"Remember what your sister said yesterday, 'a better trip than John Steinbeck.'"

Jeanne sighed. "How silly is that? I can't imagine anyone one-upping John Steinbeck. Least of all me. I only thought a brief road trip with the dog would be nice. Since I have to drive the truck to Florida anyway, that's all I had in mind. Well, I mean, if you're not available for us to do it together."

He didn't answer.

"That's what I thought."

They rode along in silence, Jeanne replaying all the comments at yesterday's barbecue over in her mind. Gary made it sound plausible. After a while, she said, "Let me think about it," but Gary's smirk made her wish right away to take the comment back.

Lou and Phyllis along with Gary's brothers, Nick and Fred and Lou's secretary, Susan, came traipsing out to meet them when they arrived. They stood around the truck watching as Gary turned the crank to raise the top, their enthusiasm somewhat less effuse than the guests at Ginger's barbecue.

Susan asked, "Are you driving it back to Florida? Peggy can stay here. We'll see to it she gets settled in college and everything. You two can drive it down together. Make a vacation of it."

Gary looked at Jeanne as he made his announcement: "Jeanne's plans have changed. She's not going to Florida. She's making a trip to Alaska."

All heads whipped around in Jeanne's direction, mouths agape, eyes amazed.

Jeanne protested. "I only said I would consider it."

Gary was already talking over her, explaining about Paul and Barbara, and what a unique opportunity it was, and how this trip was better because she wouldn't get to Florida until the summer heat had abated. He sold the idea like a used car salesman.

"Are you crazy?" Phyllis asked. "It's bad enough to have her driving to Florida by herself, let alone have her driving clear across the continent and back. What are you thinking?"

Nick pointed out, "She just said she was only thinking about it." He turned to Jeanne. "Isn't that right?" Then turning back to Gary, "You don't seriously expect her to do this, do you?"

Lou wanted to know how he planned to pay for it, and Gary had an answer for that as well. "We have more than enough money from Joey's accident insurance. Anyway, it won't be that much because the gas in Canada with the dollar exchange is cheap, and the campgrounds don't cost anything." He repeated what Paul had said almost verbatim.

The accident insurance? When did he come up with that idea Jeanne wondered.

"It doesn't sound to me like she wants to do this," Fred said.

"Of course she does. She wants to do this Travels-with-Charley trip, just her and the dog." Gary was looking at Jeanne now, willing her to back him up.

"Can't she do that on the way to Florida?"

Everyone waited for an answer, but Gary had given up trying to argue.

They had started back inside when Lou grabbed hold of Gary's arm. "Go ahead," he said when Jeanne stopped to wait. From the house, she watched them through the window, standing in the street, facing each other with matching profiles, Gary, a tall version of the shorter Lou, with the same thick wavy hair minus the gray. Lou did all the talking, pointing to the truck, pointing to the house, while Gary just stood there, at forty-five, pouting like a twelve-year-old.

He brought up the conversation on the way home. "Why did you tell Pop I wouldn't go with you for a gravestone?"

"How about because you wouldn't. Your father asked me about it one day. I told him that you were always in a big hurry to get back to Florida and that I was waiting until you had time because it wouldn't be fair, it wouldn't be right, to leave you out of it." She emphasized all the final words.

The phone rang at eight the next morning. It was Lou with a message for Gary that Greenlawn Memorials expected him at ten.

Gary sounded subdued as he talked to him. "That's okay. We can do it. You don't need to come." At the monument office, he took time going through the choices, sharing with Jeanne what he thought, asking her opinion. Jeanne could hear the lump in his throat.

In the end they kept it simple. A cross at the top, the family name below that and underneath, on the left, 1959, the year Joey was born, his name, Joseph Louis in the middle, and on the right, 1978, the year he died.

When they finished, they drove across the street to the cemetery. They didn't bring flowers, but someone had. Someone was always leaving flowers. As they stood there in the soft rain, Gary put his arm around Jeanne's shoulder and pressed her close to him. "He was such a wonderful son. I miss him so much." Jeanne could hear him swallowing his tears.

Chapter 13

Gary drove off for Florida after the July 4th weekend pulling the *Quest* behind the station wagon, the tension between he and Jeanne seemingly diffused. Or so she let herself believe.

She hadn't expected to feel so distraught watching the boat disappear down the street. She had daydreams of sailing the *Quest* down along the coast, but Gary had no time for that. With all the neighbors assembled to wave goodbye, she worked hard to put on a cheery face. She didn't fool her friend. As she turned and headed back up the driveway, she caught the sympathy in Anna's smile.

After Gary left, Jeanne dove into preparing the house to rent so she could go to Florida as soon as Peggy left for college. She and Gary had met with a realtor, but the agent put such a negative spin on the house's condition, Gary decided not to sell it. He didn't want to fly home every weekend to deal with repairs. "How about we rent it for now?" and Jeanne squelched her urge to jump up and down with glee. She had never wanted to sell the house. She always hoped Gary's assignment would change. If they held onto it, he might end up moving back.

Jeanne was carrying a box she had packed to store in the garage when her sister, Lisa, showed up at the front door. Lisa was a student at Stony Brook University, and, whenever she came home to visit their mother across the street, she'd stop to check in on Jeanne. "You know, Jeanne, if you let me rent the house with my college friends, you won't have to do any of this?"

"But isn't this a long way from the college?"

"There's nothing left near the college worth renting. And with the four bedrooms we can each have a room for ourselves. Just for that, it's worth the drive."

"And you'll need it furnished, won't you?" Jeanne counted all the things she could cross off her list. "You're sure now this will work for you, I mean, you're not just trying to make it easy for me?"

"This is perfect. I can't believe I didn't think of it sooner."

Lisa began showing up more often, ostensibly to help Jeanne pack, but she often lectured Jeanne on her trips to the beach, telling her it wasn't good to be running off by herself, spending so much time alone. "You need some company. You should come out with me some night. See people. Have a little fun."

They went to *Gunther's*, where Lisa made a few extra dollars shooting pool. She knew the young guys that hung out there were easy to beat. "I keep thinking they'll wise up, but they never turn down a game."

"Lisa, you don't see yourself. When you sidle up to them wearing that smile of yours, flashing those gorgeous blue eyes of yours, and say, 'Wanna play?' in that cajoling voice of yours, they don't care how much it will cost them."

"Oh, come on."

"Okay, maybe some of them might still think they can beat you because, you know, you're a girl, but most of them know better."

Jeanne wondered if Lisa knew she only went with her to see Joey's friends. Jeanne worried at first that it might make them uncomfortable to see her, but they always came over to say hello and fill her in on the latest gossip.

Like most others in town, they rarely mentioned Joey. Everyone acted as though his death was forgotten. People who used to cross to the other side of the street to avoid her or suddenly started searching the shelves at the supermarket when they spied her in the aisle now invited her to lunch and gave her little goodbye gifts, chatting away about her trip. Joey never entered the conversation. Jeanne had learned not to talk about him unless someone else did and that happened so seldom these days it often caught her by surprise.

In mid-August, Katy came home from her summer job in Martha's Vineyard to help with packing up the house before her fall semester began. In her organized way, Katy made quick work of the tedious job of moving anything extraneous from the bedrooms. Except for Joey's room. Without discussing it, Katy left that for Jeanne.

Jeanne came home from shopping one afternoon to find Katy kneeling on the front porch in front of a canvas propped against the wall. Bottles of acrylic paint, bowls and brushes, sat on a tray beside her. A vase of Jeanne's favorite flower, the Black-Eyed Susan, sat on a table next to the canvas.

"What are you doing?" Jeanne asked.

"What does it look like?"

"I mean, don't you need to get things ready for school?"

"I guess, but I thought this was more important. This way you'll have a memento when you move to Florida. I know how much you love these flowers."

All her pent-up emotion suddenly let go as Jeanne crumpled in tears before even trying to keep them at bay. She kept saying, "I'm sorry," as she tried to get control. The worried expression was back in Katy's eyes. She put her arm around her mother. "It's okay, Mom."

Jeanne's inner voice kept telling her to stop. Just Stop! But she continued to cry, as she kept repeating, "I'm okay, I'm okay."

A few days later, after Jeanne assured her she was perfectly fine, Katy took the train to the city to register for the upcoming semester. Peggy and John were out on the Sound, taking advantage of a sunny August day for one last outing before putting his clam boat up and heading for college.

In the empty house, Jeanne went upstairs with Gulliver behind her to pack what remained of Joey's things. She had made attempts before, but something or other would bring tears, making it impossible to get the job done. Now she couldn't put it off any longer. One of Lisa's friends would need the room.

A few weeks ago, with Anna's gentle persuasion, Jeanne had packed Joey's clothes in boxes for the thrift store. Over Anna's objection, Jeanne kept Joey's North Face jacket and the wide-ribbed green corduroy shirt. Anna had tried to dissuade her. "Don't you think they'll be too much of a reminder?" But Jeanne had learned to ignore Anna's conventional expectations. A reminder was the reason she kept them. She didn't say that to Anna, arguing instead she might have a need for something warm.

Now, as Jeanne sifted through his treasures, all the bits and pieces left behind, she welcomed the solitude. With no one in the house, it was easier to decide what to keep and what to let go. A framed photograph of Joey at his high school graduation sat among other framed photos of his friends. She remembered him in his blue cap and gown up on the stage, searching for them in the audience, and when he found them, waving his diploma over his head, beaming as though he had just won the Golden Fleece.

Jeanne sat on the bed feeling her energy drain away. Leaving the bedroom for another day, she climbed in the truck with the dog and headed for the ocean.

She and Gulliver strolled the Captree pier, watching charter boats return with their catch, a cloud of screeching seagulls welcoming them to the dock. She longed to be out on the water.

Leaving Gulliver with her mother, she flew down to Florida for Labor Day weekend. At the airport, she watched Gary come in from the street, nervously scanning the crowd looking for her, then reacting with pleasure when he saw her, relieving her worry it might not go well.

In the morning, they took the *Quest* for a sail, motoring out in a stiff breeze on a choppy sea, gulls wheeling above them, Jeanne breathing deep the sea air. They hoisted the sails and settled before the wind, all worries drowned out by the sound of halyards humming in the breeze, waves slapping the hull. She thought of Joey, lying prone at the bow watching the boat cut through the swells.

That night they had dinner on the deck at Gary's new yacht club, with the sun going down on the gulf, the red sky reflecting on the sea, the moist warmth of the air, the gentle breeze. He asked if she was getting everything done for her trip? Did the truck get a tune-up? He asked about tires? Did Tony check the tires?

"Not yet. I've been too busy packing and trying to get the house ready for Lisa. I haven't started on the truck yet."

"Do you have any idea how lucky you are? I know people who would give anything to go to Alaska. I wish I were going." He acted as though the decision had been made, ignoring the many times she had expressed her reservations.

As she listened, it suddenly hit her that he was desperate to talk her into the trip. She needed to end it. "Gary, stop. I'm not going to Alaska. That's not what I want. That was your idea, not mine. I only want to get to Florida, you know, be with you, get back the life we once had."

He slammed his fist on the table, rattling the glasses, forgetting for a moment where he was. "Damn it, what is your problem?" loud enough for everyone to hear. Startled by his anger, Jeanne leaned over with urgency and whispered. "Gary, everyone can hear you."

He looked around, glaring.

"I want to be with you, Gary. Is there something wrong with that?"

"Let's get out of here," he said, and called for the check.

The next morning he tried again to make the trip sound enticing, but his anger returned when she told him to stop trying to convince her. She wasn't going to Alaska. She had made up her mind.

His fury returned. "I'm sick to death of the constant disagreement. Why can't you do what I want? Why can't you just let me breathe?" He stormed out the door, and she heard the car race out of the driveway.

She would have called a cab and gone straight to the airport, but her flight wouldn't leave until late that night. Instead, she sat on the patio with her coffee, telling herself it was obvious he didn't want her there. She had to stop ignoring his behavior or trying to explain it away. She didn't know if he was involved with someone again, but she couldn't deny that was how he behaved.

Over the years, at times like this, she had teetered on the verge of divorce, but this time felt different. This time she meant it. She was tired of the constant knots in her stomach, afraid to speak her mind, hoping somehow things between them would improve. Having dreaded this moment for so long, it was actually a relief to have it finally decided.

She was thinking of the difficulty of telling her daughters when the sound of his car in the driveway caught her by surprise. He came in oddly subdued; the telltale knit brow, nervousness to his smile.

"I thought we might go to the beach and then get dinner at the club before your flight." He put his arms around her and told her how sorry he was about what he said. "I wanted this time together to be nice."

She didn't tell him what she had been thinking. She wanted so much to believe him. When he dropped her at the airport that evening, he asked her if everything was okay. Did she understand? If she would just take this trip, he could get things worked out. Right then, she should have asked him: what things? Susan came to mind, sitting in her kitchen, asking the same question.

On the flight home, she replayed the conversation in her mind regretting not asking him what things. There might have been a reasonable answer ending all her angst. On the other hand, she didn't think he'd tell her if there was someone else.

By the time she landed at JFK, she had decided to put the divorce on hold. She didn't want to give up on her marriage. Why not go to Alaska and give Gary the time he wanted? A cross-country road trip with the dog could be the respite she needed, an escape from the constant tension keeping her stomach in knots. From what Paul said, she could be there in ten days. If she stayed a week and spent two weeks getting back, she'd only need a little more than a month. If things hadn't mended by then, at least she could say she tried.

Chapter 14

In the days since Jeanne had returned from Florida, she had put all her energy into moving out of the house. She had just finished packing the last of her books, when an ominous clatter brought her to the bedroom window. Down in the driveway, hard drops of rain splashed white as they hit the pavement. *Damn. Why couldn't it wait until I finished?*

She struggled to pick up the heavy box. When she reached the head of the stairs, she could see that the front door in the downstairs hall was closed and uttered another quiet *damn*. She had intended to leave the door open to get through easily without having to put down the box, and then struggle to pick it up again.

At the bottom of the stairs, she moved close to the door and with both hands still grasping the box, she manipulated the knob with her fingers and freed the latch. With the door slightly ajar, Gulliver pushed with his nose to widen the space enough to squeeze through the gap. "Good Boy," she called after him as she used her shoulder to open the door wider.

Straining to carry the books in the heavy rain without slipping on the wet stairs taxed what little energy remained. She breathed a thankful sigh to find the camper door ajar. She would never have managed to open it without putting the box on the wet ground. Tired from a long day of climbing up and down stairs, she considered leaving the box on the rain-splattered camper floor, but, worried that the books might get wet, she climbed in the camper to put them away.

The camper had a perfect cubby within an arm's reach of the bed, with shelves deep enough and high enough to stand the books on end. Sliding doors would keep the books in place when the truck was moving.

From the top of the box she unpacked the blank notebooks her sister Ginger had given her to use for journals and stacked them one on top of the other. Next to the notebooks, she piled up the guidebooks, at least one for each Maritime Province and one called *The Milepost*, a guide for the Alcan, the road to Alaska.

Opposite the journals, she stood the books side by side, among them *The Spell of the Yukon and Other Verses* from her brother, Kenneth, with a copy of "The Road Not Taken" by Robert Frost tucked inside. From the bottom of the box, she took out *Ulysses* and held it for a moment, wondering if she should bother before she put it on the shelf. She didn't think she even liked it. *If I can't finish it this time, I might as well quit.*

She put the atlas and her maps in the remaining space, and then took a moment to look over everything. Satisfied, she climbed down from the camper and closed the door.

Back in the house, she changed out of her wet tee shirt and took a towel to her wet hair. She dried off Gulliver, then poured the remains of her Chianti into one of the juice glasses she had left for Lisa. With her wine and notebook, she headed to the shelter of the front porch to sit in the coolness brought on by the rain and let the tension drain away.

In his usual way, Gulliver followed her onto the porch. He never let her out of his sight these days. If he wasn't lying at her feet, he was sitting sentry at the truck door. For the past week, he had been watching the cartons going into the camper. Jeanne guessed he knew something was up and wondered if he worried he'd be abandoned. So many members of the pack had disappeared. "Don't worry, boy." She patted his head and rubbed his ears.

Resting her head on the back of the rocker she listened to the raindrops tap out a rhythm on the leaves of the trees. The pitter-patter blended with the louder tapping on the driveway and the more metallic notes playing on the camper roof. She closed her eyes to listen to the music.

A whiff of wet pavement brought memories of summers past when they gathered on the porch in the evening to watch the fireflies come out after the rain. "*Where have all the fireflies gone, a long time passing? Where have all the fireflies gone, long time ago?*" Gulliver perked up his ears as she sang; he drummed his tail on the porch floor.

"Where has everything gone, huh, boy?" Life had unraveled like a piece of sweater yarn caught on a nail, leaving a hole as it pulled away the wool that made the warmth. Empty chairs sat lonely beside her.

With little enthusiasm, she opened her notebook to her latest list to check one last time that she hadn't overlooked anything. She drew a line through *books*, and then moved to *haircut*. That didn't happen; she never found time for an appointment. She crossed off *haircut*, then circled *tires* writing *Ask Uncle Chris* on the line next to it. On her way north, she would drop her mother off in Massachusetts, and she'd then have him check their condition. If he thought she needed to replace them, she could get them in Buffalo when she stopped at Peggy's college, or maybe even in Toronto. They might be cheaper there.

Written at the bottom of the page, almost as an afterthought, *Joey's photo album* was still not checked. *Why is that not crossed off?* In a sudden panic, she ran down the steps to the camper. Unable to picture where it might be, she searched the cabinet under the sink and the one under the bench below the bookshelf. The contents, neatly organized, were easy to discern. When she opened the storage bin under the dining seat, she took everything out in the remote possibility the album lay hidden under something. It wasn't.

Back in the house, she ran to the den, her agitation mounting, in her mind, a picture of the album with the red cover. Nothing. *The garage.* She hurried down the stairs with Gulliver behind her. In the garage, dozens of boxes sat waiting for shipping to Florida, but when she took hold of the first box, she realized her mistake. She hadn't labeled them.

In one, she uncovered wine glasses, and in another, her demitasse cups. One turned out to be her art print books, among them Andrew Wyeth's. She was tempted to take it but reminded herself that, as much as she enjoyed going through the pages, it was too big for her bookshelf. She needed the space for the picture album.

With each wrong box, her panic grew that Gary might have

taken the albums with him when he drove a carful of his things to Florida. She didn't want the album in Florida. She might not end up in Florida. She often wondered if Gary would ever want her to come.

When she caught sight of the red album cover visible through the hand slot of a box in the back of the pile, she let out a shout, "There!" Gulliver followed with a short, sharp bark. A surge of energy helped her move the other cartons out of the way. She took the album out of the box and clasped it to her chest, still horrified that she might have driven off without it.

She carried the album to the camper and sat on the bench by the bookshelf, slowly turning the pages, remembering Joey's friends shyly coming toward her at the wake. Most of the funeral was a blur, but that moment remained a vivid scene: Tricia carrying the package, Vinnie with his arm around her waist, the rest of them stealing sideways glances at each other. Pictures of Joey filled the album with his delighted grin, mischief always in his eyes.

His friends had come by a few weeks ago to say goodbye. They sat on the back deck while Gulliver circled from one to the other, collecting ear rubs, his busy tail wagging. Jeanne kept extending the conversations, finding it hard to let them go.

She tucked the album on the shelf with the books and went back to the porch to retrieve her wine. The rain was letting up, the tapping intermittent. In the west, against the clouds low on the horizon, a parting burst of color streamed through the quieting rain. "Look at that, Gulliver. A red sky. We can only hope, huh, Boy?"

Jeanne woke to a raucous argument among the crows in the street below her bedroom window. "Not that again." Rolling over in her bed and clamping a pillow over her ears, she voiced her impatience with this early morning affront until a sudden thought caused her to open her eyes wide. Today was the day. Both anxious and eager to get on the road, she thanked the crows for the noisy wake-up call.

As she drank her coffee, she reread her note of instructions for Lisa, adding Gary's phone number along with a check to cover the cost of the moving van. She tried to shake off the nagging feeling that she'd forgotten something, but it wouldn't let go.

With nothing else to do, she climbed the stairs to her son's bedroom for one last look. A shaft of sunlight streamed through the bare window, falling across the empty bed, filling the room with morning brightness. She sat in the sun looking out at Gulliver in his usual place in the driveway, keeping vigil by the truck door.

After a while, she got up from the bed and opened the closet door. Not tall enough to see the top of the shelf, she stood on tiptoe and swept her hand across it. Nothing.

She crossed the room to the bookshelves. They were too high to reach the top, and when she contemplated getting the step stool from the basement, the voice in her head was back. *Enough. You know there's nothing there. Let it go.*

On the way out of the room, she hesitated at the door, resting her hand on the red wall, remembering when Joey said he wanted to paint his walls red, and she told him it had never occurred to her that he cared about the color of his walls. "I know" came back at her full of accusation and a teenage pout. Then he wanted a captain's bed.

"What's wrong with the one you have?"

"Nothing, it's just not a captain's bed," which made perfect sense to him.

Why didn't I get him the damn bed? Tears came the way they sometimes did these days, softly, without giving notice. Except for the sting, she hardly knew they were there.

The minute Jeanne opened the passenger door to the truck, Gulliver was in like a shot, forgetting he was achy with arthritis and normally needed a boost. He took possession of his space, curling up on the seat, averting his eyes. When Jeanne climbed in the driver's seat, he inched closer to her side. She sat for a moment looking at the garden steps, seeing Joey walking away, his brown jacket, his broad shoulders, his wavy brown hair, wondering still what he had meant to say.

She backed out of the driveway and continued backing up the street, far enough to position herself to see her house, and paused for one last long gaze. Pots of yellow and orange mums arranged to each side of the front door stood out in the dappled light of the morning sun. Last night's rain brought an extra luster to the mid-September green of the grass and the leaves of the oak trees climbing the hill in front of the porch.

She took one last glance at all the things that pleased her, the tieback curtains in the upstairs windows, the wrought-iron railing she painted with care, the wicker chairs with the yellow cushions. She pictured Peggy in the corner chair with her guitar on her knee, Katy in the other, lost in her latest novel, and Joey, sitting on the end of the railing his back against the post, entertaining everyone with his latest escapades. A few more minutes watching Joey on the railing and then, with a sigh, she nodded her head and put the truck in gear.

Chapter 15

Jeanne's spirits lifted when she saw Mary waiting on the landing of the front stoop beaming with pleasure, obviously excited about the trip. With lipstick on and her hair newly styled, she looked much younger than her 63 years.

Days before, when Mary had asked for a ride to Massachusetts, Jeanne had argued it was out of her way, until she realized it would put her just south of the Maritimes. Instead of going through Buffalo and missing her favorite part of Canada, she could drive straight north to the Atlantic Provinces. Her trip might be a few days longer, but she didn't think that mattered. She would start out on a happy note, pleased to have her mother's company.

Full of enthusiasm and eager to get going, Mary started down the stairs, suitcase in one hand, picnic hamper in the other, and no way to hold on to the railing. Jeanne jumped out of the truck and yelled at her to wait. "I'll get those, Mom. Stop! You can't walk down these rickety old stairs carrying all that stuff."

She grabbed hold of her mother's suitcase, but when she reached for the picnic hamper, Mary held on to it. "At least let me have one of them," she said with her customary sharp-eyed insistence.

A thumping tail welcomed Mary into the truck. "Gulliver, Gulliver, you lucky dog, you. What a trip you have in store for you. You take care of Jeanne now. You hear?"

The dog nestled his chin in her lap and looked up at her with his brown eyes in the way he had of making one think he understood every word. "Look!" said Mary, "He knows just what I'm saying, don't you, boy?"

As Jeanne pulled into the street, Mary wondered aloud where everyone was. "I guess I expected a crowd to wave goodbye."

"I'm glad no one's here, Mom." Her comment brought raised eyebrows from her mother. "I asked everyone not to come. I told them I'd be too busy. It's easier this way."

"But even the neighbors?"

"Can you imagine if everyone were here? It would take an hour to get down the block."

"Looks as though someone didn't get the message." Mary pointed at a figure at the far end of the street, waving at them to stop.

Jeanne pulled over and rolled down the window, "I thought we said no more goodbyes."

"I know, I know." Anna handed Jeanne a bottle of Chianti.

"Here. Did you think I'd let you get away without a bon voyage present? Don't open it until your first night camping. I want you to pour two glasses, one for you and one for me, and drink a toast 'To the open road!'" She finished with a flourish in her dramatic way. Then she handed Jeanne an envelope, saying, "See what it says: *Don't read until you pour the wine.* Promise."

Not wanting to get weepy, Jeanne offered a stilted "thank you." They tried to hug through the open truck window, but it was awkward, especially with Anna making an effort of her own to hold back tears. As she drove away, Jeanne glimpsed Anna in the side-view mirror, waving her arms. She stopped the truck and called back, "What?"

"Write, and I mean proper letters, and not a few quickie postcards either."

"Okay, I promise. No quickie postcards." Jeanne nodded her head and waved goodbye.

As they drove away, Mary asked if Jeanne wanted to stop at the cemetery. "I'm fine, Mom. I went after Mass on Sunday."

During the week before she left, Jeanne had been so busy with last minute errands, she had almost skipped the cemetery. She didn't think Joey would care. She always struggled with the thought that he wasn't actually there. But she set aside her skepticism and went to tell him she wouldn't be around for a while and hoped he didn't mind. She even suggested he ride along with her on her trip. She liked to think she felt his presence.

They headed east, hoping to catch the Port Jefferson Ferry to

Bridgeport without too long a wait. On the way Mary brought up the headstone. She promised to stay on top of it, to see that it got put in place, and to let Father Mahoney know when it would be installed so that he could plan for the blessing. She would let the family know and maybe one or two friends like Anna and Eileen. Jeanne was sorry she would be away for that and she could tell her mother was also.

Arriving early at the pier, they found few cars waiting to board, and no RVs in the camper lane. Safely aboard by noon, with Gulliver left in charge of the truck, they climbed the stairs to the top deck to sit in the warm September sun.

The breeze had brought the sailboats out, and white sheets chased a brisk wind in a perfect line across the water. Jeanne watched the boats tack east, mainsails full to starboard. Across the Sound, brightly colored spinnakers billowed ahead of returning boats. She thought of the Quest sitting in Florida and how great it was going to be to have the boat in the water all year always available in every season to hop on board and go for a sail.

Mary spread a kitchen towel on the bench between them and laid out corned beef sandwiches on paper plates. She poured coffee and handed Jeanne a cup, and as they drank it, Mary's expression suggested she had something to say.

"What, Mom?"

"You don't have to do this, you know. If you don't want to go on this trip, don't go."

Jeanne sighed. Now on her way, she needed encouragement, not reminders of her doubts. But it didn't surprise Jeanne that her mother knew her reservations. How could she not, with Jeanne finding excuse after excuse to put off her departure? She made light of it, playing her role of making it okay so her mother wouldn't worry.

"I know, Mom, but who gets an opportunity for a road trip like this? I have a camper to stay in, my dog by my side, and no schedule hanging over me. I can stop when I want, go when I want, and do whatever pleases me. I'm looking forward to some peace."

"But Alaska? I don't care what anyone says. That's too far. You'll be driving forever."

"No I won't Mom. If it's taking too long, I won't go that far. It's really only the Maritimes I'm interested in. You know how much I always wanted to spend time in the Maritimes. But I wouldn't mind seeing the Canadian Rockies if it comes to that."

"What I know is you'd rather be going to Florida. Isn't that true?"

"And I'll head there as soon as I think I've had enough. You know Mom, you said yourself, it was Dad's dream when he had the nine of us launched, to go on a road trip with you. Must be a part of him in me."

"You got that right." Mary looked off at the water, probably remembering Albert, who was only sixty when cancer ended his life. They never had their grand adventure.

Chapter 16

When Jeanne pulled into her Aunt Betty's driveway at three in the afternoon, Betty and Chris came down the steps with their daughter Christine to greet them. Betty's rosy Irish complexion and the warmth of her blue eyes made it easy to see she was Mary's sister, even though the two were not quite a perfect match. Betty was taller than Mary's four foot ten and her hair was short with more red than Mary's longer auburn tresses.

The family shared big hugs with Gulliver wagging his tail with excitement, his big doggy grin creasing his muzzle. He singled out Chris for attention, and Chris responded with welcomed pets.

That evening, during dinner, conversation was all about Jeanne's trip. Chris said she should go north on 89. "It's only four hours to Montreal. You can easily pick up the Trans-Canada highway there."

"But she's stopping at Fredonia to bring Peggy her things," Mary said.

"Well, then she better go straight west on the Mass turnpike, don't you think, Dad?" Christine's engaging smile and dark eyes closely resembled her father. She turned to Jeanne: "You can pick up the thruway when you get to New York."

"Actually, I wasn't planning any of that. When I leave here in the morning, I'm going straight to the Maritimes. I've got this perfect opportunity. I may never get there if I don't go now."

"But doesn't that make your long trip even longer?" asked her uncle. "It's as though you're covering half the globe. As I understand it, Toksook is as far west in Alaska as you can get. Almost to Russia, for heaven's sake. A regular odyssey, for heaven's sake."

"That's the thing, half the globe. I can't imagine actually going all the way."

"But wouldn't that be truly epic," said Christine, excited over the prospect. "Make your odyssey from the most eastern point of the continent to the most western point. Since you're going to the Maritimes, you could put your feet in the Atlantic, and when you get to this Toksook place, put your feet in the Pacific."

"You know, Christine, my friend Anna had the same idea. She thought I should collect some ocean water at each end of my trip, but what would I ever do with it?"

The family continued the conversation over the prospect of an odyssey, how many miles the trip entailed, and how many she could cover in a day, until Betty brought out the cake. The bon voyage message on the top, carefully lettered in chocolate, said, *May the road rise up to meet you.* Mary expressed her disappointment that they couldn't fit more of her favorite blessing and then recited it from start to finish putting extra feeling in *May God hold you in the palm of His hand.*

Christine gave Jeanne warm slippers for a present, telling her they'd come in handy in the camper when the weather got cold. The card she included had a copy of a silkscreen abstract by a Canadian artist of mountains rising steeply out of the water to tall craggy peaks. She said the picture reminded her of pictures of the mountains in Alaska. Jeanne read the note.

Dear Jeanne,

I'm with you on your journey. Write if you want. I'd love to hear from you. I think what you're doing is the best thing, the most courageous thing that people can do. If you ever feel too alone, you can call me reverse. I do think of you.

Christine

Jeanne felt the familiar catch in her throat. She wanted to tell her cousin how much she appreciated her encouragement, but all eyes were upon her and she was sure her voice would break. She managed a thank you and gave her cousin a hug.

When they finished their cake, Chris walked Jeanne out to the camper. "Let's check those tires. And I guess it won't hurt to check everything else. Right?"

"Sure, Uncle Chris, but really, I'm on top of it. The Skamper dealer covered everything with me, and my neighbor Tony went through everything again. I can even use the hydraulic lift to change the tire. Not that I'm expecting to change a tire, but just in case."

"I'm sure you can, but let's check to be sure nothing got overlooked. Then I can tell your mother everything is fine so she won't worry."

So that's why her mother had suddenly needed to go to Massachusetts, Jeanne thought. It was just like her to come up with such a scheme.

Chris walked around the truck, eyeing everything from front to back. "An F250, huh, looks like a '78. Pretty heavy duty, I think. Have you driven it much?"

"I went on a road trip to Quebec with my friend the summer we bought it."

"Good. How about this Skamper? A good company is it? I mean did you get what you expected? Everything working as it should?"

"It's great, Uncle Chris. It's so easy to manage."

He pulled on the tie-downs. "Glad to see these," he nodded.

"Gary had those added to keep the camper secure in high winds."

"Can you handle the propane tank?"

"Easy." She showed him how it disconnected from its port if she needed a refill.

"Promise me you'll never pull away from any place until you're sure you've turned off the propane?"

"I'm aware of that, Uncle Chris. Really."

The tires didn't impress him. "How long have you been driving on those tires?"

"Since we bought the truck two years ago. The last time I checked they have about 52,000 miles on them."

"We can go to my tire guy in the morning and replace them."

Jeanne assured him she planned to do that in Buffalo when she got to Peggy's college. When he looked at her with skepticism, she promised to call him when she had them replaced.

Inside the camper, he turned the crank to raise the roof and marveled at how easy it went up and how roomy the camper was with the top raised. "Lets in lots of light, I see." He unzipped one of the vinyl windows. "Screens, that's great, especially if it's hot and you need fresh air." He opened the refrigerator. "What did they say about the fridge? Will it stay cold without the propane running?"

"The temperature only changes about 4 degrees during the day. If it's good and cold before I go on the road, it should stay cold until I'm ready to stop for the night. At least that's what the dealer said."

"Good. I guess I can't really check the stove and heater without the propane on. Have you used them yet?"

"I did one night when I stayed at the beach."

"So they work, then?"

"Yes, Uncle Chris. Everything works."

He checked the hoses to the water tank, the tools in the toolbox, and even the first aid kit. Even the lock on the door. "Make sure you keep this locked, okay?"

Satisfied with his tour, he put his arm around her shoulder and said, "Now listen, Jeanne, if you ever have a problem, I want you to call me collect. Promise."

"Thank you, Uncle Chris, but I don't want you worrying."

"Oh Jeanne, I'm sure you will be just fine. If anyone can do this, you can."

The rest of the family joined them in the camper when they finished the dishes, and Chris assured Mary everything had his seal of approval. Squeezed around the dinette, they chatted until late in the evening.

Jeanne woke to a sunny morning in a positive frame of mind. She found her mother having coffee with her aunt at the breakfast table, watching the birds at the feeder that hung outside the window. She was disappointed to hear her uncle and cousin had already left for work. She would have liked to thank them and share a heart-felt hug goodbye.

The three of them chatted about everything but the trip until a long pause in the conversation prompted Jeanne to take one last sip of her coffee and say it was time to leave. Mary and Betty stood in the driveway, side by side, waving her off with matching smiles, their brave smiles never reaching their eyes, smiles pasted there because the occasion required smiles, but their hearts not in it; sadness filled their eyes and the ever-present apology.

Jeanne drove down the pretty neighborhood street, Gulliver sitting up tall, watching out the window with an air of alertness as if he sensed something different. The morning sun beamed on the neat suburban houses, washing them in warmth. She drove past the carefully tended lawns, the affluence apparent in the street-side plantings, the manicured driveways, the drapes in the windows. At the stop sign, she caught her mother and her aunt reflected in the side-view mirror. They had walked to the edge of the driveway and stood in matching postures with hands still raised, waving goodbye. Jeanne rolled down the window and put out her arm to wave back, then turned the corner, and they were gone.

Not long after, she came to the sign for I-95. "Here we go, Gulliver, just you and me, buddy." A few thumps of his tail told Jeanne he heard as she drove onto the highway and out of her life as it was, with only a vague notion of where the road would take her and no idea what the future held in store.

Part Three

The traveler has to knock at every alien door to come to his own...

Rabindranath Tagore

Chapter 17

Jeanne left Stow with her romantic notions of traveling only on back roads set aside. Her uncle had talked her into skipping the country roads in the Boston suburbs and taking I-95 to US-1. Farther north in New Hampshire and Maine, she was more likely to find the quaint villages with the tall church steeples and the sailboats bobbing at anchor in small, peaceful harbors: the quintessential New England images she wanted to capture with her camera.

Somehow she missed US-1. When she came to a sign for *West Beach*, the word *Beach* didn't sound right. She pulled over to check her map, and, sure enough, she had driven right past the connection. Although she had only been on the road for about an hour, she argued with herself that she had good reason to stop. Gulliver was restless and could use a walk, and here was a beach right when they needed it.

With summer over and kids back in school, only a handful of people walked along the shore. Jeanne gave in to the urge to get her feet wet in the lapping surf. Gulliver, in a playful mood, pranced alongside her. She played with him as she strolled to the end of the beach and back. By then it was time for lunch, and all she had to do was walk the few steps to her home on wheels to get something to eat.

She took the sandwich she made and her blanket back to the beach along with her guidebooks for Maine and the Maritimes. With no telephone calls interrupting and no one needing rescue from a problem, she could finally concentrate on where she was going, something she had yet to pin down.

A story featuring the Cabot Trail with pictures of high bluffs overlooking the sea made the destination number one on her list. The road headed north on the west side of Cape Breton Island, then connected with the Trans-Canada Highway going south on the east side. She imagined a feast of spectacular ocean views. As she turned the pages, she saw that a ferry went from Eastport to Deer Island, New Brunswick. The perfect shortcut.

Gulliver, who had been cheerfully clambering over the big rocks on the east end of the beach, came and spread out on the blanket beside her. The old inertia took hold as she watched the gently breaking waves. Why not stay the night?

At a campground down the road from the beach with a view of the water, she climbed into her loft bed early in the evening. With all the bustle and fuss behind her and the sea air wafting in her open camper window, she drifted into a deep restful sleep. When she headed for Maine the next morning, fresh and relaxed, she was full of purpose. "We're actually doing this, Gulliver." He moved closer to her in the seat.

North of Freeport, Jeanne followed US-1, looking for territory she recognized from her road trip with Anna in that summer before Joey died. Their first night in Maine, hungry for a special dinner, they had followed *Best Lobster in Town* signs which led them well off the main highway and down ever-narrowing country roads. Whenever she and Anna thought they were lost, another *Best Lobster in Town* sign conveniently appeared.

They kept telling themselves it must be an elegant restaurant on the water and hoped it wasn't too expensive, but when they reached the end of the road, they found a busy warehouse on a wharf piled high with lobster pots. Inside the wide overhead door sat a single picnic table covered with a red-checked tablecloth. Above the door was a replica of the signs they had followed: *Best Lobster in Town.* They fell into a fit of laughter. That night they dined on the most delicious lobster Jeanne thought she ever had.

Lost in her memories, Jeanne wondered if she and Anna might ever be as carefree as they were then. Anna was funny and had a knack for getting past Jeanne's serious nature, but it seemed since Joey died, Anna's happy disposition had disappeared.

On impulse, she turned off US-1, hoping to get closer to the ocean. Route 186 took her to Arcadia National Park at the end of the Schoodic Peninsula, where she followed the park road to Schoodic Point. Before her lay the storied rock-bound coast of Maine, framed in the iconic, tall, pointed firs.

A wide formation of smoothed, pink-tinged granite stretched toward the water, with massive slabs of the leveled plain sometimes dropping in steps until the stony floor ended at a cliff with a sheer drop to the sea. Darker, narrow rock-filled seams ran through the granite as though long-ago streamlets of flowing magma had frozen in place. At each of the far ends of the point, a wall of conifers hemmed in the rocky plain like columns of tall green soldiers marching to the sea. With a loud whump, waves crashed against the granite wall, splashing spray skyward.

Jeanne and Gulliver walked to the edge of the shelf and watched the gulls sweep, circle, climb and dive. She held her face to the blowing wind and relished the misty ocean air, the taste of the sea.

Not twenty feet from her, out over the water, a gull furiously back peddled with its wings, hovering a moment before dropping like a rock, headfirst to the water. In the next second, it came up with a crab and deposited it on a rocky ledge ten feet below where she stood. The gull stood beside its catch like a sentry, watching the crab on its back, its legs flailing, clawing the air, desperately reaching for purchase to flip itself over on its belly and scuttle to safety in the sea. Then the gull reared its head and jabbed its beak in the crab's belly, waited a moment, and did it again. Jeanne recoiled. Feeling helpless, she walked away unable to watch.

As she walked to the camper, a family with two children scrambled out of their car and headed to the cliff to throw treats to the gulls. The squabbling colony, wheeling and screeching and fighting among each other, soon had the family engulfed in a flurry of wings and noise. When they finished their happy outing, the children waved to her as they walked to their car.

Watching them drive away, Jeanne realized she and Gulliver had the whole place to themselves. "Gulliver, let's stay here tonight!" She raised the camper top, put on Joey's North Face jacket for protection from the sea wind, happy she hadn't given in to Anna's advice to give it away. She brought her beach blanket with her to spread on the smooth rock and her notebook to write letters.

Anna was first on her list, and that made her remember Anna's bottle of wine, the one she promised to open the first night. This was day two, so she returned to the camper to retrieve it. Back on her blanket wind kept fluttering the papers. She wasn't able to write withou holding the pages in place while at the same time holding her wine glass to keep it from toppling over, so she took everything back to the camper. Sheltered from the wind, she appreciated her rolling cabin. She set her writing paper aside to feed Gulliver and fix a proper supper, so it wasn't until later in the evening that she got back to the letters.

Dear Anna,

I wish you could see this beautiful spot I found. It looks like someone's ode to Maine. It's right on the water on a rocky cliff. I know you'd love it. I'm spending the night here, and Gulliver and I have the entire place to ourselves. I can't believe my luck. How many times on our trip had we hoped for a place all to ourselves?

You'd laugh in hysterics if you were here right now. In only a few hours, I have covered every available surface with clutter. The sink is full of dishes that need washing, the table covered with odds and ends of kitchen things that need a home like the lobster cutlery set someone gave me as if I need lobster cutlery. Gulliver and my clothes lie strewn across my bed. It wasn't easy to get him up there, but I piled up the dinette cushions for him to climb on and gave him a boost. He's so delighted with his perch, and it helps to have him out of my way. I am in my usual state of disarray. Why don't you meet me in Nova Scotia and come to my rescue? Kidding aside, I wish you were here. I've let "am I really doing this?" creep in a few times, but "yes, I'm really doing this" has taken over, and I'm excited to get going. Except for when I'm not, but you know how that goes. Thanks for the wine. As ever, you provided just the right touch.

Love you, my friend.

Jeanne

Jeanne had turned her attention to the job of cleaning up and putting everything in its designated place when she came upon Anna's card and remembered she promised to read it when she had her wine. Folded up inside the card was Anna's long letter.

Dear Jeanne,

I am putting down on paper what I could not say because I don't think I could get the words out. I'll miss you a lot, that's for sure. Our friendship has come a long way these last 8 years and now it's like a chapter in my life is coming to a close. I know you'll be coming back in a few months, but it won't be to the house so things will be different. I try to think our relationship will be the same, but I can't imagine how. I'm sure you will be a different person when you finish your trip, how could you not, and it will change a lot of your attitudes. Joey's death has changed your family more than anyone could have imagined. I didn't realize it myself, but thinking back on a lot of things, I can see the changes. Maybe it would have happened anyway. Sometimes I'm so sad seeing how everyone has gone in different directions with the family scattered to the four winds.

I wish you had shared your feelings with me. We never really talked about Joey, and I so wanted to do that. I can't let you go without telling you how I felt, still feel about Joey. You need to know how much I shared your grief. My heart broke that day. I've spent many days crying my eyes out until they were red and swollen, and there was no one I could turn to for help. Nothing has affected me the way this has. Ever. Ever. I'm wondering if I should send you this letter at all. I don't want to make you feel bad bringing it all up, but I just had to let you know. I had to stay up to write this because I felt something was missing. Jeanne, I want you to have a wonderful trip. You said goodbye and you're gone, and I don't want you to let this spoil your trip. Please drive slow. Be careful of people. You're too trusting. I know I sound like your mother, but you know I'm right. I hope this letter doesn't ruin our friendship. I'll never forgive myself.

Anna.

The letter left Jeanne deeply stunned. Why hadn't she recognized Anna's grief? Why hadn't they talked? She knew Anna was fond of Joey. She always doted on him. Jeanne remembered them at family barbeques, or out on the sailboat, how they'd banter back and forth, the two of them laughing at some shared amusement. How much fun they brought to everything.

Anna's words about the family brought Jeanne to tears. She never realized anyone noticed how much they had come apart.

She considered tearing up the letter she just wrote, but decided instead to add a P.S.

Anna, I wrote this letter before I read your card. I am so sorry I didn't realize how much you were hurting. How sad and inept we all were, confused about what we should say to each other. I am so regretful that I wasn't more aware. I wish we had talked. It deeply moved me when I read what you had to say. Right now I am overwhelmed but when I think my feelings through, I'll write.

Love, Jeanne

Jeanne's late-night caffeine kept her awake. She sat amid the clutter remembering the moments when Anna suddenly left the room for some vague reason, like others in her life who behaved much the same. Too sad to write more letters, she busied herself puttering about, bringing some order to her one-room space until well past midnight when she pushed Gulliver over and crawled into bed.

Chapter 18

In the middle of the night, Gulliver's barks startled her awake. He had jumped down from the bed and stood with his nose to the door. Someone was knocking, calling loudly, "Park Police, open the door." He added, "And hold on to that dog."

Jeanne did her best to quiet Gulliver while struggling to attach his leash. When she opened the door, there stood the ranger in all his impressive regalia: a handsome wide-brimmed park ranger hat, with his shiny badge, gold buttons, and black leather belt gleaming in the light from the camper. "You can't stay here. You need to go to a DCA."

Still half asleep, Jeanne couldn't understand what he said. "A DCA?"

"A designated camping area," he said, as he watched the dog who had stopped his barking and was now issuing a quieter but more menacing growl.

"Can you tell me where that is?"

A stream of directions came from the trooper, hurried by his distraction with the dog. He mentioned routes and turns and miles, all of which Jeanne missed in her sleepy condition.

"Can you show me on the map? I'm not familiar with any of those places."

He hesitated, mulling it over while keeping his eyes glued to the dog, who looked as though he might pounce at any moment. "On second thought, you probably should stay here for the rest of the night. There's a dense fog, and you shouldn't be driving around if you're not familiar with the area. Just make sure you're gone when I get back in the morning."

"Thank you. I appreciate that. I'll make sure to leave first thing." She listened as the ranger drove away, and then gave Gulliver a pet. "Good boy. Good boy."

But Jeanne didn't leave the first thing as she had promised. She was up early enough, thinking of Anna and Joey when through the camper window she saw the dawn unfolding across the sky. She made a quick cup of coffee and carried it out into the chilly morning air. The scattered clouds in the east had turned a deep pink, announcing the coming of the sun. Like a crescendo, waves crashed against the rock wall and sent spray high in the air.

Invigorated by the roar of the surf and the gulls' noisy calls, Jeanne sat on a stone step and watched the tiniest glimmer of gold on the horizon. The image expanded in slow motion as it climbed out of the sea, turning the water red and casting a rosy gleam on the east-facing facets of stone.

By the time the morning celebration had ended, cars had come, and Schoodic Point wasn't hers anymore. She made quick work of getting the camper ready to leave, then climbed into the driver's seat and got back on the road.

On her way to Eastport to catch the ferry, Jeanne saw a sign for Corea and made a quick detour. The little hamlet was on her list of memorable places to visit. She and Anna had stopped there on their road trip, and Anna was much on her mind.

When Jeanne reached the quiet village on the bay, she remembered why she and Anna had found it so charming. Well off the beaten path, Corea escaped the ugly trappings of contemporary life. She walked along the high wharf that stood tall on pilings exposed at low tide through the clutter of colorful buoys and lobster pots stacked high against sun-bleached clapboard shacks. Gulliver traipsed along by her side, taking everything in like a seasoned tourist.

In the quiet harbor, sailboats rode on their anchors. A skiff left a soft ripple in the still water, the whirring of its outboard motor the only sound disturbing the quiet. Steeped in the heavy scent of the sea, she looked across the harbor to a picture-perfect scene of white and weathered clapboard buildings randomly climbing the hill. A tall white church steeple rose in their midst.

She took a moment to savor the view before going in search of the shop with the delicious donuts she and Anna had had with their morning coffee only to find it was closed for the season.

Two hours later she pulled into the small town of Eastport, feeling as though she had left New England behind her. Gone were the picturesque, weathered clapboard buildings. On the main street, three-story structures of dark brick stood like a fortress in perfect order.

It took little time to discover the ferry office; more time to realize no one was there. From a passerby, she learned that the ferries had stopped running days ago.

Back in the truck, her momentary disappointment set aside, she checked her guidebook and saw that the nearest border patrol station was at Calais, less than an hour away, and open all day which meant she had plenty of time to explore the town and get something to eat. Still hungry for a donut, she headed back to a shop she had passed on Main Street.

The simple sign above the door said *Bakery*. Tall narrow windows lined the front of the stern-looking brick building. Behind the ornately framed panes, blue-checkered cafe curtains gave the shop a softened face. Through the windows, she could see people sitting at tables. She could get breakfast here.

Inside, sunshine streamed in the windows warming the creamy white walls. An aroma of freshly baked bread and sizzling bacon met her at the door, pulling on deep recesses of long-ago memories of her grandmother, which only strengthened when the waitress walked in from the kitchen.

Like her grandmother, she was plump with rosy cheeks and barely 5 feet tall. She wore an updated version of the housedress her grandmother had worn in the same sort of small, printed cotton with the same no-nonsense white apron; the strings wrapped around her middle and tied in front. Her flat silver hair was wound in a bun, which sat on the nape of her neck. She looked at Jeanne with her grandmother's blue eyes, only more of a search in them than a twinkle.

Jeanne was four years old again, back in Brooklyn in Mom's house as everyone called it, lying awake in the early morning dark, listening to soft murmurs of people talking somewhere deep in the house below. Inching her way to the edge of the bed, she'd take care not to wake her little sister next to her and her baby brother in his crib. She'd tiptoe down the hall, then down the first flight of stairs to the hall below with the thick carpet and then the next flight, as the smell of sizzling bacon wafted up from the kitchen. When she reached the bottom step, she'd sit to wait for her aunt and her granduncles to leave for work.

Her granduncle Corney always left first. "There ye are, me Blackie," he'd call to her when he saw her sitting on the stairs. She didn't know then why he called her Blackie, but she learned when she got older that he loved her dark eyes and brown hair. In a family of blue eyes and strawberry blonds, she and her father and her Aunt Isabel were the only ones who looked like him. When he called her Blackie, she could tell that it pleased him. She'd wrap her arms around her knees and shrink into the steps.

Out of the top drawer of the credenza, he'd take a handkerchief and stuff it in his back pocket before going down the hall to get his lunch pail out of the icebox which stood by the door to the street for the iceman's convenience. Then he'd turn back her way and give a salute.

Aunt Virginia soon followed, with her red hair piled in a high pompadour. She'd stash her handkerchief in her purse and wave as she rushed down the hall, high heels clicking on the bare wood floor. Quiet Uncle George was always last because he washed the dishes before he left. He took great pains with his handkerchief, looking in the mirror over the credenza, as he fussed to arrange the points lined up just right in his jacket pocket much the way she often watched her father do the same thing.

When they were gone, she'd tiptoe into the kitchen glad her sister and brother were still asleep. Mom would say, "Good Morning, Glory," hugging Jeanne with a warm smile. Jeanne sat in the kitchen in her grandmother's soft chair by the furnace near the coal bin to wait while her grandmother sliced thick slabs of white bread and dropped them into the hot bacon grease to fry.

She loved sitting with her grandmother at the big dining room table, just the two of them, having breakfast together, fried bread and tea, with an extra sugar cube in her cup, and her grandmother's warning with one finger over her lips, not to tell anyone. Then she'd follow her grandmother's lead, and carefully pour the contents of her cup into her saucer, from which she'd daintily sip her tea.

Jeanne considered requesting a slice of bread fried in bacon fat when the waitress asked for her order, but she let it pass. No one did that anymore. Later, on the way back to the truck, with a fresh loaf of unsliced bread, she stopped at a butcher shop to get a package of bacon and asked if they knew of a place she could park for a while with a view of the bay. She wanted to write a few more letters to mail before she crossed the border.

"You can get great views at Shackford Head State Park, but if you're heading north, there's a road on the right as you drive out of town. Drive as far as you can go and just pull over when you see the water."

High on a hill, Jeanne found a spot amidst tall firs with a beautiful view in the distance of Passamaquoddy Bay sparkling in the sun. As the day moved into late afternoon, she sat at her table writing letters to Katy and Peggy with the camper door open so she could keep an eye on Gulliver. He had settled in a spot beneath a tree where the sun came through to warm the ground, but a noisy squirrel harassed him, chattering away. Gulliver didn't treat it with the usual outrage he reserved for squirrels. Jeanne wondered if his arthritis might be a problem from being cramped up in the truck too long.

When long shadows from the late afternoon sun added to the idyllic setting, Jeanne felt the quiet peace that had eluded her for so long. Since the day had mostly passed, she didn't see any reason the border couldn't wait.

In the morning, a hint of light peaked through the canvas covering the window by Jeanne's bed, and when she rolled up the window cover, she saw the sun repeating the spectacular show of the previous morning. A blazing pink to orange sky spread across the horizon, reflecting on the water. She hated to move and spoil the moment.

Gulliver had no interest in waiting, making it obvious he wanted to go out. He was perkier than yesterday and did not appear to be in pain. When Jeanne opened the door, he headed straight for his tree and sniffed around, probably searching for yesterday's squirrel. Jeanne fussed over their breakfast, frying the bacon and then frying the bread in the bacon fat, thinking again of Mom.

She remembered how much she missed her grandmother after her father came home from the war, and they moved two hours away from Mom's house at the end of a long highway. On Sundays, they would all climb in the old Ford and head for town, Jeanne in the back seat with her sister, Ginger, and brother, Kenneth; her mother in the front seat with her new baby brother, Jackie, on her lap; her father at the wheel.

They were always running late, but that didn't stop her father's repeated escapes from the highway to find a place to quench his thirst. Back on the road, he'd speed past other cars to make up for lost time, her mother calling on Jesus, then more loudly, "Jesus" and "Jesus, Albert, Jesus!" as her father sang away.

They'd arrive to everyone there before them, uncles and aunts and new baby cousins. While everyone hugged and kissed, her grandfather led her father aside and sent him up the stairs to find a place to sleep it off.

Through the crowd, Jeanne got a quick glimpse of Mom leaning over the stove in the kitchen. Most Sundays she'd cook roast leg of lamb and serve it with mountains of mashed potatoes smothered in gravy. She'd hear Mom's laughter at the big table and wish she were sitting beside her, instead of stuck in the corner at the kids' table, in charge of her younger siblings and cousins who sat squeezed together on the ironing board spanned between two chairs to make a bench.

When it was time to go, she'd suffer the sharing of her grandmother with everyone lined up before her for hugs, waiting patiently for her turn to feel her grandmother's plump arms wrapped tightly around her, to relish a brief whiff of her sweet scent.

Gulliver's bark startled Jeanne from her thoughts. He had discovered a squirrel high in a tree and the two were having an argument. The peace and beauty of the spot tempted her to linger another day, but she had letters to mail, and thought she should shop for groceries before she crossed the border, and since all of that meant putting everything away, rolling down the top, securing the clamps and turning off the propane, once on her way, she might as well keep going.

A phone booth outside the grocery store reminded her she hadn't called Gary.

"Where are you? I've been waiting for you to call."

She covered the highlights of the past four days and for once, Gary let her talk. When he asked about Gulliver, she told him how his arthritis bothered him. "I gave him Bufferin with his supper, which helped, but too much of that won't be good for him. It's probably not such a good idea to keep him cooped up in the truck all day."

"Gulliver will be fine. He loves riding in the truck. How long will it take to get to Peggy's?"

"I'm not sure. I'm not in any hurry. I'm just getting started, and I want to enjoy every mile."

"That's what I want you to do. No need to rush." Gary reiterated his usual litany, extolling the trip and saying how happy he was for her, how he wished to be going with her, but he needed time to get everything in order, his old argument that he never fully explained.

It was still early in the day when Jeanne headed for the border. The brick gave way to clapboard, and New England returned in the neatly painted houses, the flowers still blooming in the late summer gardens. An old couple, rocking on their porch, watching the traffic go by, seemed weathered and gnarled like the spindly trees that clutched the rocky ledges along the coast. Jeanne wondered what they might think if she were to pull over to have a chat.

"Here we go, Boy," she said as they crossed the bridge over the St. Croix River and pulled up to the window at the Canadian border crossing station. Gulliver sat politely beside her. She had his health certificate ready, but the border guard said she only needed that to get back into the States. Jeanne told him she was heading for Fundy National Park, and he passed her through with hardly a word.

Chapter 19

*E*arly in the afternoon she came to the campground on the Bay of Fundy and was surprised it wasn't the natural, woodsy setting she expected. Instead, she found green lawns neatly manicured like a golf course and carefully delineated parking places, with picnic tables and fire pits arranged the same at each slot. When a park ranger came her way, she hopped out of the truck with Gulliver to meet him.

"New York," he said, acknowledging the license plates. "What brings you up here so late in the season?" He smiled with a friendly welcome.

Jeanne kept it simple. "I'm on vacation."

"Traveling alone are you?" and to Jeanne's "yes," he said, "No doubt about it, you ladies from the States have your independent ways. Look at you driving a truck no less. Well, I say more power to you. If you can drive around the likes of New York, you shouldn't have any trouble up here. I went on holiday to New York once. Don't imagine I'll go again. Those New Yorkers drive too fast. Run you off the road, they will."

Jeanne wanted to defend her fellow drivers, but he was going on about his problems with New York, and she didn't want to interrupt him.

"And the transports. If the speeders don't get you, the transports surely will, rumbling down the road the way they do, bent for hell."

"Transports?"

His strange look suggested everyone knows what transports are. "The big trucks that haul the big containers."

"Oh, the 18-wheelers."

He laughed at that. "I guess we speak different English, eh?"

Gulliver had run off to explore, and when she called him back, the park ranger wanted to know how he got the name, Gulliver. She had told this story many times. How the dog was a Christmas present for her son when he was eight years old, how he used to watch a cartoon show on TV called *The Adventures of Gulliver*, and how there was a fluffy white dog named Tagg, on the show that Joey loved. "We all expected him to name the dog, Tagg, but for some reason of his own he preferred Gulliver."

"So, how come you have the dog if it belongs to your son?"

Jeanne wished he hadn't asked that question. She felt the way she did when she was asked that other question—"How many children do you have?"—and never knew how to answer. Should she say two? Should she say three? If there were social conventions for the proper thing to say, she had never learned what they were. Although she tried to avoid making people uncomfortable, most of the time it seemed easiest to tell the simple truth. But it was difficult to say the words and it didn't always turn out well.

She took a deep breath and said, "My son died a few years ago in an automobile accident. Gulliver and I have become good friends." As she spoke, Jeanne was looking down at the dog. When she looked up at the ranger, his sunny disposition had disappeared.

He turned away, shaking his head. "It's a sad business. A sad business."

He headed back to the office, then turned back to say, "If you need anything," shaking his head again, looking down at the ground. It was all she could do to maintain her composure fighting the ache in her throat. She hadn't meant to open that door. She'd try to remember not to let it happen again.

The next morning the soft patter of rain on the metal roof of the camper woke her to a dismal day. Later, passing through Moncton on her way to Nova Scotia, Jeanne found the town dreary in the rain. Signs promoting the tidal bore were everywhere; it seemed to be the town's one claim to fame. A crowd gathered beneath umbrellas by the river gave her a clue she had found the right place to watch the event. People smiled and pointed, chatting back and forth. Places to park along the road were filling up quickly, so Jeanne grabbed the first available space.

She sat waiting in the truck with Gulliver, with passing pickup drivers giving a friendly wave much like motorcycle riders greeted each other at home. She took to waving back. In her side mirror, she watched a Winnebago that had passed, suddenly make a u-turn and come back, pulling over to park up the road a few spaces in front of her. A youthful-looking gray-headed couple wearing matching L. L. Bean red check wool shirts, made their way toward her with a big black Labrador on a leash. Their friendly smiles made her wonder if she knew them. They walked right up to the truck window as if they were long-lost friends.

"Saw your plates. We're from New York, too." Somehow, running into someone from home did away with the usual reserve of strangers. They acted like neighbors talking over the back fence. The couple, Rita and Tim Stout, had recently retired from teaching. They had deliberately waited to start their trip until after the kids were back in school.

Gulliver kept nudging Jeanne to get out, so she put his leash on and joined the Stouts walking the dogs. The black Lab's name was Morgan, and he looked just as old and as friendly as Gulliver.

The usual conversation ensued over what each was doing, and Jeanne mentioned her invitation to Alaska. The comment usually ended with one of two observations, either the dubious: "You're driving by yourself to Alaska?" or the impressed: "How brave you are to be driving by yourself to Alaska."

This time it was the first observation and came from Rita, who inserted "that big truck" in her remark. The reference always amused Jeanne, as though she were driving an 18-wheeler, or the task required a magical quality other than turning the key in the ignition and putting one's foot on the gas. Her standby answer had become, "No, not exactly. I have my dog with me," which usually left everyone with nothing else to say. This time she added, "But I probably won't go all the way to Alaska. I don't think I'll have enough time." Tim looked at her with a hint of something curious in his smile. Jeanne wondered what he was thinking.

In the distance, the burbling sound of rushing water drew the crowd closer to the riverbank. They craned to see the wave as it came around a corner into view and pushed upstream through steep mud banks. The river churned to a creamy froth. It may have been the dreary day causing Jeanne's dismal mood, but when the tidal bore rolled over the brown, silty Petitcodiac, she felt as though she had wasted her time. Not so the rest of her fellow bore tide watchers, who clapped and cheered when the wave rolled past them, Tim and Rita among them, making up for Jeanne's failure to show appreciation with their enthusiastic cheers.

When the event ended and the crowd began to thin, Rita suggested they exchange addresses promising to keep in touch as though their shared few minutes made them lifelong friends. Jeanne doubted she'd ever see them again.

Instead of getting on the main highway, Jeanne headed east out of town along a secondary road that followed the coast. She came to a small town beach with parking on a bluff overlooking the Northumberland Strait and enjoyed an early supper looking out at the sea. Later, she climbed down a long staircase from the bluff to the beach and took Gulliver for a stroll along the red sandy shore. It was the perfect setting to spend the night and then watch the sunrise over the water in the morning, but a sign said it was only available for day-use.

Jeanne contemplated camping anyway, except she wasn't sure what to expect from the Canadians. They might be fussy about tourists following the rules. When she finally got back on the road, it was already getting dark.

Driving along in the failing light, squinting to search out a welcoming campground, she was thinking of spending the night on the side of the road when a sign for Loch Lomond Campground came to her rescue.

She left early in the morning, heading for Cape Breton Island in a happier frame of mind than the day before, early enough for a leisurely drive. The truck hummed along nicely, making good time until Jeanne encountered a traffic jam just outside Port Hastings. Inching along with the tiresome upshifting and downshifting, Jeanne finally came upon the cause of the delay. On the other side of the highway an 18-wheeler lay on its side against the guardrail as though it had just decided to take a nap, the guardrail serving as a convenient pillow.

Once past the truck, the traffic thinned, the road wound around curves and climbed up and down hills. The fog that hung in the Cape Breton highlands crept its way to the road hampering her ability to see where she was going. Behind her, an 18-wheeler, riding practically on her bumper, added to her stress, prompting her to pull over to let him pass. When the big truck got in front of her, she could see its taillights better than the road, so she followed it to the Whycocomagh campground.

She couldn't believe who was there. The people she had met in Moncton, with Morgan beside them, stood by their Winnebago waving hello. Rita and Tim, delighted to see her again, invited her to park right next to them, but she had her eye on the lane that meandered up to the top of the hill. "Thanks, but I wanted to be up high. I bet I have a view of the water from up there. Why don't you join me?"

Tim shook his head, "We're already hooked up here. Maybe we'll walk up later and say hello."

Jeanne found her spot on the hillside more to her liking than Fundy Park. Her door opened onto a path, which wound through a grove of old apple trees and led to a mountain trail. With Gulliver leading the way, Jeanne worked her way up Salt Mountain through the hardwood forest on a trail edged with woodland ferns, relishing the earthy scent of the woods. Patches of leaves had taken on autumn colors, hinting at the beauty to come.

Gulliver diligently moved up the hill before her, often stopping to wait for Jeanne. In time, they came out of the woods to a lookout on the edge of a slope with a breathtaking view of the blue water of Bras d'Or Lake. A moss-covered rock provided a place to rest. Gulliver stretched out at Jeanne's feet, catching his breath as she stroked his back.

Hours later, on the way back to the camper, watching Gulliver's easy trot, she saw how happy he was in the woods instead of cooped up in the truck where he had been every day for almost a week. Tomorrow she'd hang around for a while and treat him to another excursion.

Chapter 20

In the morning, planning to stay put for the day, Jeanne lingered over her coffee before heading out with Gulliver to climb the trail. They stopped only briefly for the beautiful view of Bras d'Or Lake before continuing along the loop which brought them back to where they started. Jeanne had been tempted to take the extended route to the top of the mountain, but she worried the steepness might be too much for Gulliver.

With the rest of the afternoon ahead of her, Jeanne got out her big pot planning a proper dinner for a change. She was standing at the stove, stirring spaghetti sauce, watching all the comings and goings down the hill through her camper window, when a brand-new-looking 1980 two-tone brown Chevy pickup came up the drive. A sleek blue kayak stretched across the top from the cab roof to the tailgate.

The truck passed the cut-off to Jeanne's camping spot and continued around the curve to park at the picnic shelter where a young man with a beard got out and unloaded his gear. He had a dog with him. "Company, Gulliver; let's go have a chat."

She walked down the lane and as she got close, it occurred to her the dog might not be friendly, so she put Gulliver's leash on, just in case. About 10 yards away, she stopped in her tracks, feeling the old rush, the weakness in her knees. His brown wavy hair brushed his dark brown leather jacket. Taking a deep breath she deliberately ignored the sensation and continued down the lane.

He turned when he heard her coming and, after her polite hello, he introduced himself with a warm smile. "Hi, I'm Sean. Nice dog you have, part German shepherd, I'd guess."

"Yes, he's a collie-shepherd cross. And yours?"

"Oh, he's just a mutt, you know, Heinz 57 varieties, that's him." They talked about their dogs, how old they were, how long they had them, their charming idiosyncrasies. Eventually, they got to the dogs' names.

"Heinz. How clever." She laughed, but he didn't remark that he noticed anything odd about Gulliver's name.

"Just to let you know, I haven't taken over the picnic shelter. I just parked here because it's cold and windy on the mountain, and I only have a tent. You're welcome to use the shelter for your dinner. I mean, don't let me get in your way." And without skipping a beat, he said, "Come by later and join me for a drink."

Jeanne surprised herself when she said she would. "And I'll bring my wine." She was pleased that she hadn't yet had more than a short glass of the Chianti.

Back in her camper, she cooked the spaghetti to go with the sauce, wondering if she should share it with her new neighbor. She finally walked over to ask him. She had given a fleeting thought to the Stouts, but quickly dismissed it. There was only enough for two.

While she and Sean talked about dinner, Gulliver, walked up to Heinz, intending to be friendly, but Heinz promptly snapped at him with bared teeth. Sean and Jeanne reacted to the ugly growls each grabbing hold of their dog. Jeanne held on to Gulliver, talking softly, trying to soothe him, while Sean put Heinz in his truck, then walked Jeanne and Gulliver back up the hill. "I hope this hasn't changed your mind. I mean you'll still come by for a drink. Yes?"

"I will, and, like I said, I'll bring dinner, but I need to be sure Gulliver is okay."

The dog curled up on his blanket without complaint. Jeanne sat by him for a time, stroking his back until he settled and fell asleep. She decided he'd be fine if she didn't stay away long. She mixed the sauce with the spaghetti to make it easier to carry and put the wine in her brown tote with her tape player and some tapes.

Jeanne thought her spaghetti sauce was especially good, and Sean apparently agreed, not turning down a second helping when Jeanne offered it. After dinner, he got a leather-covered traveling bar from his truck, something you'd expect in a limo, not a pickup. He offered her Amaretto, then Drambuie, saying he'd get ice if she'd like a Rusty Nail, but she stuck with her wine.

While they sipped their drinks, they shared little bits of themselves. He owned a farm on Prince Edward Island where he had a pottery workshop, and also worked metal. He showed her a silver clip with a gold spring he had made and laughed when she asked him what it was. "I'll show you." He opened another handsomely tooled expensive-looking leather case retrieved from his truck and rolled a joint. "See, a roach clip. I have another one. Can I roll one for you?"

Jeanne declined, thinking it was an opportune time to head back to Gulliver.

"Don't go yet. It's still early."

"I should get back to the dog."

"Listen, I have these great tapes. You didn't bring your tape player not to use it, eh?" From his truck he retrieved yet another leather case. "This guy is from your part of the country. Do you know him?" He put Mose Allison in the tape player, and when the lyrics started, Sean sang along.

Look out, stand back, I'm just a wild man on the loose. He sang the jazzy tune as though he were Mose himself.

Lock up your wives; hide your daughters. He was having fun playing the role and Jeanne smiled at his antics, the hint of mischief.

After Mose Allison, Sean wanted to hear one of Jeanne's tapes, so she played the Keith Jarrett tape Katy had given her. They both sat back and got lost in the soft melodic piano playing of *My Song*. Sean listened somewhat more subdued. "That was beautiful. Jazz, huh? I'm surprised. I'd guess you'd be a country fan."

"Oh no, not country." Then she remembered Willie Nelson. "I do have one country tape though, Willie Nelson."

"Let me guess. 'On the Road Again.'"

"Yeah, someone thought it the perfect gift for my trip. I didn't even know who Willie Nelson was until that movie came out. Now I love to listen to him sing."

Without missing a beat, Sean presented the famous line with a perfect impression of Willie's accent. *I'm gonna get me a bottle of Tequila and find one of them Keno girls that can suck the chrome off a trailer hitch and just kick back.*

"Why is it everyone likes to quote that line?" Jeanne laughed. "Yes, well, I guess I like Willy well enough, something engaging in his voice, but I'm not a country fan. All that twang and sentimentality doesn't do it for me. I prefer Simon and Garfunkel or maybe James Taylor."

"Hey, I've got a James Taylor tape." When the music started, Sean's style had completely changed. *"When you're down and troubled, and you need a helping hand."*

It must have been the wine that helped Jeanne find her voice. *"And nothing, nothing is going right. Close your eyes and think of me, and soon I will be there, to brighten up even your darkest night."* She stopped, feeling the tears on the way.

"I can tell that one is special for you," he said.

Jeanne thought of Peggy singing the song with her sister Catherine at a family barbecue, how heartfelt the two of them sang together. It was that first summer after they lost Joey and everyone was in tears. She kept the memory to herself nervous about where the conversation might go. She smiled and nodded at his comment then said she needed to get back to her dog.

In the morning, Sean knocked on the camper door. "You forgot your tape player." He seemed older, a heaviness in his eyes; his playful demeanor had disappeared. Jeanne offered him breakfast, but he said he needed to catch the ferry. After he left, she noticed the note tucked in the tape player.

Thanks for dinner. It was delicious. You must come to Prince Edward Island and meet my wife, Alice. Let me return your hospitality. It was nice to meet you.

Sean

He included an address with directions. How perfect, thought Jeanne. She'd never been to Prince Edward Island. And from there she could get a ferry to Newfoundland Island, the farthest point east she could go.

Chapter 21

Jeanne took Gulliver for another hike to the Bras d'Or Lake lookout and by noon she was on her way to the Cabot Trail, thinking if she finished her drive that afternoon, she could head for Sean's the next day. She dismissed her reservations about dropping in on him. He must want her to visit, or he wouldn't have invited her.

Driving away from Whycocomagh, she saw a sign for gloves on a store window and remembered she hadn't packed any. The nights had been cool. She might need them soon. No one was inside except for the two ladies standing behind the counter. From the hint of resemblance in their posture, the shape of the brow, Jeanne conclude they must be sisters although something set them apart, as though they were geraniums on a porch, with the one in front of the other getting all the sun. The bright one wore a multicolored knitted sweater. Her bright red lipstick stood out when Jeanne walked in the door. The quiet one wore a simple grey cardigan over a plain white blouse with a tweedy skirt.

On her way to the gloves, Jeanne stopped at a case of souvenirs lured by a beautiful needlepoint of a colorful bird. The quiet sister came up behind her. "That's a yellow-rumped warbler. I made that one myself." Her soft voice matched her looks, but her smile brought life to her face, and Jeanne knew she had to buy the bird or watch the smile go away.

The bright one began a barrage of questions as she placed Jeanne's items in a bag, asking Jeanne where she was from, where she was going, and what she was going to do? "Traveling all by yourself? Oh, you poor thing. How lonely for you." Her words came with a corresponding sympathetic expression; her brows furrowed her mouth in a grim pout.

Discomfort took hold of the quiet one's eyes. In a more mellow voice than her loud sister, she said, "Oh, I don't think that's true. It's a wonderful idea. I wish I could do that. Someday I want to do that. Drive across the country by myself."

To Jeanne, she sounded as if she wanted to escape. "Yes, you should," Jeanne said. "The best thing is you don't have to please anyone but yourself."

"Oh, that would be so wonderful," said the quiet one. "And I'd bring my cat."

The bright one rolled her eyes.

"There you go," said Jeanne. "Pets are the best company."

Jeanne headed for the Cabot Trail, thoughts of the two women traveling with her. The quiet one looked as though she'd thrive if she got out from behind her sister's shadow.

A few miles down the road, Jeanne came to the small hamlet of Belle Cote on the north side of Margaree Harbor, where the Margaree River runs into the Gulf of St. Lawrence. Lured by a sign for Beach Cove Lane, she followed it to a long narrow spit separating the harbor from the gulf and parked at the end of the drive to let Gulliver out for a romp. Lobster pots stacked high along the road and lobster boats tied up at the dock reminded her of Maine.

The sound of a pounding hammer came from a beached boat, which Jeanne had first assumed was abandoned until she saw the old man hard at work. His attention was fixed on the hatch of a gray painted box in the middle of the open deck. He hammered on the hatch, then lifted it and dropped it and hammered on it again.

Jeanne thought he would soon have a fine working hatch, but why he needed it on this ragged old boat mystified her. She wanted to ask what he was doing, but he was so engaged in his work, she hesitated. Squelching her reluctance, she worked up enough courage to say hello. "Hi, are you fixing up the boat?" What a dumb question, she thought.

"Yup, just took her out of the water." His "out" had that neatly clipped Cape Breton sound to it.

She thought, my God, he's been going out to sea in this. How does he keep it together? Weathered and peeling, paint on the boat was long forgotten except for the newly painted box.

The old seaman stopped what he was doing, sat on a bench, and took off his old blue seaman's cap. He pointed to a place for her to sit and politely gave her his attention. Bent and wiry, he reminded her of people on their porches back in Maine. He lit up a smoke and offered one to Jeanne, looking at her with something going on in his eyes when she didn't accept.

"Ten years I've had her." He looked at the boat with satisfaction. "I've had lots like her. Been a lobsterman for 50 years, myself." He turned to Jeanne, "I gather you're here from the States. On vacation, eh?"

When Jeanne said she was from Northport, Long Island, his eyes opened in surprise. "Have a sister on Long Island."

Jeanne hadn't expected that response. He took a long puff on his cigarette while gazing out at the bay. "Don't know where," and after more sitting and gazing, he turned to give Jeanne a look full of resentment. "Haven't heard from her since she got married and moved away."

He turned his gaze back to the water and seemed lost in his thoughts. Why do people lose each other that way, Jeanne wondered. It only takes a phone call.

Jeanne struggled for a way to continue the conversation and finally asked to take his picture. He politely obliged, even offering to pose at the wheel. He asked if she were traveling alone.

"Yes, just me and my dog."

"He's a friendly dog. Keep you safe, I imagine." With that, he had nothing more to say. He gathered his tools, picked up his hammer, and saw and climbed out of his boat. Gulliver hopped up and trotted right after him. With Jeanne and the dog following, he headed for an old truck parked in the opposite direction of hers.

Not wanting to let him go, she continued talking. "I have a boat, a sailboat, but not wood like yours," with apology in her voice because she thought he might be a purist who might not appreciate a fiberglass boat.

"Nothing wrong with that. There's one at the dock over there."

He pointed Jeanne in the opposite direction while he continued on his way and Jeanne realized he was trying to politely take his leave.

Later, as she drove by, she saw him back by his boat, cutting up a fish. She wanted to ask him for another picture, one of him cleaning the fish, but decided against it, hesitant to intrude any further. She honked the horn and waved goodbye as she drove away, but when she barely got a discernible nod back, she sighed with disappointment. Here was someone full of stories of the sea she'd love to hear. But why would he tell them to her? She should appreciate that he spoke to her as much as he did. *I wish I had asked his sister's name. Maybe I could find her.*

The day slipped away as Jeanne continued to the Cabot Trail. Cottages facing the setting sun dotted the hillside, aglow in yellow light. With the day's light waning, Jeanne crossed a small bridge and came to Cheticamp Campground. She pulled in for the night, putting her Cabot Trail drive on hold until morning. She hadn't calculated the extra time for taking pictures and meeting people, but the last thing she wanted was a mad dash every day from point A to point B, skipping moments like her brief conversation with the two sisters and the old lobsterman.

The rumble of trees thrashing in the wind and the rattle of hard rain hitting the roof woke Jeanne in the middle of the night. Gusts howled from far off, long before they hit, buffeting her little home on wheels. There would be a pause for a minute before the next blast came roaring towards her and pounded against the camper's thin metal walls. Gulliver stood anxiously looking up at her, so she piled up the cushions for him to climb up to her bed to sleep at her feet. With the windows zipped closed, the canvas shades secured, Jeanne pulled her quilt around her and felt sheltered from the storm.

In the morning, all the fury of the night had disappeared. Jeanne woke to the quiet patter of rain on the camper roof. At times she found it soothing to listen to the rain while snug in her warm camper bed, but today the sound filled her with disappointment. Out her window, the fog hung heavy in the hills. Driving the Cabot Trail with its views shrouded in mist was not what she had in mind. She had her heart set on moments that took her breath away when she came over a hill or around a curve and caught the sun glistening on the sea.

In the hope the fog would lift, Jeanne waited out the morning, washing dishes, and putting every little mislaid something in its place. And when the sun still hadn't come, she took her laundry to the camp washing machine and even ironed her clothes, but as morning became afternoon with no end to the rain, she became discouraged with little hope for better weather if she stayed another day.

By two in the afternoon, she gave up waiting, rolled down the camper top, and headed north, hoping for some magical moments.

A few miles north of Cheticamp, the Cabot Trail ran along the coast high on a ledge, a tumble away from the sea. Enough fog had dissipated that she could see all the way to the horizon. Even in the rain, the magnificence of the vast gulf astonished her. Jeanne was glad she hadn't waited for the sun.

She drove along a ribbon of road carved out of the hills following the coast for miles enthralled with the view until the road moved inland, heading east. When later the road turned south, the sea reappeared in quick glimpses between the trees, treating her to momentary thrills all the way back to Whycocomagh Provincial Park. She found the same spot up the hill she enjoyed the last time she was there and settled in for the night planning on treating the dog to another hike in the morning.

Before she went to bed, Jeanne filled pages in her journal with her encounters of the past few days. She checked her ledger where she logged the mileage each morning before she got on the road. The day she left Northport, the odometer read 52,541.4; now, it was 53,817.2. That's 1,275.8 miles in 9 days, about 140 miles per day. She didn't see how she could go to Alaska. "We'll never get there at this rate, Gulliver."

Chapter 22

Jeanne moaned when she woke to another day of rain. There'd be no hike up Salt Mountain today. It took most of the morning to conquer her reluctance to get out of bed.

Ordinarily, she'd scan the view as she rode along, but the gloomy day left her indifferent to the landscape. She might have missed the hitchhiker had the sign for Port Hastings not jolted her out of her lethargy. This was the spot where she had passed the truck accident on her way to Whycocomagh. She had slowed down to avoid a similar fate when he came unexpectedly into view, sitting on the guardrail, casually thumbing a ride.

As Jeanne rolled by him, he looked right into her eyes. Immediately she had a stark and unwanted image of him crushed beneath the 18-wheeler. She felt the old weakness in her knees, an icy shiver through her body. When she pulled over to calm herself and catch her breath, she saw him in her side-view mirror running toward the truck.

Gulliver's angry barks startled the hitchhiker when he opened the door. He jumped back saying, "Does he bite?"

Holding tight to Gulliver's collar, Jeanne said, "I'm sorry, but I didn't stop to give you a ride. It shook me up to see you sitting on that guardrail. I needed to pull myself together."

Puzzled by her comment, he asked, "You're not giving me a lift?"

"No, I don't pick up hitchhikers, but I'm glad you're here because someone should tell you not to sit on that guard rail. It's dangerous."

With his mouth ajar, his puzzled expression was more acute. Jeanne tried to explain. "I guess you aren't aware of the truck accident. It was lying on its side on that guardrail exactly where you were sitting. Why don't you move up the road? At least on the shoulder where the road isn't curved." Even as she spoke, Jeanne could tell he wasn't listening.

Eyes squinting, he was looking back at the guardrail and Jeanne could see the wheels turning in his brain. When he looked back at her, Jeanne guessed he had come to some conclusion because his expression had morphed to a hint of self-satisfaction. Pleasure, mixed with a hint of mischief, filled his warm brown eyes. He tilted his head, and with one of those cajoling smiles known to charm mothers into doing what they know better than to do, he said, "Well, I guess you'll have to give me a lift then because it would be too dangerous leaving me out here on the road. You don't want me to get killed."

Jeanne shuddered at his comment. Despite her discomfort she treated his question lightly. With a laugh she said, "Really? Do you think you can guilt trip me into giving you a ride? Really?"

"I'm only going as far as Halifax," he said in a more sober tone, "and your ferocious friend there will make sure I mind my manners, not that I wouldn't." His grin gave way to a plaintive look, and he added: "I'm soaking wet."

"I wasn't planning to go to Halifax. I'm getting the ferry for Prince Edward Island."

"Today? I hate to tell you this. Not today, you're not. You'll never make it."

Jeanne half expected she'd miss the ferry when she left Whycocomagh so late in the day, but she still had hope. She sat back and heaved a sigh. "Darn, Oh well, I wanted to visit Halifax too. I guess it's not that far out of my way if I have to wait until tomorrow anyway."

"If you want, I could get out in Truro."

"Let me think about it. Get in. You can put your pack behind the seat."

For a moment, Anna's admonition came to mind—*you're too trusting*—but Jeanne didn't think so. She had always been good at sizing people up and didn't remember ever getting it wrong. Besides, in this situation it would be better to give him a lift than to drive off without him and have to cope with the horrible image of him crushed beneath a tractor-trailer.

He sat in the truck, all smiles, animated with his success, petting the dog who had quickly warmed to him. "For a minute, I was afraid you wouldn't stop. I mean, at first, when you looked at me as you drove by, I was sure you'd stop, but then you kept going. So when you finally did stop, I said to myself, 'I knew it.'"

"But you didn't know it, did you? Because that's not why I stopped."

"My name is Jeff, by the way."

"Jeanne. Hi."

"What was that you called the dog, Gulliver? That's original. What prompted that? *Gulliver's Travels?*" He laughed.

Jeanne kept the story short, hoping to avoid awkward questions. He simply nodded. He sat quietly for a few minutes before he said, "So, let me see if I understand this. You didn't want to pick me up. You just wanted to tell me what? Move my hitchhiking someplace else? It bothered you that much?"

"You didn't see that truck the other day. What were you thinking anyway on a curve like that? In the rain, no less. You should be more careful."

Jeff looked at her with a bemused smile. "I have to say, I don't know why it's so important to you, but I won't ask. Whatever it might be, it got me a ride. Look at that rain. And here I am, not out in it getting wet."

Jeanne was so enjoying Jeff's company she never noticed the turn for the ferry. As they got close to Halifax, he told her of a café he thought she'd like and offered to buy her coffee. "They have great cinnamon buns. I bet you could use a break from driving. I'd like to say thank you."

It wasn't only coffee that tempted Jeanne. Her pleasure in the company of her passenger made her reluctant to let him go. The café sat in an old downtown neighborhood where the ornate molding framing the storefront windows reminded her of Eastport, Maine. The only thing missing was the brick. Along one side of the dining room, a bar-like counter stretched the length of the restaurant. Customers occupied most of the stools as well as the bentwood chairs around the dark oak tables. Jeff asked the hostess for the table by the window. He had that comfortable demeanor of familiarity with home ground.

A new shyness developed between them in the first awkward minutes of waiting for their coffee. Jeanne began the conversation by asking him why he was sitting on the guardrail, risking his life. He laughed at the inference and seemed to enjoy the opportunity to explain himself. He was from Minnesota, had graduated from the university in the spring, and had taken a year off to figure out his future.

He knew what he wanted to do: go on long expeditions in the wilderness, live in a tent, canoe the Boundary Waters, go up to the Canadian Arctic, and cross-country ski across the Pole. He just didn't know how he could manage it. "There's this slight inconvenience; I have to eat. That means I have to earn a living, and I can't figure out how to earn a living and still live in the wilderness and do the things I want to do. I had this idea that maybe if I wrote about my escapades like John McPhee or Sigurd Olsen I might make it work. Unfortunately, I'm not a writer. Not like them."

Jeanne settled into the comfort of hearing him talk, listening to the earnestness of his romantic hopes, his youthful ideal of a life well lived coming to grips with the practical realities. She wanted to encourage him. "Oh, you'll find a way. You're so passionate about what you want to do. That's the important part. Your passion."

He ran his fingers through his brown hair, brushing the errant curl back from his forehead while he shook his head, a humble "no" in the face of a compliment.

Jeanne continued. "You should keep a journal of your experiences and pictures to go with it." She had to smile at herself, telling this total stranger the same thing her sister had told her. She shared the story of her journals with Jeff. "My sister gave them to me to document my trip to Alaska."

"Alaska. Wow. Wish I could go with you." He had that wistful look Jeanne had seen before in everyone who wanted to ride along with her. There was a lull in the conversation then, and he looked at her with a more quizzical expression. After pausing a moment, he asked, "Mind if I ask you what you are doing in Nova Scotia?"

"Yeah. Not exactly on the way, is it? It's just that if I were driving through Canada, I didn't want to pass up the Maritimes. They're the best part of Canada, or at least from my point of view." And Jeanne was thinking to herself that it would satisfy her to finish her exploration of the Maritimes and head for Florida, but she didn't share that with Jeff. Enthused about her trip to Alaska, he was telling her all the things she should do on the way—canoe the Boundary Waters and drive the Icefields Parkway in Alberta. "There are so many places I could show you." He sighed. Quiet now, he sat for long minutes looking out the window.

When he picked up the conversation again he said, "So you said you wanted to catch the ferry."

She told him about Sean and his farm on Prince Edward Island, and for a minute thought he'd invite himself along, but he told her she should wait for the weekend.

"There's this fantastic fiddle concert in Truro. You don't want to miss it. It's the best thing in Nova Scotia. Mostly farmers and fishermen, and they're better than the professionals."

As he talked Jeanne realized the tables around them were empty. They had spent a long time dawdling over their coffee and never even noticed the crowd clearing out.

"I'll think about it," she said, "but right now, I have to find a place to spend the night."

"There's this great place you could stay right on the water and it's easy to find. Just follow the main street out of town and go east on the shore road. Murphy Cove. You can't miss it, and you'll probably have the place to yourself."

Jeanne found Gulliver sitting up tall, watching for her. She was apologizing to him for taking so long when she saw Jeff coming towards the truck. He waved at her to wait.

"In case we miss each other at the fiddle concert, here's my address. Will you write to me? At least let me know when you get to Alaska."

"You mean *if* I get to Alaska." She wrote her address for him only to cross it out and write her mother's address instead. "It's my mother's address. I'm not sure where I will be."

Jeanne watched him walk back to the café, then started the truck. With her mind full of Jeff, she didn't realize she was going in the wrong direction. She should have turned back the way she had come. An hour later, she arrived at a pretty little place called Peggy's Cove.

Chapter 23

The quaint hamlet reminded Jeanne of Schoodic Point with its extensive rocky outcropping of granite stretching to the water. Atop the massive stony mounds sat an iconic octagonal lighthouse, three stories high, painted a clean white with the lantern room atop the structure painted a bright red. Jeanne imagined the view from the top had to be spectacular, but the lighthouse was closed to the public.

From tourists taking pictures, she learned she'd have to go back through Halifax to get to Murphy Cove. They told her of a campground not five minutes away, and she pulled in there for the night. With Gulliver curled up beside her, she sat on the small camp beach sipping her wine and listening to the softly lapping waves, thinking she couldn't have hoped for a better trip. The setting sun reddened the sky, ending the day in quiet wonder.

In the morning, Jeanne had coffee on the deck of a small cafe near the sunny harbor while she watched the boats get underway, after which she walked up the road with Gulliver to a high vantage with a picturesque view of the charming village. Houses painted in bold colors bore little resemblance to the weathered clapboards along the Maine coast. The yellows, reds, and blues of the buildings so closely matched boats along the quay that Jeanne wondered if houses and boats were painted with the same paint. She sat enchanted, thinking Peggy's Cove the prettiest village she had ever seen.

Later she headed for Murphy Cove, happy for a ride in the country without rain. As she rode along, the shadow of her truck followed alongside her. It reminded her of a turtle traveling along with its house on its back, which pretty much described her current condition.

Around a curve past a welcome sign for the hamlet of Murphy Cove, Jeanne came to the campground sign just where Jeff had said she'd see it. She turned into the road, drove past a few houses, across a small bridge, and came to a driveway that ran between broad, green lawns dotted here and there with evergreen trees. A small house sat back from the drive with country charm in its pyramid roof and the small crisscross grilles in the upstairs windowpanes. The place felt like someone's front yard.

Further along the driveway, a wharf extended a hundred feet perpendicular from the bluff. Three buildings, weathered gray, stood in a line on one side of the wharf, leaning against each other, appearing to hold each other erect. The squat shed at the far end, seemed to be sagging into the wharf probably from long years of settling in its place. Squeezed between the shed and the more recently built two-story structure was a smaller building with lobster pots piled high by its door. She was looking for a clue where to register when she heard a noise coming from the tall building closest to the shore and headed that way.

Inside the open warehouse-sized door, a fisherman was busy filleting fish. His white hair and beard belied his youthful vigor. Behind him, lobster pots stood one on top of the other, almost to the ceiling. A cement tank reminded her of the big tubs she saw in pictures of peasant women crushing grapes with their bare feet to make wine, except the briny odor meant it must have something to do with fish. "Can I camp here for the night?" Jeanne asked.

"Sure can. Give me a minute." His youthful voice fit his lively demeanor. He splashed water on his hands, then dried them and came out the door. In the bright light, his eyes were the blue of the water on a clear day.

"Is that Murphy Cove?" Jeanne pointed.

"No, no, no, no, that's the Tickle."

"The Tickle?" She laughed. "How did it get a name like that?"

He looked at her for a moment as though he hadn't noticed her before. Then he threw his head back and nodded. "Ah well, that's what it is you see, the Tickle. It's like a straight, you know, a narrow waterway between two islands, or in this case, the land and the outer islands. It's a channel, you see, a place to get your boat through to the bay."

"Well that's a new one. Don't think I ever heard tickle used that way." She pointed out over the water, "What about all those islands. Looks like they block the ocean."

"Oh, no, no, no, no. You sail around them. It's easy-going out there."

"No, I meant the view, you know, to watch the sun come up over the water."

"Ah. Trust me, you'll have no problem with that. We have more than our share of breathtaking sunrises. Moonrises too. But you'll want to get out of bed." Then he looked at the camper. "Or maybe not with the top up, eh?"

He led her over to a small building on the other side of the drive, and while she filled out the register, the nudge of a dog's nose startled her. "Oh my gracious you look just like Gulliver."

The camp host looked around the end of the counter. "Are you talking to the dog? Because, if you are, her name is Murph. Looking at the register, he read her name. "Jeanne? Hi. I'm Murphy."

Jeanne laughed, "Oh, like the dog?"

"No. No, no, no, no. Murphy. She's Murph. How long are you staying?"

"Just the night. Where should I park?"

"Suit yourself, but if it were me, I'd pull right up to the edge of the rocks at the top of the hill there, get as near the sea as I can."

Back at the truck, Gulliver was on his feet watching her through the window, crying to get out. He had spotted Murph following behind her. Jeanne grabbed his collar when she opened the door, telling him to stay, but she let him go when she saw both dogs wagging happy tails. He and Murph checked each other out as though they were long-lost friends.

If it wasn't obvious Gulliver was older, they might have come from the same litter. Murph had the same German shepherd coat, the black back and brow with the brown legs. She had the same brown muzzle, but without the gray. Satisfied with whatever they were sorting out, the two dogs ran off together, Murph leading with a determined trot.

Close to the sea, Jeanne felt at home. She raised the camper top, then rolled up the window covers for the full panoramic view and unzipped one window to let in the sea air. Later she was strolling around the campground, taking pictures of Gulliver and Murph together on the rocks and of the old pier, the weathered buildings, and the fir-covered islands in the distance with their mysterious allure when she heard her name called and turned to find Murphy waving her over to the tall building.

"Come on in here a minute. I have something you'll want to see." He pointed to a bench. "Sit. Sit." From an old, galvanized pail, he splashed seawater onto his worktable. Then he readied his knife on an old grindstone. He retrieved a fish out of a bucket and held it up for her to see. "Now here's a fine haddock for you. See how it gleams, and, here, take a whiff. Smells nice and fresh, doesn't it."

He plopped the fish on the worktable and got down to business. "First, I slice the head under the gills, flip it over, and get the other side." He pushed the head off the table, into a pail. "Then one neat, clean slice along the backbone, clearing the ribs and a neat trim around the belly. Flop it over and the same." He paused for a minute, "Now watch. A nice neat push of the knife," his words slowed, matching the tempo of his movement, "and we separate the fillet from the skin. He did the same with the other half. "And there you are, two neat fillets, just like that." He looked at Jeanne for a minute—from his expression, thinking something over—then wrapped one fillet in brown paper and handed it to her.

"I'd wager you never get the true flavor of fish fresh out of the water back in New York. That stuff you buy frozen is no good. They bring them in after being out there a good ten days or more. Old they are, and the stench comes at you from a mile away. When they get them to shore, they dump them in formaldehyde they do, and clean them up, and make them as white and pretty as can be, and freeze them in your

14-ounce packages. You think you're getting something for your $2.49 because you never tasted a fish fresh out of the water, mouth-watering good, with the smell of the good clean sea in it." Murphy put his hands on the table and leaned her way, his gesture an exclamation point.

She thought of the charter boats back home at Captree, the fresh-from-the-sea fish people brought in from their day on the water, but why tell him and spoil his self-satisfaction with having a monopoly on fresh fish.

That night, on her way back to the camper from the shower, a bright light sitting on the water at the far end of the bay caught her attention. She sat on the camper doorsill and watched the brilliant silver glow take on a rounded edge. The straight line of the horizon across the bottom of the light made it appear someone was pulling it ever so delicately out of a slot in the sea. As it rose, the glow threw a silver pathway across the water right to her door.

Joey took over her thoughts. She always felt his presence on beautiful moonlit nights. The silver pathway reminded her of the night she drove over the bridge to Gilgo. Sometimes she squelched her skepticism and let herself think Joey sent the moonlight to show her the way. Through the night, the white light of the late September moon kept her company, shining in her camper window, throwing patches of moon glow on her quilt, and on Gulliver curled up on the lower bed.

Gulliver's little whines woke her in the morning announcing his impatience with waiting to get out. Jeanne opened the door to see Murph looking frisky, bowing and tossing her head, inviting Gulliver to join her. He jumped out and ran off with her, not bothering to wait for Jeanne to put the step down for him.

She cooked bacon and eggs and took her breakfast out in the clean morning air with just enough of a nippy bite to make one hungry. A sizable boulder, near the edge of the bluff, provided a perfect seat. Near the top of the bluff, weeds grew in the crevices between the rocks. It was easy to see where the high water line was. Below it, barnacles and seaweed covered the boulders that spent their life in the coming and going of the tides. Over the years, the water had smoothed their rough quarry-cut edges.

As Jeanne enjoyed her breakfast, two kayaks came along the Tickle, the voices of the paddlers amplified by the water, calling to each other as they headed for one of the spruce-covered islands. She longed to be out there on this perfect autumn day.

In her comfortable spot, Jeanne watched Gulliver and Murph gambol over the boulders. Full of youthful exuberance, Murph clambered over the rocks and splashed in the water at the bottom of the bank where the low tide had exposed a narrow strip of beach. Gulliver gamely tried to follow, struggling to keep up with Murph, jumping from rock to rock on shaky legs, his old joints and unsteady legs showing his age. Determined to catch up to Murph, he worked his way to the bottom of the steep bank on his own. Together, they splashed back and forth along the sandy strip, Gulliver wearing his big doggy grin, his tongue flapping from his mouth.

She left them to play and returned to the camper to get ready to leave. As she lowered the top, Murphy came by and said he would take her fishing if she stayed another day. He tempted her with descriptions of the beauty out around the islands. She looked out over the little bay, torn by a wish to stay and a need to go, but if she stayed, she would miss the fiddle contest, which meant she would miss Jeff.

"Thank you, Mr. Murphy, but I can't. I'd love to, but I can't. I promised to meet someone in Truro."

Gulliver was reluctant to come when Jeanne called. He kept looking back at Murph. As they pulled out of Murphy's yard, he sat up straight, looking out the truck window with sad little whines, craning his neck to keep Murph in his sights as long as he could. When they reached the road, he gave one bark of displeasure and plopped down on the seat. "I'm sorry, buddy," she said, "I wish we could stay too, but we can't stay forever." She rubbed his ears, explaining in a consoling tone. "It's not our place. The longer we stay, the more attached we'll get. It will only get harder to leave, and we'll never get anywhere if we keep not wanting to leave."

They were on the road for a good hour before she realized she hadn't called Gary.

Chapter 24

Jeanne found the red brick Legion hall on Brunswick Street in Truro faster than she anticipated, but she hadn't expected so much traffic. Along both sides of the street, as far up the road as she could see, earlier arrivals parked bumper to bumper. The line of cars trying to inch back into traffic from the parking lot confirmed the lot was full.

She turned into a side street, hoping to find parking in the back of the building, but found no hope there either. Continuing up the residential avenue, she headed for spots that looked open, only to discover they were driveways. Three blocks away from the hall, she finally squeezed into a vacant space.

Not comfortable leaving the dog in the truck that far from the Legion Hall, she considered putting him in the camper but worried his consequential barking might invite an interloper. Better to leave him with his blanket in the cab where he could watch anyone going by. "Okay Gulliver, I'm counting on you to mind the store." She locked the door and hurried to the Legion Hall, telling herself she'd stay only long enough to find Jeff.

Fiddle enthusiasts moved slowly up the front stoop one step at a time and then milled around in the front lobby, saying hello to friends. Jeanne purchased her ticket, and snaked through the crowd into the auditorium where she stood surrounded by others like her without a seat. Weaving through fellow concertgoers, she worked herself to the side of the room to get a better view. Bundles of corn stalks provided the stage with an autumn backdrop. Scarecrows sat on bales of hay among big feedbags labeled Circle F Feed. A grand piano, with its top raised, occupied one side of the stage.

The noise quieted when a lone figure strode to the microphone. "Woowee, do we have a crowd! It looks as though no one stayed home. We have great fiddlers for you tonight. Lots of old-timers you know well, and a few new fiddlers, coming up the pike."

He introduced a petite young girl casually dressed in blue jeans with a red sweater. She had the lightest of blond hair. The announcer asked how long she had been playing.

Pulling herself up to her full 4 feet, she noticeably took a deep breath and said, "Since March." The crowd reacted with a giggle, which appeared to confuse her. She turned towards them with a furrowed brow.

"Do you enjoy it?" he asked.

Again, pulling herself up, taking a breath, she said, "Sometimes."

More twitters from the crowd, louder this time, even a guffaw or two. The young girl gave a startled look at the audience then followed with a barely perceptible shrug of her shoulders.

When she played, she was all business, and any concern the concert was amateur hour soon disappeared. She stood straight as a rod, moving her bow neatly with precision yet without body language other than a perfunctory curtsy when she finished. If she hadn't said she had only been playing for six months, Jeanne wouldn't have believed it.

From her position against the wall, Jeanne scanned people sitting in seats, beginning to fear she might not recognize Jeff without seeing his face. She continued to search the applauding audience, until the adult contestants took over the show. The first wore work overalls over a blue cotton shirt and when asked what he did, he waved a dismissive gesture at the audience. "Everyone knows me."

"Well, for the record."

"Ok, I'm a farmer." He looked at the audience and repeated with emphasis, "a real farmer." The audience responded with loud applause, and Jeanne wondered what she missed in the exchange. He was big and burly, but he played the sweetest music as daintily as anyone, with one pinky held straight up like a duchess drinking tea.

The next fiddler played a Brahms waltz in a slight crouch, pure pleasure on his face, then clicked his heels, stood up straight, and switched to a jaunty reel, finishing with a quick elbow dip and a deliberate stomp.

An older fiddle player with a raspy voice and friendly banter said he had been playing since the first contest in 1932.

"And you're still playing?"

"How old you got to be before you stop looking at women? Well, I haven't got that age yet. So yes, I'm still playing. And I plan to keep playing as long as the Dear Lord lets me breathe."

Jeanne noticed a comfortable camaraderie between the fiddlers and the hometown crowd, as though they grew up together and still lived in the same neighborhood. She imagined them on a first-name basis when they ran into each other in the supermarket or church.

There was a fiddler who grew award-winning Christmas trees and another who made violins. Jeanne expected something classical from him, but he played a sailor's hornpipe, followed by an Irish jig, and members of the audience joined in the dancing in front of the stage. Watching the happy dancers bouncing up and down, arms stiff by their sides, she momentarily envisioned her mother and her aunts at any family gathering. Jeanne had a sudden realization she should have brought her mother on the trip. *Darn, why didn't I invite her to come with me?*

Just as the emcee announced intermission, Jeanne saw someone in a brown jacket sitting near the stage. Thinking it might be Jeff, she worked her way along the wall toward the front of the room, but she couldn't see through the crowd that filled the aisles. She couldn't find Jeff anywhere, and as much as she hated to give up her search, she left the auditorium wondering if she might have better luck finding him at the campground. Walking to the truck, her disappointment shifted between not finding Jeff and not bringing her mother on her trip.

Gulliver's peaceful greeting when she opened the truck door relieved her regret over leaving him by himself for so long. She drove to the campground in a light but steady rain past a hitchhiker holding a sign for Playland Park and was half a block up the road when it occurred to her it might have been Jeff. Pulling over, she watched in the side-view mirror as he ran towards her, just like the last time she passed him on the road.

Jeff opened the door wearing his wide grin. "Here you are coming to my rescue again. And in the rain again. Maybe you should follow me around Canada, eh?" He laughed, and Jeanne's pleasure at seeing him cut through her anxious mood. Gulliver licked Jeff's face, as happy to see him, as Jeanne. "Were you at the contest?" Jeff asked.

"I was, I kept looking for you, but there were too many people."

"I was looking for you too. I left at intermission so I could get a ride. Smart, don't you think? Here we are!"

Jeanne declined Jeff's invitation to join him for pizza. She wanted to phone her mother before it got too late, and she still hadn't called Gary. "Why don't you leave your pack and pick it up later?"

She called her mother from a payphone in the campground office.

"Oh, I'm so glad you called. Where are you? At Peggy's?"

"I'm still in Canada, Mom." Jeanne gave her mother a lengthy report of the past ten days before getting to the fiddle contest and the Irish dancers. "You'd have loved it, Mom. I wish you had come with me."

"What, all the way to Alaska? That's much too long a trip."

"We'd be good company for each other. I had everyone making hints to come with me. Why didn't you say something?"

Mary's continued insistence that she didn't want to go relieved Jeanne's remorse until she hung up the phone and had second thoughts. It would be just like her mother to want to protect her from pangs of regret.

When she called Gary, the phone rang and rang.

Jeanne was snug in her camper, writing a letter to her mother when Gulliver's wagging tail told her someone was approaching. Since he wasn't barking, she assumed it was Jeff.

"I have a spot to pitch my tent right next to the shelter. I'd like to make breakfast for you in the morning if you'll let me?" His pleased-with-himself smile was back.

Only in the morning, it was still raining, so Jeanne invited him to the Skamper instead. She made him pancakes and they sat in her small dinette listening to rain patter on the roof.

"Hear that? It sure is nice sitting in here with the rain pouring down and not getting wet."

They grinned at each other for a while, enjoying each other's company, making small talk. "I've been thinking about writing a small article about winter camping and snowshoeing up north around James Bay. I'd like to capture how my friends and I share the same feelings being out there together without having to define it. You know, show the experience we've had and not get overly wordy with too much self-reflection."

He paused, looking out the window again before he continued, "It's pure wilderness up there. The days are short in winter, but when it's dark, the stars fill the sky. You can't imagine so many stars. Sometimes we even see the aurora."

"You should write about it, Jeff. Do it. If you don't, it will just bug you all the time."

"I've thought a lot about it, you know, being a writer, but it makes me cringe to think of depending on an income from selling what I write."

"Just do one piece and see how it goes."

"But it's so unsettling. I wish it were easy and I could always depend on an audience to read my books, you know, like Sigurd Olson or John McPhee."

One more time, he looked out the window. Jeanne could tell something had occurred to him when he looked her way again. She didn't want to press, and it wasn't necessary.

"Do you ever wonder if travelers don't breathe some rarefied air that lets them experience things more intensely? Or if two people who meet while traveling would like each other as much if they lived down the street from each other?"

Jeanne wondered if he was thinking of her. "No, I wouldn't say that exactly, I mean, I get what you're saying about the rarefied air, or something akin to it, that makes one want to connect with strangers, but it has a different effect on me. I just want to get a person's phone number so I can call sometime, find out what they're doing, what's going on in their life. It's not so much would we get along if we were neighbors, but how I can fix it so we can be neighbors. It's a silly notion, I guess. I can't collect people like driftwood on the beach."

"Yeah, but look at us, we're having this great conversation, but if we were neighbors, would we even talk to each other?"

"I'd like to think so. But it probably wouldn't happen. To you, I'd be that old married lady down the block, always rushing off somewhere with things to do."

He smiled stirring his coffee then looked up and sighed a deep sigh. "Did you ever wonder if you met yourself on the road in a strange place, you'd recognize who you were? I think I'd know if I came across myself in the woods. When I'm hiking or camping or canoeing, it feels like me. It's where I belong in this life."

"I don't know how to respond to that. To meet yourself, I mean. How can you meet yourself, unless you have a twin, in which case you would still be meeting someone else?"

"Don't be logical about it. It's just you. Would you know it was you? Or would the place you're in make you someone you didn't know? Does everything depend on where you get planted in this world? Suppose you got planted here in Truro. Would you be a fiddle player?"

"I doubt that very much, Jeff."

"But, why?"

"Jeff, did you notice one woman fiddle player? Did you not notice they were all men? No, I wouldn't be a fiddle player. I'd be a fiddle player's wife. I'd cook and clean and keep everything together while he fiddled his days away."

Jeff laughed. "But how about that girl?"

"Different generation, hope for the future, I guess. I don't know how to answer your question, Jeff. People are who they are, but I can understand how you might be a different person if, as you say, you got planted in the wrong place. I mean, I wonder if any of those fiddlers would be fiddle players if they didn't live their life in Truro? Would they be busy doing something else, always wondering what they were missing?"

"Right. That's what I'm trying to say. I'm not in the right place for who I am, and I wish I knew how to fix it." With another deep sigh, he looked out the window. "Looks like the rain is letting up. I should go."

Jeanne watched him get ready to leave, feeling a sudden pang. Tomorrow he'd be gone, but she couldn't just adopt him and take him home. "Why don't you join me for dinner tonight? Mr. Murphy gave me this wonderful fish fillet. It's way too much for me."

Chapter 25

Jeanne followed Jeff's advice to take the ferry from the town of Caribou instead of driving through New Brunswick to Cape Tormentine. While waiting to board, she kept thinking of him, so much like Joey in his youthful angst and romantic hopes for the life he wanted, his quest to find a place where he knew who he was. *I can't believe I'll never see him again.*

The old exhilaration took hold when the *Prince Edward* sounded its horn. They were underway on a gray sea beneath gray clouds. Jeanne climbed to the top deck with Gulliver on a leash to watch the wake churning behind them. She wondered where the sailboats were. Except for the ferry, the sea was oddly empty.

A stiff wind soon chased her into the lounge where she found a place to sit with Gulliver stretched out at her feet thumping a loud greeting on the deck whenever a fellow passenger came their way. He soaked up attention from total strangers who rubbed his ears and said pleasant things to him. Jeanne enjoyed the conversations that automatically followed once Gulliver broke the ice, until someone said the ferry was pulling in, and everyone went out to watch it dock.

The boat maneuvered into the small harbor at Wood Islands heading for the slip. From the deck, Jeanne looked across a broad plain, flat and treeless, above sharp banks of brick-red earth. A Canadian flag, with the iconic red maple leaf, fluttered in the breeze. Three lighthouses sat on the bluff, about 20 yards from each other, the tallest attached to a small house, the smallest atop a shed, and the third standing off from the other two with its four walls inclined like a pyramid. Their clean white walls, the red roofs, the red-trimmed pediment windows with decorative flared cornices, the crisscross design of the railings around the lantern rooms all testified to excellent care and appreciation.

She took Route 1 to Charlottetown hoping for glimpses of the water, but saw nothing through the curtain of trees until the woods opened to quaint farms, some with green fields and others with bare red dirt, whatever they had produced already harvested. Set back from the road, white clapboard farmhouses with wrap-around porches stood near large white barns with curved eaves at the edges of metal roofs.

Jeanne pulled over when she saw a large sign that said *Potatoes.* Brown paper bags filled to the top sat on a table beside a large pickle jar stuffed with Canadian bills. In front of the bags, a sign read—*$1, pay here.* She waited for someone to show up, but when no one came, she put her dollar in the jar and took a bag, feeling like a thief even though she knew she wasn't. "Imagine that," she said to Gulliver when she climbed back into the truck.

Following Sean's directions, she came to a long driveway, which ran between a field of fat orange pumpkins, and a fenced meadow dotted with sheep made even more picturesque by the golden yellow birch along the periphery. Just short of the end of the lane, she pulled into a parking area beside the house. "You better stay here, Gulliver. We don't want any trouble with Heinz."

The two-story colonial with cedar-shake siding and large picture windows would blend in nicely with the homes on her Northport suburban street. An imposing, heavy oak wood front door seemed most likely handcrafted, with a stained-glass window featuring birds in jewel tones.

Jeanne rang the bell.

A shadow behind the stained glass moved toward the door and a woman opened with a friendly "Hi" as if she were expecting someone else, but when she saw Jeanne, she asked, "Can I help you?" with more of a questioning scowl than a smile.

"Hi, I'm Jeanne. You must be Alice."

"No," she shook her head, "I'm her friend, Patti," and she called, "Alice!" as Jeanne continued speaking, feeling the need to explain.

"Sean invited me to stop when I was on the island. I should have called first, but I didn't have a number."

Jeanne didn't know why, but a sudden coolness came into Patti's face. Someone asked who it was and Patti's comment, "Someone Sean knows," sounded disdainful. Jeanne wondered if it was something she said.

Alice arrived at the door warm and welcoming, full of smiles, her blond hair pulled back in a youthful ponytail, more in keeping with the image Jeanne had in mind than Patti's bangs and straight black hair. "You came! Sean wasn't sure you would." She led Jeanne into the kitchen where a group of women sat around the table paring vegetables. Someone pulled up a chair, someone else poured coffee, and Jeanne answered questions about how she had met Sean until interrupted by a loud slam of a door somewhere in the back of the house.

Heinz came running into the room, soon followed by Sean. Even in her delight at the sight of him, Jeanne sensed something different. He seemed somehow subdued. He hugged her and quietly said he was glad she came. "C'mon, I'll give you a tour."

Jeanne followed him to a small corral across from the barn, where he stopped to introduce Matilda, a mare with a white streak stretching from her forehead to her muzzle. When Sean whistled, the stately chestnut trotted up to the fence, nodding her head.

After a few moments sweet-talking and patting her nose, Sean led Jeanne to a small barn, which provided housing for one enormous pig. Jeanne never knew pigs could be so huge. Sean beamed as he introduced Rosy. "Isn't she pretty?" The pig waddled Sean's way, seemingly as fond of Sean as he was of his pig. She rested her chin on the railing of her pen, letting out little grunts of greeting. Sean scratched the pig behind the ears as though she were an oversized puppy, and like a proud father recited a list of prizes she had won. When he finished with the pig, he led Jeanne to a circular metal staircase that led to the loft. Curling fronds designed as balusters for the handrail prompted her to ask if he made it himself.

"I did. Welded it from scrap metal. The corners were tricky, but I love the way it turned out." At the top of the stairs, they entered the workshop that Sean had mentioned in Whycocomagh. Light from a large, opened loft door at the far end of the room bounced off a mobile that hung suspended from the ridgepole. The mobile moved in the currents of air wafting in through the open loft door. Stylized sea birds, like the birds in the stained-glass door, glided in slow motion.

Sean explained how he made the mobile, covering all the details of where he got the copper, how he punched out the forms, his challenge to construct it in a way that balanced the weight, but Jeanne was distracted by bundles of greenery with string around the stems, hanging upside down from the rafters. "Oh, you have an herb garden," she said.

Sean followed her eyes, then threw his head back and surprised Jeanne with a delighted laugh. There was a slight glimpse of the Sean of Whycocomagh. "Yeah, I have an herb garden. C'mon, I'll show you."

They stopped to collect Gulliver, whose enthusiastic tail wagging showed he remembered Sean. The dog pulled on his leash as they walked along a driveway in front of a long white barn.

Around the corner of the big barn they came to a narrow footpath, which entered a thick wood. Since she always envisioned neat little herb gardens in tidy, square plots right outside the kitchen door, Jeanne thought it odd to be entering the woods. She mentioned that to Sean who laughed again. "Parsley, sage, rosemary, and thyme maybe; not what I have."

They soon came to an acre-sized clearing hemmed in by tall trees along the perimeter. Rows of stalky plants stood taller than Sean's six feet.

"Ta-da! My herb garden." He watched for a reaction then said, "You don't know what it is, do you?"

"Well, I never saw it before, but I would guess marijuana. Why else would you hide it deep in the middle of the woods like this?" She walked up to the plants for a closer look. "Isn't this risky?"

"Oh no, no risk, not here. Nobody cares." As they walked back to the house, he talked about his crop as though he needed to explain. "I can't keep the farm with a few cows and a patch of pumpkins. With the potatoes, I'm lucky if I break even. Without my, uh, herb garden, I'd go bankrupt, have to sell the farm, and then what? Get a nine-to-five job? I can tell you that doesn't sound appealing."

"What about your artwork? It's very distinctive. Can't you sell it?"

"It takes time to make a mobile. I'd have to turn one out every week and get a good price to earn what I earn from, uh, my herb garden. That's not art. That's manufacturing. It wouldn't be fun anymore."

Jeanne had an unpleasant picture of him losing everything: the sheep in the meadow, the cows in the barn, the lovely chestnut, the prize-winning pig. She thought of Jeff trying to find his own comfortable arrangement, a way to have the life he wanted without "selling out," as he said. Sean seemed to have succeeded, however unorthodox his solution.

That evening the "few friends" turned into a crowd, and Jeanne was the center of attention. Alice had introduced her saying, "Sean's friend from the States, they met camping, she's on her way to Alaska," putting extra emphasis into *Alaska* which made Jeanne uncomfortable. It sounded so definite.

Guests at the dinner table fell into opposite camps discussing her trip. The why-bother crowd told her she was wasting money on gas if she weren't going to Alaska for a job. The other bunch, with the same expression in their eyes as their counterparts in Northport, made varying comments, which, summed up, meant, "I wish I were going with you."

When dinner was over, the discussion continued about how long it might take, the best route to follow, some guests sharing their favorite place to stop, others arguing over whether she should stop at all. Jeanne sat back and let the conversation float around her until Patti interjected.

It might have been the marijuana they passed around or a few too many beers, but her voice was thick. "If you're supposed to be going to Alaska, what are you doing in Prince Edward Island?" Aren't you a bit lost? Alaska is west, you know, as far west as you can go. That way." She turned around to point the direction. "You're all the way east."

Patti seemed to be itching for an argument, but Jeanne made an effort to remain pleasant. "I know, I keep telling myself the same thing. But Alaska is only a remote possibility. It's the Maritimes I didn't want to miss. Who knows if I'll ever have this opportunity again?"

Patti wasn't hearing it. "Did you make a wrong turn? Don't you have a map in that truck you're driving? Or maybe you're not even going to Alaska, and you're just like the rest of your crowd. All talk."

An awkward silence took over the room as Jeanne kept her composure hoping her embarrassment didn't show. She saw Sean's discomfort as he threw a glance toward Alice. Everybody's eyes had turned from Patti to Jeanne. As calmly as she could, in a light-hearted voice, Jeanne explained her invitation from Sean "I didn't want to just not show up without an explanation. That would be rude."

"Oh, that's a new one. An American, from New York no less, minding her manners."

Stung by the insulting words and deriding tone, Jeanne couldn't understand what made Patti so hostile. She could see from the expression on Alice's face that she was clearly disturbed. Going on as though she hadn't heard Patti's insult, Jeanne said, "And I sort of had this plan to start from the most eastern point before I go west. Put my feet in the Atlantic, and then, if I get there, in the Pacific. There's a ferry from here to Newfoundland Island where I can get as far east as I can."

There was an immediate chorus of "You don't want to go to Newfoundland."

"Oh honey, there's nothing there."

"The ferry is expensive."

"You're wasting your time."

"I guess I should think about it some more," Jeanne said.

During the exchange, Alice deftly maneuvered Patti into helping her in the kitchen, and Jeanne found herself surrounded by a small group of enthusiastic supporters taking turns expressing encouragement, but Jeanne found it difficult to talk. Patti had her completely rattled.

At the end of the evening when the guests had left, Alice invited Jeanne to park in the driveway for the night, saving her the trouble of searching for a campground. She had just emerged from bed in the morning when she opened the camper door to Sean's knock. He held a shopping bag and seemed his more serious self again. "Alice is sorry she missed saying goodbye. She had to go to work. She wanted you to have these for your trip." He took out a jar of honey from his beehives behind the barn, a jar of raspberry jam Alice had canned, and a fresh loaf of bread he had baked that morning. As he described his offerings, he apologized for Patti. "You won't let it ruin your visit I hope."

"I had a wonderful visit, Sean. I'm so glad you invited me."

Jeanne offered him coffee, but he said he had a long list of things to do. "I better get going. You probably need to get going yourself. I thought when you leave you could drive up to the Stanhope beach. Take a drive along the Gulf Shore Parkway. It's just as easy to put your feet in the water there. I know the map says the Gulf of St. Lawrence, but forget that. It's all the same water, just the ocean with a different name."

They looked at each other, caught in that moment when there's nothing left to say, but so much left unspoken in their eyes. Then he leaned over and gave Gulliver a pet. "Have a good trip, Boy."

She drove to Stanhope beach, as Sean suggested. With Gulliver beside her, she walked to the water, took off her shoes, and got her feet wet. Since everyone, even Sean, advised against it, she had decided to skip Newfoundland Island, hoping she wouldn't regret it. She had promised Anna she'd step in the Atlantic as far east as she could. She didn't want to disappoint her.

Looking out at the blue water stretching to the eastern horizon, she saw what should be the start of her odyssey, but she couldn't muster any enthusiasm. She couldn't get Patti out of her mind.

Chapter 26

Onboard the *Prince Edward*, Jeanne headed for Cape Tormentine across a turbulent Northumberland Strait through white-capped water with ever-deepening swells. She stood astern, under cloudy skies, defying the breeze, clinging to the rail, inhaling the clean scent of the sea as she watched the island slowly fade in the distance.

Patti's taunting voice echoed in her head. *Aren't you a bit lost? Did you make a wrong turn? Are you really going to Alaska, or is it all big talk?* She couldn't stop thinking about her. She realized how it must look, why someone might wonder what had her meandering around the Maritimes if she was supposed to be on her way to Alaska.

Jeanne admitted to herself there was some truth in what Patti said. She never really wanted to go to Alaska. That was everyone else's romantic notion. Anna, the girls, her sisters, everyone acted as though it was just what she needed, so she'd vacillate between going and not going and telling everyone including herself she might or she might not.

She had mostly avoided everyone's magical thinking until Gary insisted, even pleaded, that she give him time to get things squared away. In the back of her mind she thought she wouldn't need to go to Alaska for that. Now she realized she should have been more definite about that from the start.

She needed to make Gary understand the Alaska trip was not going to happen. She wanted her life back or at least a semblance of it. Florida would never have been her choice, but that was where Gary was, and she would make the best of it. If she camped with the dog along the way, enjoyed the mountains and the beaches, she could be in Florida in a week, maybe ten days. Gary should be satisfied with that. When she got to Fredonia, she'd make sure she got him on the phone. She'd make him understand she was tired of waiting.

At Cape Tormentine, she found a campground that let her park for the night even though it was closed for the season. It was still dark when Jeanne left the campground early and headed to the highway. She stopped for a quick breakfast in Moncton and was drawn to a display case in the restaurant lobby that featured brochures of the Gaspé Peninsula. They stood out from the others with pictures of high bluffs looking out on a silvery sea. She dropped a few brochures in her purse and headed back to Gulliver with his treat.

After hours on Route 11, she pulled off the highway at Campbellton and wound through the village streets looking for gas. She took a break at a small café and while drinking her coffee, she looked through the Gaspé brochures. She found reference to a provincial park at the end of the peninsula, with a point marked Le Bout Du Monde. Imagine that, she thought, the end of the world, and only a day away. She couldn't pass that up. She asked the waitress if she would recommend the Gaspé Peninsula.

"Gaspesie? That depends on what you're looking for."

As Jeanne considered her answer, the waitress said, "Beautiful views of the water if it's pictures you want."

"How long does it take to drive?"

"Depends on how long you want it to take."

And while Jeanne hesitated again, the waitress added, "You might do it in three days, out and back, maybe two with steady driving, but add a few days if you plan to stop any place; you know, get out and stretch your legs, take in the views. They have whales, you know."

Later, when the waitress came with her check, Jeanne asked for directions to the Trans-Canada highway.

"Make a left and go over the bridge. You'll see the signs."

"And the Gaspé?"

"Same thing. Over the bridge." She called to Jeanne as she headed for the door, "They speak French, you know."

Not five minutes after she crossed into Quebec, Jeanne came to a T in the road. Two arrows on a sign pointed in opposite directions—one left to Amqui and places west, and one right to the Gaspé Peninsula. She dismissed thoughts of Patti's barbs and her conflicted intentions. If she passed up Le Bout Du Monde, she'd always wonder what she missed. With a sudden burst of determination, she took in a deep breath and turned right.

Except for the French signs, there was little to distinguish Route 132 from a country road on the north fork of Long Island. Occasionally, a brief glimpse of the water came through the trees. Then just as the view opened wide to the Gulf of St Lawrence, the windshield showed the first drops of rain. She ignored it, driving towards Gaspé, through village after quaint village with causeways across picturesque inlets where fishing boats bobbed on their lines. A roadside field filled with cows brought a yip from Gulliver, who was sitting tall in his seat watching the passing countryside.

Late in the afternoon, a subtle change crept into the landscape. Signs touted whale watching and Perce Rock. Restaurants advertised lobster for dinner. Tourist walked with umbrellas along the road. Jeanne kept driving, her mind set on getting to her destination.

Soon after she crossed the bridge at Gaspé, she came to the Forillon Park campground. It was already getting dark.

She woke late in the morning, her deep sleep helping her recover from a long day of driving. She listened carefully while the camp host gave directions to Le Bout du Monde. "The walk is about three kilometers from where you park. That's about two miles. Most people take about an hour."

On the road to the parking area, she ticked off the landmarks the park ranger had given her—Hyman's store, then the cemetery with the cross—and shortly after that, she came to the pull-off for parking. "Here we are, Boy." He sat up and looked out the window, ready for action. According to the host, this was the only place with easy access to the water. Everywhere else, the bank was too high.

Jeanne followed Gulliver down the trail to the crescent-shaped beach hemmed in at each end by high bluffs. Water lightly lapped the shore where pieces of driftwood, and the remnants of good-sized tree trunks, lay strewn across the sand near the high tide line. With its surface of rocks and pebbles, the beach wasn't the smooth walking of Long Island sand, but Jeanne didn't mind. She took her shoes off and waded in the shallow water, standing for a moment despite the cold. She had no idea if she were further east than the Stanhope beach, not that it mattered anymore, but she found the moment satisfying, all the same.

Gulliver found a large branch he could barely carry in his mouth and held his head high as he ran her way to drop it at her feet. To indulge him, Jeanne picked up a smaller piece of driftwood and played a game of toss and fetch before putting on her shoes to leave.

At the east end of the beach, the trail went up the hill and proved more rudimentary than Jeanne expected. They crossed a small footbridge over a shallow brook where Gulliver stopped for a welcomed drink, then followed the trail along a high grassy ridge with a stunning view of the Gulf of Saint Lawrence. Further on they entered a thick wood where the overhead branches formed a dark tunnel. Rays of sunlight streamed through the trees. She could see the light gleaming at the end of the canopy.

They came out of the trees, where the trail ended abruptly on a high, sheer cliff—Le Bout du Monde. Looking out at an open sea all the way to the horizon, she felt like she stood at the edge of the earth. Under a reddening sky, a rosy sheen splashed on the water. She stood with Gulliver in the quiet beauty, thinking of Joey and the pleasure that came over him watching the sunset.

How often, when they were out on the *Quest*, he insisted they drop the sails and sit quietly rocking on the water, long enough to watch the stars appear as the night took over the sky. Almost two years had passed since he left them, but at moments like this she felt him beside her, and thought if she just reached out far enough, she could touch him. *Can you see this, Joey? Are you here?*

In the waning afternoon, Jeanne began to worry they might not make it back to the truck before dark. Reluctantly she left, hurrying behind Gulliver, who trotted along, leading the way. With his steady, relaxed gait and no sign of wariness in his perked ears, he relieved her worry of what might lurk in the dark woods. He stopped once where the trail forked and looked back for advice. Jeanne told him to go on, and he confidently trotted ahead, picking the route that soon led directly back to the truck.

At first light, she took the dog for his walk in the chilly morning air before making quick work of driving away. A few miles from the campground, the road came out from the trees on the north side of the Gaspé to the eye-catching view of whitecaps on a choppy sea, sparkling in the sun far out in the Gulf. Now and then, she'd come to a hamlet not situated according to any plan, just strewn across the landscape as though someone threw out seeds, and houses sprung up wherever the seeds fell.

According to the camp host at Forillon Park, Quebec City was about eight hours away. Jeanne hoped to reach the city by nightfall, but she had only reached Riviere Du Loup when she gave up for the day and pulled into a campground. She took Gulliver for a long walk along the St. Lawrence River and thought about Patti, still troubled by her words.

She was glad she decided to put Alaska to rest. The colors in the trees meant the end of summer. Last night the heater in the camper worked all night to hold off the chill. It had to be clear to everyone that it was too late to be driving into snow country.

Jeanne took time to get the camper in order before leaving for Fredonia at midday. Rolling along the highway, caught in the flow of 18-wheelers and commuter traffic, she sped past Quebec City with pangs of guilt for not stopping. She skipped Montreal and stops for coffee. It still took seven hours or more after leaving Riviere du Loup before she drove over the Thousand Islands Bridge. Well after dark and fighting sleep, she gave up on Fredonia and pulled into the first truck stop she came to, just off the highway in Watertown, New York.

The next day, over three weeks from the day she left home, Jeanne arrived at Peggy's dorm. She sat in the truck, thinking of what she would say to Gary. Until now he had thwarted all her efforts to join him. She would give him all the arguments. It was too late in the season to go to Alaska. It was too long a trip for the dog. It would cost more than they expected. She wasn't sure which argument would convince him, but she had to make him understand.

While going over her options, an approaching campus officer drew loud barks from Gulliver until Jeanne rolled down the window and the officer's friendly voice calmed the dog. "There, there, good boy." He told Jeanne she needed to park in the visitor's section at the Round Road parking lot if she wanted to stay overnight. She was so relieved he didn't tell her to leave. Before moving to the lot, Jeanne called Peggy from the dorm lobby.

"Mom, Where are you? I've been expecting you for weeks."

Jeanne took pleasure in Peggy's voice. "I'm here, Peggy, in the lobby. Is there a nice place nearby to go for dinner and talk?"

Gulliver jumped to his feet when he saw Peggy coming. For a minute, he looked uncertain. He stared intently and then trembled with excitement, little yelps leaving his throat. When Jeanne let go of his leash, he ran to Peggy in a full gallop, then jumped all over her, licking her face, rubbing against her, trying for hugs. His sharp barks mixed with excited whines. On her knees, trying to hug him, Peggy kept saying, "Gulliver, Gulliver."

Chapter 27

Gulliver scrunched up against Peggy, settling his chin in her lap as they rode down Central Avenue, with Peggy chatting excitedly about her job at the local pub, her latest role with the drama club, her music, the band, John, mostly John, in between giving Gulliver pets while talking puppy talk. Jeanne marveled at her enthusiasm, gratified to see her so upbeat.

They went to *Aunt Janet's*, Peggy's favorite restaurant in the nearby town of Dunkirk and sat opposite each other, enjoying their hamburgers and fries. Jeanne gazed with pleasure on her daughter's smiling face. Her thick brown hair hung long and loose. Jeanne couldn't remember when she last saw her so carefree. They were eating ice cream sundaes when Jeanne brought up her plan to forego Alaska.

Peggy put down her spoon and leaned back in the booth with eyes wide. "Are you serious? Why?"

"I just want to get to Florida."

"But I thought you liked road trips?"

"I do, I do, and this one has been the best. Wait until you see my pictures. But you know, I don't think right now is a good time. If they don't already have snow up there, they will, most likely, by the time I get there. Not the best camping weather, is it? And something tells me Toksook might not be the best place in winter."

"See, I knew you should have left sooner. Not in October. You were supposed to be coming back in October."

"You know how busy I was. It couldn't be helped."

"What did Dad say?"

"I haven't told him yet."

"Mom." Peggy shook her head and frowned. With a slight pinch to her eyebrows, her enthusiastic smile became more subdued.

"And it's not only the weather. Gulliver worries me. He's getting old, you know, and he gets achy from sitting too long in the truck." With a deep sigh, she hesitated for a moment, wondering if she should get to the crux of the matter.

Peggy guessed she had more to say. "What, Ma?"

"I met this person in Prince Edward Island who wanted to know what I was doing in the Maritimes if I'm supposed to be going to Alaska. It made me question it myself. I never really wanted to go to Alaska. Everyone around me just got carried away, especially your father, and whenever I tried to resist, I always lost the argument."

"I think everyone thought it would cheer you up. You were always so sad."

"I know everyone meant well and if there were nothing else in my life, I could travel around the Maritimes forever, but I have this nagging feeling that I shouldn't be playing hooky when so many things need my attention."

"Like what, Ma? You see that's your problem, always worrying about taking care of things. In case you didn't notice, we're taking care of ourselves just fine. Can you worry about yourself for a change?"

"Peggy, how can I enjoy a road trip with this constant worry in the back of my mind?" Jeanne hesitated to mention her other worry, but did, anyway. "You know, your father and I have been apart too long. It's been two years.

"Well, everyone will agree with that."

Jeanne was about to ask her what she meant, when Peggy said she had to get back. "Can we talk about this later? John and I have to practice for the show tonight. Wanna come?"

"I'd love that, Peggy, but I need to call your father first. Get things worked out."

"There's plenty of time. We don't go on until 10."

Jeanne dropped Peggy at John's and went to the dorm to call Gary on the hall pay phone. When he didn't answer, she luxuriated in the dorm's free shower before trying Gary again. Still no answer. She wondered where he could be. He never worked late on a Friday night. Could he be out on the boat? After the third unanswered call, she gave up trying to reach him and drove to the pub for Peggy's show.

She arrived to a crowd hovering at the front door, and Peggy's powerful voice blasting into the street. Jeanne stood for a moment relishing the sound of it before working her way into the pub and up to the front of the stage. Peggy was belting out "Proud Mary" with everyone on their feet, singing along, arms in the air, clapping a single beat between the words.

Rollin' (clap), Rollin' (clap), Rollin' on the River.

She was back to the old Peggy, full of energy, capturing the audience, with no sign of the grief that once took all the life out of her.

In the morning, Jeanne tried Gary again, and when he still didn't answer, she told herself he must be out for a weekend sail. Where else would he be?

She drove to the nearby Lake Erie Park to spend the weekend and welcomed the change from the college parking lot. A mix of red, orange and yellow colored the leaves edging the camping spaces. No one was around. On a nearby bluff, looking out on the lake, she found a bench under a maple tree to sit and watch Gulliver as he ran off to explore.

He found his way to the water and splashed in and out, playing a game of his own until he stopped, raised his nose, ears pointed, peering intently up the beach in the opposite direction of where Jeanne was sitting. Jeanne tried to see what had his attention. When he took off running away from her at a brisk pace, Jeanne wondered if he was looking for her. Can he not see me? She called his name, and he stopped short, looking her way with an oh- there-you-are expression, then trotted up to her and put his paw in her lap. "I'm right here, you silly dog. What's the matter with you?" She thought she saw the signs of cataracts. "I need to get you to a vet, Puppy. We need to get home."

Monday morning, she rose early, hoping to catch Gary before he went to work, only to be frustrated by another unanswered call. He couldn't have left this early, she thought. It was only 7:00 am.

Jeanne drove to Dunkirk pier and sat in the truck with her coffee and her fried egg sandwich watching the morning bustle of people getting ready to sail. She was mulling over the arguments she would use with Gary when a sloop in full sail came along the dock for a landing. Caught by the wind, it was dangerously close to slamming into the pier. She sat up straight in her seat shouting, "pull up, pull up!" then sat back and breathed a sigh of relief as the sails dropped and the sailboat glided along the dockside without a disaster.

A vivid memory of Gary and Joey arriving at the Northport dock in a stiff wind took over her thoughts as though it just happened there before her. It was *Quest's* maiden voyage and the whole family was there, Anna and Tony, with them, waiting to board. When Joey tried to jump from the boat to the dock to secure the line, he fell in the water between the boat and the pilings. By some miracle, Tony had found the strength to grab him and pull him out. In her mind Jeanne saw Joey standing there soaking wet, laughing it off, while everyone else tried to recover from panic. "You live a charmed life, young man," Tony had said. Remembering his words brought the welling of tears.

Jeanne walked with Gulliver along the pier looking over the boats before heading to Peggy's dorm to call Gary and this time, to be certain to reach him, she called him at work. The agitation in his voice came through the phone as soon as he answered. "Where have you been? I've been waiting for you to call."

"The question is: where have you been? I've been calling, but you haven't been answering."

"I told you, you can always get me here at work."

"On the weekend? I don't think so. Besides, you never have time to talk if I call you at work. You only take the call to tell me not to call you at work. Look, can we start over and have a friendly conversation? I'd appreciate a friendly conversation right now. Can you try: 'It's so good to hear your voice,' or 'I've missed you?'"

A sigh from Gary, followed by a quieter "Where are you?"

"Fredonia. I'm with Peggy. I got here Friday night."

"Fredonia? But it's been three weeks. You should be halfway to Alaska by now."

"If I recall, you said not to rush. Remember? Look, I need to talk to you about things, but first I've got a problem."

"Now what."

"I need to replenish my cash, but I can't get Traveler's Cheques with a credit card, and I wanted to talk to you before I wrote a check.

"How much do you need?"

"I'm thinking $500. I can use the credit card for tires, but I need cash for everyday expenses."

What happened to the Traveler's Cheques you took with you?"

"That was three weeks ago before I drove more than a thousand miles paying for gas because no one would take my Amoco card. So can I write a check, or do you need to make a deposit?"

"You drove 1,000 miles! And you're only in Fredonia? Where have you been?"

"The Maritimes, Gary. I sent you postcards."

"Postcards?" He seemed not to know. "Look, don't cash a check. I'll send a Western Union. I'll get back to you."

"Wait, we need to talk."

"I told you I'm busy." He hung up the phone.

Jeanne's stomach was in knots from trying to work up the courage to tell him about Alaska, and to have him hang up on her only made it worse. She spent the night in the Round Road lot and in the morning Peggy came to the camper to tell her Gary wanted her to call. Jeanne phoned him from the dorm lobby; he was almost friendly. "I'm going to send a Western Union money order on Thursday for $1,000, and I'll put money from the savings account in the checking account. That should be plenty for good tires and for winterizing and whatever else the truck needs. Now here's the thing. I'm sending it to a Western Union in Buffalo. Can you pick it up there?"

"There has to be one in Dunkirk, but okay, that might be better because I need to go to Buffalo for tires. Gary, I need to talk to you. Can we do that without you cutting me off again?"

"Okay. What?" with a sigh.

"See, it's much better if we don't snap at each other. Give me time to explain things before you hang up on me."

"Jeanne, you don't know what it's like here. I'm under a lot of pressure."

"That's why I should be there, Gary, to help. When I talked to you yesterday, I wanted to tell you I wasn't going to Alaska. My guess is I could be in Florida in a week. Joey's anniversary is coming up. I really think we should be together, don't you?"

It was as though Joey's anniversary was never mentioned.

"What are you saying? You're not changing your mind again, I hope."

"Try to listen without getting upset. I'm not changing my mind. I tried to tell you all along I only wanted to go to Florida. It's been two years Gary. Two years." She covered all the points she had discussed with Peggy, but he only zeroed in on one.

"What's this two years stuff? It's not like I never was in Northport. And you were here in August, remember?"

"Gary, we've only seen each other for occasional visits. For two years, Gary, just visits."

"Let me try to explain it to you again. Hold on, I'll be very cool. You need to finish this trip because you'll never let me hear the end of it if you don't."

"I don't know why you say that. I swear I'll never mention it."

"You didn't let me finish. I'm not ready to have you here because things are too involved here. I can't be dealing with getting ready for you to come here while I'm dealing with everything else."

"Gary, you're not listening. I said I'm not going to Alaska. I think I've driven far enough."

"No, you're not listening. I said you're not coming to Florida." He was back to the squelched voice, yelling under his breath. "You're not coming here now. Not now. I'm not ready for that."

"What am I supposed to do? I can't go home. Do you want me to throw out our tenants?" She realized she was losing it, her throat tightening, making it difficult to speak.

"You know what, I don't care where you go, you're just not coming here."

"So that's it? We're finished?"

"No, God, that isn't what I meant. Why don't you listen? I'm just telling you to wait. Just wait."

She felt the telltale ache in her throat. "I can't talk anymore. I'm saying goodbye." This time Jeanne hung up the phone. She leaned her back against the wall and slid to the floor, overcome with sobs, until she suddenly realized where she was and the thought of Peggy finding her there got her to her feet. Peggy didn't need to see this. How would she explain?

Chapter 28

Jeanne drove to the Lake Erie campground, rolled up the top and crawled into her bed. Curled up in her quilt, she listened to the world outside her door, soothed by the gentle splash of small waves on the beach, and the rustle of leaves when the wind moved through the trees. A truck passed on the highway, children shouted far off, and in the shelter of her peaceful haven, only the ticking of the clock and the quiet breathing of the dog. The autumn sun streamed in the windows, warming his bones as he slept. She was grateful for Gulliver's company.

She wanted only to sleep and put Gary out of her mind, but she kept hearing Gary's angry words: *I don't care where you go.* Gulliver's pestering to go out rescued her from her melancholy. She got out of bed and walked him to the lake, thankful for his lively trot. She didn't want him to get old.

That night, a strange nightmare of a ghostly figure hanging suspended in the middle of an enclosure woke her in a panic. She had a vague sense of other images in her dream, but the memory was opaque. She thought the figure might be herself.

Trying to ignore it, she wrestled over what to do. Waiting Gary out was no longer tolerable. It rendered her unable to function. She had been doing that too long. "Just wait," he had said. Well, she had waited long enough. She couldn't live this way any longer, suspended, with no direction.

She considered going back to Long Island and parking in her mother's driveway, but what would she tell everyone? And she couldn't just stay in Fredonia. What would she tell Peggy?

The need to pick up her money order in Buffalo pushed her to close up the camper and get the truck moving. On the way out of town, she stopped by Peggy's dorm to tell her she wasn't going to Florida. "Not yet."

"Why not?" Peggy asked, searching Jeanne's face.

"Your Dad and I talked it over, and he wants me to wait a few weeks. He still wants me to go to Alaska."

"Didn't you explain it to him?"

"He wasn't hearing me. He kept saying now was not a good time to come down there."

Peggy didn't appear convinced. She gave her mother a long hug. "Call me, okay? Let me know where you are."

In Buffalo, Jeanne picked up her money order at the Western Union office, then spent much of the afternoon sitting in a grubby service station, waiting for the truck to get winterized and fitted with new tires while Gulliver sat patiently at her feet, checking every new arrival, appreciating whatever attention came his way. With nothing to do but wait, she ran over in her mind all that had happened in the last two years, trying to figure out what was nagging her about Gary. She had been blaming his angry moods on Joey, but now she couldn't help wondering if it was something else. She hadn't wanted to believe Susan when she tried to warn her. She kept pushing away the thought there might be someone else, but it kept coming back.

While she waited, she wrote Gary a long letter. Telephone conversations never resolved anything. She could never find the right words. In her letter she brought up his leaving for Florida the way he did, hardly ever coming home, insisting she take this trip even though she told him she didn't want to. Not caring that she wanted to be with him. She thought about mentioning Joey, but left it out. She couldn't put the words on paper.

She was glad she hadn't called her mother about going to Florida. She wrote her a note as though everything was normal telling her she was getting new tires and to let Uncle Chris know. She wrote Anna and Lisa she was having a great trip.

When the truck work was completed, Jeanne found a motel to spend the night and snuck Gulliver in when no one was watching. He settled on the soft bed with his big doggie grin as though it was a special treat just for him. She still wasn't sure what to do. She didn't want to go home, but she didn't want to sit forlorn in some campground dwelling on her sorry life either. More of Canada might help her escape her dismal state of mind.

For the second morning in a row, Jeanne woke from the same haunting nightmare. She tried to block it from her mind by turning her attention to her letter to Gary, but after rereading it, she was glad she hadn't sent it. Too often in the past, any confrontation with Gary ended up with nothing accomplished. He always had a reason everything was her fault. Nothing really changed. Deciding to give it more thought, she put the letter in her purse.

Later in the day, Jeanne crossed the border, with none of the excited anticipations of her original crossing back in Maine. With winter on its way, she headed for Toronto to buy a warm coat. The noisy street traffic and high-rise buildings of the city reminded her of New York. People rushed along the sidewalk in smart-looking outfits with the same slick cosmopolitan air.

In a fashionable department store a floor display reminded her she needed winter boots. She bought a pair of Sorels and a Bill Blass down-filled coat, maxi length, with a hood draping to her shoulders. "You look like a Russian princess," the saleslady said. She looked at herself in the full-length mirror, swaddled in black almost to her ankles, and saw only her doleful expression. She hadn't realized she looked so sad.

On her way out of town she drove passed St. Michael's Cathedral and gasped, suddenly remembering that tomorrow was October thirteenth, Joey's anniversary. How had it gone so completely out of her mind? She stopped to light a candle and sat for a long time in prayer, tormented by the thought that she might have forgotten him.

Back on the highway, Jeanne drove through a dreary landscape barely discernible from New York, the same ribbon of concrete, same malls, same franchise alleys, and same subdivisions. She went as far as Sudbury where once again, she stayed in a motel.

The next morning the nightmare woke her again. The figure

seemed to be hanging in the shower. She gave some thought to its persistence wondering what it was about, but with no answer that made sense, she tried not to dwell on it.

With little enthusiasm she opened her guidebook for Ontario to plan her route and was intrigued with a picture of James Bay. Jeff had talked about how beautiful it was and how he planned to go again. She could take pictures and send them to him.

There wasn't a road on the map, but she found a reference to a train from Cochrane. She headed north, hoping the railroad station had a safe place to leave the truck. She didn't think there'd be a problem taking the dog on the train. It never occurred to her that the ticket agent would flatly refuse to sell her a ticket.

"Why do you want to go up there?" he asked. "We only go as far as Moosonee and there's nothing there."

She wondered why she had to explain it. "I hear James Bay is very beautiful."

The agent gave her a skeptical look. "How do you plan to get there? The bay is twelve miles from the town. To actually see it, you'd have to hire a plane."

"I guess I didn't know that. Are there planes to hire? I can hire a plane if I have to."

"Listen, I hate to tell you this, but you can't go up to Moosonee by yourself. It's not safe. I wouldn't sleep at night if I sold you a ticket. You need to be part of a group or a scientist from the university or something. Not a woman all by yourself."

Jeanne walked out of the railroad station wishing she had gone west from Sudbury instead of this wasted detour. Tired and emotionally drained and frustrated, she pulled into the first motel she came to for the night. Before going to sleep, she read her letter to Gary again. This time she tore it up and wrote a new note:

Dear Gary, I'm going on with my trip in Canada. One week from now, I'll be in Calgary. I will have reached the Rocky Mountains. That is as far as I intend to go. At that point, I will head to Florida. I estimate it will take two weeks from Calgary. That gives you three weeks to take care of whatever that problem is causing you so much stress. If you haven't solved it by then, I'll assume it won't get solved. I won't wait any longer.

Jeanne.

She knew he never liked ultimatums but this one was as much for her as it was for him.

She was just about to fall asleep when she remembered her nightmare and got back out of bed to check the shower. Just as she thought, there was no way to suspend a rope in the middle of it.

In the morning, she dropped the letter in the mailbox with fresh resolve. There was no going back now. As she drove out of town, the early morning sun cast her shadow on the road before her. It wasn't until she was well on her way that she realized her nightmare hadn't returned.

She had picked Winnipeg as her destination for the night and thought with steady driving, she could put real miles behind her. The gas station attendant laughed when she told him that.

"You need two days to get to Winnipeg unless your partner there can help with the driving. He nodded toward Gulliver and laughed. "Bet he's a first-rate traveling companion. But yeah, you'd have to plan on at least fifteen or twenty hours. Maybe less if you drive real fast and never stop. You don't want to do that, do you? Your best bet is Thunder Bay."

"I want to get to the Rockies a week from now. How many days to Calgary?"

"Oh, five days is plenty for an easy drive. Not much between here and there, eh? But your first stop should be Thunder Bay.

Chapter 29

Not an hour out of Cochrane, Jeanne came to Smooth Rock Falls, where a small bridge crossed a narrow river jammed with logs. She assumed the factory-like building on the far side of the river belching white smoke was a pulp mill. Yellow foamy material floating among the logs convinced her some foul run-off from the factory was polluting the river. She pulled over to snap a picture.

She had just focused her camera when she heard a sharp yelp from Gulliver. He had run out on the logs and his hind legs had slipped into the water. His eyes were wide with panic. With his front paw nails wholly extended, he desperately clung to a log.

Filled with horror, Jeanne ran his way, sharply calling, "Gulliver! Come!" He was only a few feet from her, but beyond her reach. She looked around, frantic to do something, while continually shouting at him to come. He would only whimper.

Three logs extending out from the shore floating side by side made her think she might use them to get near him. But when she stepped on one, water spilled over the top. She jumped back onto land, fearing she'd end up like the dog.

Desperate to get to him, she took off her coat, lay prone on the ground and inched carefully out over the logs all the time praying Hail Marys. The logs stayed afloat just barely at the water line. She tried not to panic when she felt the cold water seeping through her sweater and continued pulling herself forward, hoping to get to him before he could no longer hold on. When she got alongside the dog, it took all her effort to stretch out her arm far enough to grab his collar. At first, he wouldn't budge, but a hard tug helped him scramble up beside her. Jeanne inched backwards, holding his collar as he followed along with one shaky step at a time until she came to the end of her makeshift raft, and he pulled away making a desperate leap for the shore.

Shivering in her wet sweater, Jeanne got into her coat, and sat on the ground beside the dog, trying to soothe the poor limp creature. With all her attention on Gulliver, she hadn't noticed a man in an orange vest coming her way until he stood beside them and said, "Are you alright?"

Still overwrought, she blurted out, "My dog fell off the logs. He could have drowned." If she expected sympathy, she didn't get it.

"Well, why the hell did you let him walk out there? That wasn't too smart now, was it?"

"I didn't let him. It never occurred to me he would do that. He was out there before I knew it."

He didn't seem to notice her defensive tone. He put his rifle down, which Jeanne hadn't noticed until that moment, and knelt beside the dog comforting him with a more sympathetic tone in his voice. "How you doing there, Boy?"

Gulliver whimpered and looked at him with pure pathos in his brown eyes.

"Scared yourself, eh? Your lady should take better care of you." From his pocket, he produced a piece of jerky and watched Gulliver demolish it in his usual two-gulp manner. He continued his friendly chat while he rubbed the dog's ears and patted his head. The quiet tone of his voice soon had Gulliver relaxed and himself again.

"What are you doing here, anyway?" he asked Jeanne.

"I was going by and saw the debris from the pulp mill and stopped for a picture."

He looked at the logs for a moment and then at the mill. "No, whatever it is, it's not from the mill. The river flows north here. Any mill run-off would be further upriver. I can't say for sure what you're looking at, but it's not from the mill."

His stern expression had softened to a friendly smile as he turned the conversation to where she came from and where she was going. Without thinking, she said Alaska, but when she heard herself, she tried to correct it. "Well, I might. It depends."

"Alaska, huh? Well, you'll need a decent coat. That one is not what you want walking around in the Bush now, is it? Unless you only plan to go to Anchorage, which would be a real shame." He left with a wave. "Gotta get back to my hunting buddies. Have a good trip. Oh, and trust me, you don't want to waste your time in Anchorage, eh?"

Jeanne watched him leave, disappointed to see him go. She wished she had invited him for coffee, but he was yards up the trail by the time it occurred to her to ask. Back in the camper, she dried Gulliver and turned the heater up to warm him. She changed out of her wet sweater then sat on the dinette bench petting Gulliver while she shuddered at his ordeal and the chance he could have drowned.

It was hours before she felt comfortable enough to get back on the road, so it was dark when she pulled into a truck stop just outside Thunder Bay and parked for the night between two tractor-trailers.

An 18-wheeler laboring to turn over its engine woke Jeanne early. Finally, the engine caught, and while it hummed at idle, another joined in the noise. In the next minutes, engines turned on one after another. Jeanne heard the big trucks pull out and then engage their brakes when they stopped at the exit. Now fully awake despite it still being dark, she decided she might as well get out of bed.

She went to the truck stop café for coffee, and when she returned, Gulliver was not in his usual spot at the cab window, anxiously watching for her. He sat tall, looking the opposite way at the Winnebago parked on the other side of the camper. The RV seemed vaguely familiar. As she got closer, Jeanne saw the black lab looking out the window. "Morgan," she said. "I don't believe it."

A cheery "there you are" came from behind her. "I knew it had to be you. What are you doing here? I thought you'd be in Alaska by now? Or are you already on the way back?"

"Hi, Rita. I took a few detours, I guess. I only got this far."

Tim sat in the RV while Jeanne and Rita walked the dogs at the edge of the lot, Gulliver and Morgan walking side by side like comfortable old buddies. Rita invited her to come with them to see Lake Superior, "It's just up the road at Silver Islet. There's this nice tearoom in the back of an old general store. Not real fancy, but right on the water. They have fabulous cinnamon rolls. C'mon, you want to see Lake

Superior, don't you?"

Jeanne drove behind on a road that felt carved through the middle of the woods. Other than a stretch of lake, they encountered nothing but trees until they came to a sign that said Sleeping Giant Provincial Park with an arrow pointing to a turn for a campground. Jeanne rued her decision to stay at the truck stop. She wished she had known the campground was so close.

She had just began to think the side trip to the lake was taking too long when the trees gave way to houses, and the water came into view. She followed the Stouts into the lot of a tall building on the lakeshore. Two large storefront windows were covered inside with sheets of paper, which gave the place an unoccupied look. Above the large entry door, a simple sign said, *Store*.

Tim stood with his head against the door window, his hands on each side of his face shading his eyes. "It doesn't look like anyone's there." He turned the knob, but the door was locked. "Bummer, I really wanted a cinnamon roll."

They stood in the parking lot in quiet disappointment until Rita suggested they go to Thunder Bay. "It has the best view of Sleeping Giant."

"You know, I wanted to get an early start for Winnipeg. I was planning to stay on the road and skirt by Thunder Bay. Why don't you go ahead? I can see a beach up the road where I can give Gulliver a nice romp before we get on the highway."

They said goodbye with the usual promises to keep in touch. Jeanne followed a narrow lane across a small bridge and past a few old log houses probably built in the last century. The lane continued between the beach and cottages tucked up against an imposing rock wall. Her mother would have called them bungalows. Except for the unique colors of royal blue and purple and mauvish crimson, they had the Rockaway Beach look to them with banks of windows across the front of closed-in porches. She imagined herself living on the edge of the lake, reaping all the bounties the water would give, not just the fish, but the chance to go for a sail, the lovely feel of the water in early morning swims, the dazzling moments of beauty when the rising sun glistened on the water or even when the clouds filled the sky and stormy weather stirred up whitecaps on an angry sea.

When the road turned away from the lake, Jeanne made a U-turn and went back a short way to park by the beach and let Gulliver run. A man walking toward her from the far end of the beach gave her a wave. He had the deep tan of a person who spent his days in the sun. Even in October, he wore khaki shorts. His Boonie hat reminded her of the hats her yacht club friends wore on their sailboats. As he came near, he extended his hand. "Hi I'm Dave. What brings you to our little neck of the woods?"

She turned toward the lake and stretched out both hands, "This. It's beautiful. And I heard they had good cinnamon buns at the store, but it's closed."

"Ah, yeah. We're not too happy about that. It's supposed to reopen soon. I hope so. It's like the heart of our little community."

"I gather you live here then."

He pointed. "That's my place with the blue trim."

"Oh, how lucky you are. I'd love to live here, looking out on the water. I bet it's exciting when it gets stormy. And the sunsets, I bet you get magnificent sunsets."

"Oh yes. No question the sunsets are beautiful. The way it colors the sky can take your breath away."

"Do people sit on the beach with their wine and watch it?"

"Sometimes. Particularly in summer, we get lots of campers from the Sleeping Giant Camp Ground up the road. But when you live across the lane there, you can just as easily watch from your front porch." He scanned the sky. "Should be beautiful tonight. You should stick around."

"Oh, I'd love to but I'm hoping to be in Winnipeg tonight."

"Winnipeg? Why's that?"

"I'm heading west. I once had a vague notion of going to Alaska, but now I'll be happy to just get to Calgary." *Alaska* was all he heard.

"Alaska, huh. I always wanted to go there."

"Well, that might have been the plan once, but it's too late in the season for that, now."

"Hey, do you think we could trade? You like it here so much, you take my house for a while, and I'll take your truck and go to Alaska."

She didn't know how to reply. She knew his comment was meant in jest but she stood squinting up at the house, thinking how she'd love it there. Her expression brought an "I was just kidding," from the beachcomber.

"Oh. I know, but I actually like the idea."

Driving away later, she imagined herself living in this little hamlet. She could end her trip right here. Move into a house by the water and sit on the beach every night watching the sun set. She'd get a sunfish to sail, and she'd paint her house canary yellow. She didn't expect any neighborhood busybodies would object.

She thought about how it would be if life worked that way and a person could find someone to swap places for a different life when the life they had disappointed them. She should tell Jeff she found a spot where she wouldn't mind being planted. She didn't think she'd be a different person, only more of who she was, which would suit her just fine.

Past Thunder Bay, the road wound through open fields interspersed with commercial enterprises displaying farm equipment and trucks. Occasionally, an ordinary ranch house or two-story colonial in neutral colors sat well back from the road. In almost every yard, an RV or camper trailer sat parked along the driveway as if the owners were members of a secret army of road warriors waiting for the signal to walk out the front door, turn the key for the last time, and make their long-awaited escape down the highway.

Later in the afternoon, she drove through a world of trees, mile after mile of them, standing toe-to-toe, arms reaching out to touch their neighbors. They spent their entire lives in one place wherever the seeds that sprouted them happened to fall, with their feet tucked firmly in the good earth, and nothing to do but breathe in and out and clean the air.

Now and then, the lush forest gave way to twisted, emaciated trees, their stubby green arms like clumps of green bushes hugging their trunks. With few neighbors to keep them company, they stood with their feet caught in the wrong place, lacking the sustenance they needed to flourish. Saddest of all were the dead leafless poles that had tried to grow for a time, only to succumb one day to their hostile world.

Because of rest stops for Gulliver and leaving late from Silver Islet, Jeanne still faced two hours to Winnipeg when she felt weary from the long drive. A sign for RV camping at the turn for Kenora brought her off the road. She had just finished raising the top and was getting Gulliver's leash to take him for a walk when a knock started him barking. She told him to stop as she opened the door.

"Bonjour." The woman's long curly hair was a match for Jeanne's, and she had to be about Jeanne's age. Jeanne responded with a "Bonjour" of her own which caused her visitor to switch to English when she heard Jeanne's pronunciation. "Oh, Welcome. I came to invite you to join us by the fire."

Jeanne thanked her for asking but explained she was tired from driving all day.

"Oh, you don't have to stay long. Just say hello to everyone. We watched you drive in. They'd all like to meet you."

Not wanting to offend, she left Gulliver in the truck and joined the group of campers sitting in a circle on folding lawn chairs around a fire in a fifty-gallon barrel. The place had the nostalgic rich aroma of Girl Scout camp in the morning when dew moistens the matted vegetation and the woodsy scent mixes with the smell of smoke from the campfire. Behind the gathered circle of campers, a line of RV trailers looked permanently fixed in place with built-in decks by their side doors. Chrysanthemums grew in boxes sitting on the decks. A few plots had detached sheds. Boats on trailers sat in the driveways.

They spoke French, which made it awkward when everyone

laughed, and Jeanne had no idea what they had said. Someone asked a question, which her hostess translated. "Where are you going, they want to know?"

"I'm heading for Calgary. I thought I might go to Alaska, but I got hung up in the Maritimes and now it's too late." Her comment brought laughter from her fellow campers, who made comments all in French. Her hostess, looking uncomfortable, caught her eye, then turned to the campers, shaking her head no, like a warning. She said something, which caused them all to stop talking and look at Jeanne. They're talking about me, she thought, and although she wished she knew what they were saying, she decided it was a good time to leave.

She hadn't been ten minutes in the camper when someone knocked. Her hostess stood outside her door with a young man by her side. She introduced him as her son, Michel, and asked if Jeanne would give him a lift to Saskatoon. "He has a job waiting for him."

"I wasn't planning to go to Saskatoon."

"Oh, I thought you said Alaska."

"I really don't know why I said that. I'm really just hoping to get to Calgary."

Mother and son looked at each other, the son shrugging, his teenage expression the same as Joey's when he'd just as well have his mother disappear. Unlike the rest of the men at the campfire, he wore his hair long, parted in the middle like a musician leftover from early hippie days. Jeanne thought he was only seventeen or even younger. After a pause, his mother said, "Well, if you could drop him at the intersection in Regina, I'd be so thankful."

Chapter 30

With plans to drive for at least eight hours, Jeanne left Kenora early with her charge, wishing she had found a way not to take him. Anxious about her upcoming call with Gary, she wasn't in the mood for company.

Michel had arrived that morning eager to get going, which surprised Jeanne, given his indifference the night before. He settled beside Gulliver and looked around filled with excitement. "Hey, wow, you have a CB,"

"I never use it. It doesn't work."

Without asking, he picked up the speaker and began turning knobs saying, "Skamper truck here. Anyone on?"

Jeanne thought he was only pretending until a voice startled her with a response.

"Blue Chevy here. I passed you a minute ago. Where're you headed?"

"Regina, how about you?" The conversation had Gulliver looking around confused, unable to find who was speaking. He let out one quick bark to make his point.

"How did you do that?" Jeanne asked when Michel's conversation ended. "I'm astounded."

"Easy. See this button here? You have to press it like this."

Jeanne didn't care for his smirk. He sounded as though he was giving instructions to a six-year-old.

Finished with the CB, he turned his attention to the tape player. "Got any music for that?"

"There's a case in the glove compartment."

He let out a shout when he opened the tape case. "Oh, wow, Willie Nelson!" He soon had *On the Road Again* blaring at full volume while he sang along with Willy. Jeanne warmed to his company, smiling at his enthusiasm.

They had just passed a sign announcing Regina when Michel sat up and turned off the tape. Jeanne noticed his initial enthusiasm seemed to have worn off. A new urgency took over his light-hearted demeanor. "You think you could take me with you?"

Jeanne wasn't sure what he meant. "What was that?"

"To Alaska, take me to Alaska with you. I have money. I could help pay for gas."

"I told your mother I'm not going to Alaska, Michel. I couldn't do that anyway. I promised I'd drop you off at the crossroads for Saskatoon. Don't you have a job?"

"I don't want that job. I can get a job in Alaska. They need loggers up there too, I bet."

"Michel, I told your mother I'd drop you off in Regina. That's what she expects. That's what I'm going to do."

With a teenager's pout, he slumped in his seat, turning his face to the window. Jeanne tried to soothe his feelings. "You know, if you want to go to Alaska, why don't you take this job and save your money. Then you can head up there with a plan. Maybe pick up an old car. Take a buddy with you. Share your trip with a friend, not a stranger old enough to be your mother."

He never said another word. When they got to Regina, she dropped him at the Route 11 crossroads where he could hitch a ride. He didn't even say "thank you" when he got out of the truck.

Even before Jeanne got back on the road, Michel had a lift, which relieved her worries about abandoning him in what felt like the middle of nowhere. She told herself there was nothing she could do for him. He'd be fine once he met other young people at his job. Gary took over her worries instead, but there wasn't much she could do about him either.

Tired from the eight-hour drive from Kenora, Jeanne turned into the first campground she saw in Moose Jaw and parked as far from the road as possible. On crisp leaves crunching beneath their feet, she walked Gulliver along a trail leading to the river. High on the opposite bank, a freight train, rolling west, sounded a lonesome whistle.

On the road again early, she rode beneath an endless violet-blue sky dotted with billowy clouds. Farm fields extended for miles in patches of brown and green. The lush woods of Ontario were long gone; the only trees here planted in single straight rows, their upper branches permanently bent to the prevailing prairie wind.

As she rolled along, a curious sight in the distance caught her attention. Stretching the full width of the far horizon, a bank of white clouds appeared to be emerging from the ground. The clouds kept rising as she continued west, until she had gained enough miles to put them high overhead. Broken now into separate masses suggestive of flat-bottomed barks with billowing sails, they headed south with the wind and floated away.

She popped the Willie Nelson tape into the cassette player saying, "Let's have a little country, huh, Gulliver?" He looked around the cab, in his usual way, to see what he was missing. "You're such a smart dog," she said and got a few thumps from his tail.

Jeanne drummed her fingers on the steering wheel as she sang along to the lively rhythm of *On the Road Again.* In the distance, the sun glinted off tall silos, sparkling silver against the big sky. She traveled on enthralled with the countryside until the punchy notes of Willie's guitar brought her back to the music. She had a fleeting thought to turn off the tape to avoid Willie's sad songs, but a passing scene grabbed her attention.

Out in the middle of an otherwise empty field, two barn-like structures stood side-by-side leaning toward each other as though they had spent years trying to bridge the small gap between them. As she rode past, absorbed and intrigued, she missed her moment. Willie was well into *Angels Flying Too Close to the Ground* when mid-song, the familiar refrain grabbed her in the throat.

I knew someday you would fly away.

Tears welling in her eyes, she pulled to the side of the road caught in that terrible moment the last time she saw Joey. Gulliver tilted his head, looking at her with his curious eyes, questioning with his soft little whines. Jeanne patted the seat, telling him to lie on his blanket.

Over the years since Joey died, she had learned to take some time for her emotions to settle. This time it wasn't working. Deep embedded memories of the early days after he died wouldn't go away. The longer she sat the more her thoughts moved to Gary. Was he the one she always knew would some day fly away?

How many times in the past had she thought their marriage was over only to have him charm her into putting it all behind them because it was so much easier than contemplating a divorce? Everything would be fine for a while. He'd be his charming self. She'd convince herself she did the right thing until, once again, it would all start tumbling down.

Right then, she recognized she had no reason to do this anymore, no reason to pretend, no reason to walk on eggshells trying to keep their marriage together.

Gulliver, who had been sitting quietly beside her, sat up and hit the door with his paw, announcing his need for a walk. Jeanne put on his leash and got out with him on the passenger side of the truck. They walked along a ditch separating the road from the flat prairie that surrounded her. She turned in a circle, looking across the landscape at the sky touching the earth in every direction. It was as though a gigantic blue dome covered the world, trapping everyone underneath it. Down the middle, the long road stretched before her in a straight line, all the way to the horizon.

She got back in the truck with new determination to move down that road and get to the Rockies, to call Gary and get things settled once and for all. She was beginning to accept that their conversation would end badly, but she wanted it finished.

She spent the night in Swift Current and was on the road when the sun came up. Traveling the long, straight highway, she noticed a subtle change in the landscape. A slight roll had taken over the once flat pastures, and barbwire fenced in the once open prairie. Out in the fields, cattle grazed in scattered bunches.

Not long after, a hint of white on the horizon made her think clouds were coming her way again, but the images disappeared when she started down an incline. Near the bottom of the short slope, the road spanned a cattle crossing and then climbed back up the hill. As she rode over the crest, the hint of white appeared again. She let out a shout when she realized what it was. "Gulliver!" He jumped up to look out the window. "It's the Rockies, Gulliver." The sudden hint of snow-covered peaks filled her with energy. The mountains kept rising as she traveled west, higher and higher, like a beacon leading her forward.

In a small café outside of Calgary where she stopped for coffee, a radio played in the background and Jeanne listened to Stevie Nicks as if she were singing *Landslide* just for her.

Well, I've been afraid of changin'
'Cause I've built my life around you
But time makes you bolder
Even children get older
And I'm getting older too…

Jeanne stayed the night at a campground just off the highway and then went to Banff the next day to check into a motel to have a phone available that didn't need quarters. The following morning, she called Gary. Listening to the phone ringing on the other end, she had a sudden thought—what if he didn't get my letter?

She needn't have worried. "Where have you been? I got your letter and I've been waiting for you to call."

"I said I'd call in one week. It's one week."

"It might have helped if I knew what you meant. Wait; let me read it. Okay, it says *at that point, I will turn around and head for Florida.* What's that supposed to mean? I thought you understood I'm not ready for that until after you go to Alaska. Are you telling me you're not going to Alaska? Well, let me tell you again. You're not coming here. Not yet. Not for now."

There it was; what she had expected. In a way she was disappointed, but it wasn't as though it came as a surprise. Nothing had changed. Anger still filled his voice. A moment of quiet hovered on the phone line until Jeanne found the courage to ask her question. "What's her name, Gary?"

A long pause and a sigh followed as Jeanne waited. Gary spoke with a subtle change to his voice and a small diminishing certainty. "Who told you?"

"No one told me. I finally remembered those other times you constantly spewed anger, with me trying to figure out what I did to upset you. It always turned out that you had somebody else. I should have figured this out long ago, but I kept blaming it on Joey. In my mind, you were bitter and angry because we lost our son. Perhaps that's still true, but I started getting this nagging feeling it might be something more. It wasn't lost on me that this is your classic behavior whenever you have someone on the side. But for a long time, I couldn't believe it. You were so remorseful the last time, so sincere in your promises. So what's her name, not that it matters to me anymore."

The angry, accusing voice took on the practiced tone of apology. "Rose, her name is Rose. I've been trying to break it off, but I can't just put her out on the street. She has no place to go. And she has a son. I'd be putting them both out on the street."

"She has a son?"

"He's twelve. He helps me with the boat. He really likes sailing."

"Is that what this is about, Gary? Her son?"

"No, no, I said it's only temporary."

"Does Rose know that?"

"She knows I have a wife."

"So, let's see if I understand this. You're telling me, your wife, you can't put your girlfriend out on the street just yet, even though that's exactly what you're doing with me, your wife, leaving me on the street where I've been for almost two months now, and where you insist you want me to stay until you tell me otherwise. 'I don't care where you go,' you said. Remember that. The thing I can't understand is how you ever imagined that would be okay."

"Jeanne, you know I care about you."

"Can't you see how ludicrous that is?"

"Jeanne, I'm trying to fix it. I'm trying. It's got more complicated than I expected. I need you to understand."

"So tell me, Gary, was this Alaska trip all a ruse to keep me away from Florida?

"No, nothing like that. I thought it would be good for you."

"Remember what I said the last time you got involved: there wouldn't be another chance? It won't work this time, Gary. You let it go too long. There may have been a point we might have survived this, but I don't want to anymore. I can finally stop hanging suspended and figure out what to do with my life."

"Don't say that. Look, we can sort it all out. Just finish the trip and we'll sort it all out."

"I'm going to hang up now, Gary. It's useless to talk anymore. When I figure out what I'm going to do, I'll let you know."

"Wait. Wait."

"Goodbye, Gary."

Part Four

A journey is a person in itself; no two are alike.
The certain way to be wrong is
to think we control it.

John Steinbeck

Chapter 31

Daylight seeped through the gaps between the canvass window shades waking Jeanne to an odd sensation she couldn't name. She sat up in alarm to check the dog, but he lay asleep where she had left him, under Joey's coat keeping him warm.

She listened for the pleasant babble of the brook outside her door. When she arrived late in the night, the sound of rushing water, had given her something to look forward to in the morning. Now, only the faintest murmur came through the stillness as if she had stolen away in the middle of the night to camp by a quieter stream.

She pushed aside the window's canvass, but unable to see through the frost on the vinyl, she climbed out of bed and opened the camper door. The countryside before her filled her with awe. White Christmas trees covered the valley, bunching together along the rolling plains and climbing the foothills, where they disappeared in the haze high on the slopes. Snow had come in the night, muffling the brook and filling the stillness with a palpable quiet.

"Gulliver, it's snowing," she whispered. He lifted his head and perked an ear. She hurried to dig out the boots she bought in Toronto and grabbed Joey's North Face jacket from Gulliver's bed. With the dog right behind her, she jumped from the camper. Snowflakes fluttered around her. She raised her face to the sky and enjoyed the frosty sensation of falling snow settling on her tongue.

Gulliver stood a moment, unsure what to do, before taking off like a jackrabbit alive with fresh energy in his old bones. He pushed his nose in the snow and whipped his head back and forth, then rolled on his back, kicking his legs in the air. Jeanne threw a snowball his way, and when it disintegrated in his mouth, he looked confused. She threw another, and when that one also fell apart, he gave a sharp bark. They played in the snow on the way to the washroom, and when they finally returned to the camper, Jeanne decided to stay put for the rest of the day.

Gary came back to mind with her coffee. It startled her. How had he slipped so completely out of her thoughts? Why wasn't she mourning her marriage from the minute she woke?

She had lingered in Banff after their phone call, unable to find the impetus to get back on the road and when she finally left late in the day, she drove until dark not really knowing where she was going. She couldn't stop dwelling on the sudden conclusion of twenty years together. Today, with some time to recover, she realized it wasn't sudden at all. Their marriage had been creeping away for years, and she had become inured. The eighty percent figure made new sense to her. Those were the marriages already broken and waiting for the final death knell.

From the moment they tore asunder the night Joey died, she and Gary never mended. She had tried to wait him out, telling herself he needed time to get over his grief, but she couldn't alleviate the repressed rage that came through the phone. Now she understood her efforts to have been useless. They were too damaged to help each other. They each needed to find their own way. It was time to step aside and wish him well. Time to pursue her life as best she could on her own.

In the afternoon, Jeanne took Gulliver out in the snow again, but her morning euphoria had disappeared. The trees wept in the warming air. Back in the camper she sat at the table and stared out the window thinking how everything she had known her entire adult life had melted away. She climbed into bed and let herself cry quiet tears.

When Gulliver's whines called to her under her quilt, she looked down to see his urgent gaze asking to join her, so she piled the dinette cushions on top of each other and helped him climb up to the bed. He lay with his front paw curled around her arm. Tomorrow she'd try to come up with a plan, but tonight she wished only to sleep.

She woke to a new awareness that she was no longer weighed down by the pressure to fix their broken life. She could finally stop the daily argument with herself to turn her wheels around and head south. Like an epiphany she suddenly realized she could do whatever she wanted. Go where she wanted when she wanted with no one to answer to and no nagging concern weighing on her mind.

She rejected returning to Northport. That would mean explaining to everyone, which was something she'd rather avoid until she knew what she wanted to say. Since she wasn't ready for Northport, and no longer needed to go to Florida, the only choice she could see was to go forward. Why not keep driving until she figured things out. Who knew what the road had to offer?

She headed north on the Icefields Parkway, winding her way through scenic mountains with craggy peaks rising above her on both sides of the road. Now she understood why Jeff had said not to miss it. Towering walls looked as though a sculptor had used a giant chisel to carve their faces. Some slopes appeared layered, tier upon tier in different shades of stone, hinting at different ingredients in their making. Every time she came around a curve, another piece of spectacular beauty lay framed in her windshield, as though a master road builder had deliberately engineered the parkway to maximize every scenic moment. Her doldrums slowly faded as she became more and more enthralled with the majesty of the country around her.

Midday, Jeanne came over a hill to the long white expanse of a glacier glistening in the sun. She wasn't prepared for the enormity. She pulled over to join other travelers standing beneath the massive face, but soon shivered in the frigid air. "Brrr, Gulliver, isn't it chilly?" With his tail pulled in, and his ears pinned back, Gulliver appeared to agree.

Jeanne continued up the highway, lecturing herself that as much as she wanted to sample every scenic marvel, she'd get nowhere if she succumbed to every temptation.

Or so she thought until she came upon the quiet hamlet of Jasper. Tucked amidst snow-capped mountains, the alpine town's quaint shops and cafes intrigued her. Why should she push past it? Where was she trying to go? With nothing to stop her, she could indulge her whims, have a nice long hot shower and put on a dress for a change for dinner in one of the charming village restaurants. At the first hotel she came to, she pulled in for the night.

Before going to bed, she gathered all her travel guidebooks

to sketch out some plan for the following day. *The Milepost*, her guide to the Alaska Highway, showed the Alcan just a day's ride away at Dawson Creek. She checked the index for the distance and time and found it would take three days, maybe four, to get from there to the Alaska border.

She was so close. Could she actually do it? Nothing on the map intrigued her more, and the worry of getting caught in the snow no longer mattered. The snow had already caught her, and the Skamper weathered it just fine. She shouted to the dog. "We're going to Alaska, Gulliver! Do you believe it?" She could hardly believe it herself.

In the morning she strolled through town with Gulliver on his leash, using every bit of his doggie charm to garner attention at every encounter. She bought a dozen postcards with pictures of the Icefields Parkway and took time to write quick notes before leaving town.

To Jeff, she wrote: *I can't convey in words the wonder I feel driving this road. Thank you for telling me about it.*

In her note to her brother Kenneth, who had given her Robert Frost's "The Road Not Taken," she wrote: *I'm finally continuing up the road to Alaska. This way, as the poet says, "somewhere ages and ages hence" I won't be looking back wondering what I missed. Will it "make all the difference?" I guess I'll find out.*

She considered sending a long letter to Anna but settled for a brief note about her last conversation with Gary, asking her not to mention it to anyone, particularly her mother. *I'll tell everyone the complete story when I get back.*

She sent a card to Sean and Alice and to each of her daughters and sisters, and to her mother, telling them that by the time they got her card she would be in Alaska, adding descriptions of the beautiful highway and leaving out everything else. There was so much more she could say, but it would take pages.

Her final postcard went to Paul and Barbara although she wasn't sure they still expected her. *I didn't think I would make it but I'm working my way to Toksook Bay. When I get to Alaska in a few days I'll call to see if the invitation is still open.*

With new resolve she headed for Dawson Creek with plans to check out the truck before heading up the Alcan. The next day she was at a garage when it opened. "How long will it take to service my pickup?"

"Depends on what you need. Is there a problem?"

"No problem. I had it winterized in Buffalo, but I'm heading to Alaska, and I thought I should have everything checked. I don't want any surprises."

"You're going up the Alcan? In case you hadn't noticed it's the first day of November. I hate to tell you, but the tourist season ended. Everyone is coming back." He had one of those grins that made her think he was teasing or maybe even ridiculing. "Of course, if you're planning to stay in Alaska, that's different."

"No, I'm just visiting. So, how long to check it out?"

"It depends on what we find. If you like, you can wait across the street in the coffee shop. I'll come get you when we're finished."

With no objection to his presence from anyone in the restaurant, Gulliver lay quietly at her feet. The waitress had gone behind the cash register to take a drag on a cigarette before coming to Jeanne's table with the menu. She asked Jeanne if she was getting her car fixed.

"It's my pickup. I have a pickup."

"I wondered. Harry sends everybody over here to wait. Not that I'm complaining." She was plump and fifty-something, with a smoker's gravelly voice, and whether out of nosiness or boredom or just being friendly, she seemed to want to chat. Jeanne asked her if there was a place to camp up the highway.

"Up the highway? The Alcan? You're not doing that, I hope. It's winter. Nobody's driving the highway now, not with snow on the way. Well, unless you count the semis." She cocked her head towards the window where three tractor-trailers sat side by side in the parking lot, ready to pull out.

"They like to brag about how tough they are. You know, look macho."

"I had planned to do it earlier," she said, "but I got delayed." She thought how lame that sounded.

"I'm afraid you'll find everything closed. You might have to sleep in your pickup. Does your truck have a cap?"

"Better, I have a camper."

"Oh, that's smart. I guess you could stay at the Hot Springs. Most likely won't be anyone there. You could take a dip in the pool, even if it's cold, I mean, especially if it's cold. The water is warm. If you want my opinion, it's the only thing to recommend driving north right now."

Jeanne had just finished her second cup of coffee when the mechanic popped his head in the door and interrupted their conversation. He nodded at the waitress and waved to Jeanne to come.

"Truck's all set," he said. He filled her in as they walked back to the garage. "Since you had it winterized, there wasn't much to do. Antifreeze is full. I checked the battery and oil, and both look good. Glad to see you have new tires. I replaced your wipers, but everything else is good."

He reached his arm out in front of Jeanne to stop her from stepping into the street as a car passed. "Oh, and I greased your hubs. They should be easier for you to turn. My guess is you'll need 4-wheel drive, maybe after you pass Fort Nelson." Back at the service station he said he had filled the gas tank and the extra gas can she had. "Glad to see it because you might need it. I didn't see a pour spout. You have a funnel, I hope."

"Of course," she said, remembering when Tony dug one out of his garage for her. She made a mental note to find it.

"Good. You don't want to run out of gas and end up with a long hike to a gas station. You should make a point of filling up at every road stop." He had a habit of studying her face between comments.

As he filled out the invoice, he told her she should prepare for snow.

"I'd sell you chains, but I doubt you could get them on by yourself." He paused again as he searched her face before continuing. "If it snows hard, the best thing to do is pull over and wait. Make sure you pick someplace flat. You don't want to drive into a ditch. With that neat little camper you have, you can hang out for days until a plow comes. Just get on the road and follow behind the plow. You should be fine."

On her way to the door, she turned to ask how far the hot springs were. "I mean driving time. How long a drive?"

Again, the curious look. She wondered if she reminded him of someone he knew.

"You mean Liard? It's a full day's drive. I'd say a good 8 or 9 hours. You'll get there in time to sleep. That's if you don't stop anywhere. Except for gas. Make sure you stop for gas."

Jeanne waited to leave because she could see he had more to say.

"The Hot Springs, eh? That's an excellent choice. I'd guess by now everything is closed, most likely to Whitehorse, and that's at least three days away." She thanked him and was turning to leave when he called after her. "You know what would be nice." His smile was different now, not so smart-alecky. "Could you stop on the way back and let me know how it went. I mean, I don't know how long you plan to visit, but I'd like to know everything was okay. Wouldn't be much trouble. You'll have to pass through here to get back to New York. Right?

Chapter 32

Well after dark, Jeanne pulled into the parking lot at Liard Hot Springs, wanting only to sleep after ten hours on the road. In the morning, she stepped out of the camper to discover she and Gulliver had the whole place to themselves. She grabbed her towel and put Gulliver on his leash, just in case.

Snow had fallen lightly in the night dusting the ground with a new white blanket. She found a path at the end of the lot that led to a narrow raised wooden walkway traversing a snow-covered marsh. In the distance, the walkway disappeared into the woods, luring her onward. An aura of mystery filled the landscape. She hesitated, not knowing what lay ahead.

Steeling herself against her fears, she followed the walk and entered a wintery fairyland shrouded in mist rising from the green water of a rock-bound pond. The subtle scent of sulfur filled the air. Everything was white with frost—the spindly evergreens, the curling branches of the leafless trees, the smaller bushes.

She left her clothes on the bench and sank in the lovely warmth. Gulliver lay by the pool with his chin on his front paws, sulking because she wouldn't let him join her, but she worried his wet coat might freeze when he got out.

The warm spring waters caressed her skin. She swam a gentle breaststroke then floated on her back, looking up into feathery snowflakes slowly twirling out of the sky, melting away as they reached the warm air above the pool. Tension drained from her body. Enchanted and filled with peace, she hated to leave.

It was well past noon when she headed back to the truck with Gulliver padding behind her, her body warm in the frigid air. In the quiet, the only sound came from the crunch of the snow as she walked on the snow-covered path.

Then something else, a strange and subtle beat somewhere far off behind her. She thought at first it might be the wind, until she remembered there was no wind. And the steady beat was far too rhythmic for wind. She came to a complete halt thinking to quiet her racing heartbeat; her rising panic dampened somewhat by the lack of any concern in her usually watchful companion. "Do you hear that?" Jeanne whispered, but Gulliver merely wagged his tail and tilted his head.

She hesitated to look back toward the drumming, steadily coming closer, fearing what she might find. But she needed to know. As she twisted around, she followed the sound to a solitary raven high in the sky, his wings beating a steady *whoosh, whoosh, whoosh*. He flew above them, his head cocked just enough to view the small tableau on the ground. For a long moment, she stood transfixed, watching the raven, listening to its wings as he flew off into the trees.

When she started out again, the awe of that moment went with her. She couldn't recall ever hearing the wings of a bird in flight. How to explain it? The full measure of quiet didn't fit well into words. Words were inadequate to touch the feel of it, the palpable presence, the emanation of something alive. She thought it ironic that silence was spoken of in terms of the sounds it brings to the ears. The drop of a pin, one's own breathing, and yes, the rhythmic beat of a bird's wings in flight. She would write in her journal: *"Today it was so quiet, I heard a raven fly."*

Back on the road, she drove in wonder at the ever-changing scenery. The need to keep going took hold of her, to see what spectacular delights lay around the next bend. She didn't stop at Watson Lake or Swift River. The day had begun to lose its light when she first noticed the gas tank on empty. She guessed she still had ten miles to Teslin and was praying she would make it when the truck bucked and stalled. With the power steering gone, she held the wheel steady, struggling to coast off the road until the truck slowly rolled to a stop.

Reflected in her headlights, the relatively flat stretch of ground with no ditches or trees in her way gave her reason to celebrate. Had she run out of gas ten minutes sooner, the high-cut road bank would have forced the dangerous predicament of stopping on the highway.

The difficulty of fumbling in the dark convinced her it would be better to wait for daylight to fill the gas tank. She climbed in the camper and cranked up the top with smug satisfaction. Although stranded in the middle of nowhere, she had no reason to worry with the Skamper providing everything she needed to spend the night.

The next morning an orange sky gave a warm backdrop to the far-off snow-capped mountains. Jeanne jumped from the camper, relishing the clean air. Out on the road, Gulliver trotted back and forth, his nose high, sniffing the breeze, getting his doggie bearings in a new place.

Having to resort to her extra can of gas proved more difficult than Jeanne had expected. Just lifting the heavy container out of its bracket on the back of the camper was difficult enough, but trying to balance it to pour the gas into the tank took every bit of strength she could muster. Just as she felt she had the task under control the gas bubbled back out of the funnel. She tried repositioning it only to have the same thing happen when she poured again.

Despite knowing the gas meter registered empty, she climbed back in the truck to recheck it. The engine cranked strongly when she turned the key in the ignition, but the truck wouldn't start. Pumping the gas pedal didn't help. She made another attempt to fill the tank, only to see the gas bubble out once again.

She tried to think what could be blocking the gas from going in. There didn't seem to be anything stuck in the tank. The funnel went in easily enough. Not understanding the problem or how to fix it, she sat trying to puzzle out what to do, vacillating between waiting for someone to come along the road or walking to find a gas station with a mechanic, hoping it wouldn't be too far away. Since she couldn't estimate how long she might wait, she headed out on the road, hoping a car would come along and give her a lift.

With Gulliver pulling on his leash, she was praying for a gas station around the next bend when a blue 18-wheeler passed by pulling a double load. She had heard it coming behind her for a while but didn't consider flagging it to stop. "We can't expect a big truck to pull over, can we pup?"

That's when she saw it pull to the side of the highway, coming to a stop at a good distance up the road. Presently a tall figure came out from in front of the truck. The man wore a light tan field coat, unbuttoned, and no hat.

He stood looking her way with his hands on his hips and then waved, beckoning her to hurry. "I take it that's your rig back there," he said when she arrived. He opened the passenger door and scooped Gulliver up with ease, placing him in the cab as though he were a small puppy.

"You're giving us a lift?" Jeanne asked, surprised.

"Why else would I stop?" He gave her a boost to the running board. Back in the truck, leaning over the wheel, he was checking his mirror, steering the big rig out onto the highway when he said, "So let me guess, you ran out of gas."

"Well, yes and no. The truck ran out of gas, but I have an extra can, only when I tried to pour it in the tank, it just came bubbling back out."

"Damn, I could have fixed that. It sounds like your tank's not venting properly. Damn, there's no way I can turn around now. I'll get Jesse to do it."

He picked up his CB. "Roy here. Coming in with a customer. We're twenty minutes out. I think she may have an airlock; can't get gas in the tank. Can I leave it to you?"

Jesse's voice came through the crackling in the speaker. "Yeah, I'm here. Only twenty minutes? I might as well wait until you get here."

Jeanne couldn't believe her good luck, not only her rescue, but here she was riding in an 18-wheeler, bouncing along to the steady hum of the throbbing engine and the wheels rumbling on the road. She sat in the big truck cab, looking through the big window, taking in the countryside from her high perch, feeling like a kid with a new toy.

To make small talk, she asked the trucker if he drove the road often. "I've been driving the highway off and on since 1959," he told her. "I quit a few times, once for five years, but I always came back." This time he intended to stay. "I'm never happy doing anything else."

She told him about the waitress in Dawson Creek who said the drivers who haul the big trucks up the Alcan only do it for the danger.

He laughed. "What sense does that make? That shows how much she knows. Let me ask you something. Have you noticed what beautiful country you're in? Some stretches of this road take my breath away. There are days I get so carried away I just want to bring everything to a halt and settle here in the peace and beauty forever."

Jeanne took a long look at this slightly balding man. She would never have imagined him a romantic, full of poetic ideals. Here he was guiding all this diesel power between mountains, around sharp curves, and she imagined probably sometimes on roads slick with ice or through blinding snow, and according to him, all for inspiring wilderness moments that filled his soul.

They traveled on in silence until Jeanne remembered she hadn't thanked him.

"I have to say you surprised me, stopping for me the way you did. I mean it must be a real bother with this big truck. I really appreciate it. Thanks."

He laughed, with an added glimmer in his blue eyes. "Believe me, sweetheart, it's no bother. I'll tell you what would be a bother—if I had to sit in Whitehorse tonight and listen to the guys coming behind me rag me out for leaving you on the side of the road. If I didn't pick you up, one of them would have. I'd never hear the end of it, and every time another trucker showed up, I'd have to sit there and listen to them tell the story over again."

"Wow, I never realized truckers were such good Samaritans."

He laughed even harder. "Good Samaritans, oh, that's funny. You don't get it, do you? Think. How many hot chicks are just strolling along the Alcan in the middle of nowhere, looking to get a ride? That's every trucker's daydream."

Jeanne returned to watching the far-off mountains, hoping she wasn't blushing. She couldn't remember anyone ever calling her a "hot chick."

Water soon appeared in the distance spanned by a bridge with high arched trusses on each side that gave it a scalloped look. At the bottom of the hill, they came out of a curve and headed for the bridge, which looked only marginally wide enough for the truck and only if one approached it right on target. Jeanne grabbed the edge of her seat, wanting the driver to slow down, but when the 18-wheeler rolled onto the bridge perfectly lined up in its lane, she relaxed, impressed with how the guy beside her made driving his big rig seem so easy.

The truck driver pulled into the gas station on the other side of the bridge and waved to Jessie waiting in his pickup. Jeanne was thankful for the 18-wheeler. She would have had a long walk. With some regret, she got out with the dog.

"Hey, what's your name?"

"Jeanne, and thanks again for the rescue."

"Listen. Tell you what. When you get to Whitehorse, come by and let me know you made it. Okay? You'll see my truck on the way into town. I'll be in the truck stop with the rest of the guys."

"With the rest of the guys? Oh, sure. I'll do that." Jeanne smiled.

Roy laughed, knowing she was on to his little gambit. "Promise?"

When Jeanne and Jesse reached her stranded camper, he used a different funnel and had the truck started in minutes. Jeanne was back on the road following him to the gas station to fill the tank wondering how long it would take her to catch up to Roy. In Whitehorse a few hours later, she saw the blue truck with its white stripe across the door parked on the edge of the lot near the road where she would be sure to see it. With Roy's truck were at least five more. No way was she walking into that.

Chapter 33

The promise of a long hot shower led Jeanne to pass up the RV Park for a motel. Late in the evening, she walked Gulliver in the woods in the back of the building, and on the way back to the room, he suddenly retched as though he was trying to throw up. "What's the matter, pup?" He looked at her with sad eyes. Back at the motel, he retched again. Hoping it would help, Jeanne filled his bowl with water and put it on the bathroom floor.

Listening to him lapping, she concluded he must be thirsty until loud agonizing yelps, like someone kicked him, or he was hit by a car, sent her running to the bathroom. Gulliver staggered toward her with panic in his eyes, his gait so stiff he could barely walk. When she knelt on the floor beside him, he pawed at her arm and tried to get into her lap. She did her best to comfort him. "What is it, puppy? What is it?"

A loud banging on the door startled her. Before she could respond, a young man walked into the room without waiting for an invitation. She had seen him earlier, going into the room next to hers. The beret he wore looked noticeably foreign and his accent confirmed that observation when he spoke. "I heard your dog. What happened?" With brows knit in concern he knelt at Gulliver's side.

"I don't know. He had been drinking water and suddenly started wailing. He can't walk very well, and his belly is all swollen."

Jeanne's visitor gently talked to Gulliver in what she guessed was German and then told her to call the front desk. "Tell them your dog needs a veterinarian."

"But where will they find a vet at this hour. It must be ten o'clock?"

"Call! Call! Tell them it's an emergency." Gulliver was lying on his side now, his panting labored, each breath bringing a painful moan.

To Jeanne's surprise, the front desk gave her two numbers, telling her to first dial 8 and then 0. When neither answered, she called the front desk again.

The desk clerk gave Jeanne a third number. Maddeningly the line was busy. Gulliver was yelping in pain again while the motel neighbor tried to soothe him. She called a second time and found the number still in use.

Frantic now, she called back to the front desk and got a fourth number. This time an answering service operator asked her for her name and number and the nature of the problem. Jeanne described the situation, emphasizing the emergency. She had little faith in a prompt response, but only minutes after hanging up, the phone rang. "Dr. Kilpatrick here. I don't like the sound of your message."

When Jeanne described Gulliver's condition at the moment, the heavy sigh on the other end of the phone wasn't encouraging. The vet told her to come straight to the office. "The sooner you get him here, the better." He gave her directions, which she wrote on the phone book cover. She read them back to be sure they were correct. Gulliver was now letting out intermittent yelps, trembling with his eyes wide. Without waiting for Jeanne's consent, her motel neighbor picked Gulliver up and started for the door. "I know where that is. Come."

He placed the dog gently on the seat and squeezed in next to him. The vet was waiting at his office door in his slippers with rumpled hair, looking as though he had just woken. "Excuse my appearance," he said, "I've had a long day of emergencies." He looked the dog over quickly and then told Jeanne that Gulliver had bloat. "He's in a lot of pain. I see he's an old guy, eh? I can euthanize him for you."

Jeanne looked at him, speechless, a chill rushing through her body, trying to adjust to what he had said.

"Look, I'm sorry, I know it's hard, but you have to decide. I haven't much time. I have two hours at the most if you want me to help your dog. I need to get started, or I might as well euthanize him."

"I can't just put him to sleep. I can't. I need to get him home."

The vet nodded in resignation. "Okay, I'll need to keep him overnight. I'll be putting a tube in his stomach and he'll need anesthesia." In a gentler tone, he said, "I should tell you, his chances are not good. Even with the best of care, the percentage rate for a good outcome is low, and with an old dog, it's even less likely. You need to prepare. You understand?"

Jeanne fought tears as they drove back to the motel, trying to keep her composure in front of a stranger. His name was Bernd, and she was right about Germany. He was on a semester break from law school, spending the time hitching across Canada. He said he had a dog at home like hers and tried to assure her that Gulliver would be fine.

In the morning, Bernd knocked on Jeanne's door early. "I should go with you to the vet. You should have someone with you."

On the way Jeanne drove past the truck stop and noted the blue truck had left. She hoped Roy had seen her pickup at the motel and at least knew she had made it, but she couldn't worry about that now. Gulliver was her only concern.

At the vet's office, Dr. Kilpatrick led Gulliver into the waiting room and Jeanne noticed immediately the dog's normal if unsteady gait. She knelt by his side and looked into his face, as he leaned against her, a few limp wags of his tail, about all the energy he could muster.

"It went better than I expected," were the first words the vet said. He seemed pleased, less intense than last night. Jeanne stifled tears of relief.

"He's okay for the moment. Now I have to tell you bloat tends to recur. I'd give him a few days to recover before he does any activity. Let him sleep today, okay. And don't give him too much water; say a cup at a time. Okay?"

"Can he eat?"

"You can offer him a little, but he may not have much appetite. You said you wanted to get him home. What part of the states are you from?"

"I'm from New York, but right now, I'm actually on my way to Alaska."

"Alaska, good. New York is a good ten days from here. I'd rather he have a follow-up sooner. Fairbanks is better for that. You can be there in two days driving straight and they have excellent vets. I'll give you my number in case they want to call." On the statement he wrote: *remove sutures Nov. 19 or thereabouts.*

Bernd lifted Gulliver onto the seat in the truck and stroked him gently while they drove. At the motel, he carried Gulliver into the room and laid him on the bed. As Jeanne covered the dog with the spread, Bernd stood back and watched. "I will go with you to Fairbanks when you leave. Yes?" He had decided, nodding his head, as though confirming it for himself. "I can help with your dog. What if he gets sick again? You'll need my help. I'll go with you."

Jeanne considered his offer, tempted to take him with her. "Let me think about it. First, I want to let Gulliver rest like the vet said and make sure he's okay."

That afternoon Jeanne called Gary. She had planned on giving it more time before she talked to him again, but she had to tell him about the dog. He was a different Gary when he answered the phone: none of the squelched anger she had grown to expect in his voice.

"I've been waiting for you to call," he said. "We have to talk."

"I know, but not now. I'm only calling to tell you Gulliver had a medical emergency. I'm in Whitehorse waiting for him to get his strength back."

"Whitehorse? So you're almost there. Good."

Jeanne wanted to avoid that conversation. "I only called to tell you I had to write a check to the vet for $300. He said adjusted the amount from Canadian dollars as close to the exchange rate as he could.

"$300. What happened?"

Jeanne explained the problem, talking as though nothing had changed between them, and they were still who they always had been.

"That must have been awful for him, poor guy." He spoke with genuine sympathy. "Look, I realize things are difficult. Just try to take things easy. Get your trip done and come home. I'll come up to Northport for Christmas, and we'll work everything out then. Just take care of Gulliver and don't make any big decisions until we talk, okay?"

It used to be the moment she waited for, the accommodating voice, the charm turned on, which usually meant the latest episode of disenchantment was ending. She'd seize the opportunity to get everything back to normal. This time she couldn't bring herself to pretend.

"So tell me, Gary, what's your friend doing for Christmas? Will she be coming with you?"

He sighed before he answered, trying to cover the irritation in his voice. "I told you, I'm working on it."

Gulliver slept through the entire day, not eating or drinking, getting up once for a brief walk, after which Jeanne struggled to boost him back up on the bed. She sat beside him, ever watchful, fearful, praying his problem wouldn't return.

The following day Gulliver appeared stronger with notably more spring in his step. He ate a little breakfast, and when Bernd came by, Gulliver walked over to him with a wagging tail. "How are you doing, Boy?" Bernd said.

"I think he looks a lot better, don't you."

"He does look better. I'm glad. Now I don't feel quite so bad to tell you this. I know I said I'd go with you, and I wish I could, but I'm afraid that's not possible. I found out they don't have any buses. Is this not ridiculous? No buses. How can that be? Alaska is America. No?"

"I know you want to help, but I don't think it's necessary. We should easily get to Fairbanks without a problem. I hate to think of you going all the way out of your way for nothing."

"I wanted to help, but I'd have no way to get to British Columbia. I have mail waiting for me there. I could hitch, but I think it might be colder than I'd like. I don't mind the rain, but I'm not good with the cold."

The next day Jeanne drove away from Whitehorse, determined to follow Dr. Kilpatrick's advice to have Gulliver checked by a vet as soon as possible. She'd split the 600 miles to Fairbanks over two days. She didn't think she could manage a ten- or eleven-hour slog and she knew it wouldn't be good for the dog to be cooped up in the truck so long.

She missed Bernd. He had come early that morning to help her get Gulliver into the truck. He wanted her to promise to write, telling her she must come to Germany. When she dropped him off at the intersection, where he hoped to get a ride to Victoria, he surprised her with a gentle hug, a brotherly kiss. She watched him waving in her side-view mirror as she drove off to get gas. After she filled the tank, she drove back past the intersection, hoping to thank him one more time and wish him well, but the empty corner saddened her to the point of tears. *How silly. I should be glad he got a ride.*

Chapter 34

Leaving Whitehorse, Jeanne continued up the Alcan Highway determined to get to Fairbanks and find a vet. Gulliver slept beside her curled up on his blanket. She listened to him breathing, her hand gently stroking the back of his head.

Anxious about her dog, she rarely noticed the mountains in the distance, or the trees, or the sky. On another day, she might have enjoyed the long road along Kluane Lake, but today, it seemed endless. She wondered when she'd ever get past it. Even caribou crossing the road only momentarily distracted her.

Repeatedly checking her odometer for how many more miles, then calculating how many more hours that meant, only made the trip more tedious, the monotony of the road broken only when she stopped to top off the gas. She spent the night at a truck stop in Beaver Creek, thankful the border was less than an hour away and although it was late in the day when she got back on the road, she had confidence she'd get to Fairbanks by dinnertime.

When she crossed the border, Gulliver's situation stifled any eagerness for celebration. She drove on disappointed that the moment went sadly unsung.

Four hours later she drove into Delta Junction with the tedious day on the road wearing on her. More hours of driving in the waning daylight suddenly felt overwhelming. When she came to a large parking lot with trucks and campers lined up as though they would stay the night, it looked like a promising place to stop. At the far end of the lot, an *Open* sign blinked in a café window. Without further thought, she pulled in a spot between a small sedan and a Winnebago.

Biting cold hit her the minute she opened the truck door. She hurried to unlatch the propane compartment and turn on the gas, then grabbed Gulliver's step stool from behind the seat and helped him down from the truck. When she entered the camper, it felt like a walk-in freezer. Everything had frozen: water, milk, Gulliver's canned dog food, fruit and vegetables in the refrigerator, onions, and the last of her Prince Edward Island potatoes.

She turned on the heater and pressed her hands against the grill for warmth. There was no way she could cook. The café held her only hope for refuge from the bone-chilling cold.

She got Gulliver into Gary's old navy sweater, putting his front legs through the sleeves and using a belt around his middle to keep his improvised coat from dragging on the ground. From the look on the dog's face, he didn't approve, but he practiced his usual tolerance, sitting patiently with his eyes averted. For extra warmth for herself, she put on her long Bill Blass coat over the North Face jacket, wrapped her scarf around the hood and over her face, and then headed across the lot, hoping the café welcomed dogs.

A waitress behind the counter smiled at Jeanne when she walked in the door. "Sit wherever you want," she said.

"Can I bring in the dog?"

"Oh, God, yes. You can't leave him out in this weather." When she brought the menu, she said, "Cold enough for you out there?"

Jeanne nodded. "How cold is it?"

"Twenty-eight below zero last time I checked, and it's going down even more tonight."

Jeanne didn't think she had ever been in temperatures that cold. Not even at their upstate cabin in New York. "But it's only November. If it's this cold now, what are January and February like?"

"Cold. You have to dress for it. It's the only way to survive."

Jeanne ordered hot chocolate and wrapped her hands around the hot cup to warm them. She let the waitress refill her cup and sipped it slowly, making it last until she finally ordered dinner, her usual hamburger and fries. Hours later, when the waitress brought the check, she realized she couldn't stay any longer. She ordered another hamburger in a takeout container for Gulliver, worried about his stomach, but with his canned dog food frozen, she had nothing else.

Outside the cafe, darkness had fallen, and the night sky was sprinkled with diamonds. Jeanne had never seen so many stars. When she looked straight up, the sky appeared to have no ceiling. Stars upon stars glistened deeper and deeper into space. A momentary euphoria tried to take hold, but the bitter cold kept her from savoring the moment.

A dim yellow glow inside the compact sedan parked next to her truck led her through the dark lot back to the camper. Left to whirr away while she and Gulliver warmed up in the café, the heater had taken off the chill, yet with all its effort, it didn't prevent a thin layer of ice from coating the interior walls.

In the middle of the night, Jeanne woke to the humming of the heater laboring to warm the camper, clicking off when the thermostat reached the required temperature, only to click back on in minutes when the camper lost its warmth. She had let down the canvas window covers, hoping the added barrier might help keep in the heat, but now she thought it might be better to lower the top.

She got out of bed and spread her sleeping bag and quilt on the lower bunk next to the dog, then cranked the camper roof closed. Through the long night, she often woke, thankful that her heater kept them both warm, but fretting every time the heater clicked on that she might run out of propane.

The smell of fresh, perked coffee welcomed her into the café for breakfast. Fellow travelers were thawing out from a long, chilly night. It was easy to pick out the truckers, sitting together in animated conversation. She recognized the family from the Winnebago; the kids with hunched shoulders, still looked cold. She wondered what they were doing camping in the middle of the school year. The young couple from the compact sedan looked as though they hadn't slept.

With the second order of scrambled eggs and bacon in a doggie bag for Gulliver, Jeanne paid the check and got back on the road, heading for Fairbanks just as the morning dark gave way to daylight. Had she planned for breathtaking vistas of the Alaska wilderness, this morning's drive would have disappointed her. Fog shrouded the landscape, limiting her view to the immediate surroundings. She felt as though she was driving through an opaque wall of mist. Unnerved by her inability to see the road, she turned off the highway in Fairbanks at the first sign she saw glowing through the fog. In neon orange it blinked *Ranch Motel*.

Jeanne got the name of a local vet from the motel manager when she registered. She called immediately on the manager's phone and made an appointment for nine in the morning. Then she asked if she could use the phone to call Toksook. She wanted to see if Barbara still expected her to come. "Sure, call wherever you want. I'll just add it to your bill."

Barbara couldn't wait for Jeanne to get there. "It's so good to hear from you. I didn't get your card, but I talked to Ginger. She told me you were on the way. I'm glad you didn't give up." With summer long gone, Jeanne would have understood if Barbara had changed her mind about the visit, but she was glad she still expected her. Had she come this far and not gone to Toksook Bay, she'd rue the decision all the way back to New York. How would she ever explain it?

Jeanne learned from Barbara that Wien Air was the best way to get to Toksook. A few things that Jeanne hadn't considered surfaced when she called to book her reservation. She needed a dog crate, and Gulliver needed a parvovirus vaccine shot. Also, if she flew from Anchorage, she would pay less for the ticket and because there were more flights she'd probably get there sooner.

Fog still blanketed the town when Jeanne headed to the vet in the morning. If anything, the fog had thickened, encasing everything in rime. Jeanne couldn't open the frozen truck door. The motel lady came to her rescue using a hairdryer on a long extension cord to defrost the door latch.

The vet looked Gulliver over as Jeanne explained his history in Whitehorse and showed him the note from Dr. Kilpatrick.

"Given his history, he looks good to me. Maybe a little dehydrated. His stitches are nice and clean."

Jeanne asked for a parvovirus shot explaining Wien Air required it for the dog to fly. "I'm going to Toksook, and they won't take him without it."

As the vet got ready to give the shot, he seemed reluctant. "Are you sure you want to take him to Toksook?"

"I thought about skipping the trip, but they're expecting me, and I've come a long way."

"Well, I was thinking about the dog. Why don't you board him at a kennel? It won't cost much more than a plane ticket. The flight to Toksook is long. He's an old dog. Right? It might be hard on him. But, if you're determined to take him, at least wait until he has his sutures removed."

Jeanne left the vet's office, worried now about taking Gulliver on the plane. She'd have to let Barbara know she'd be delayed a few more days.

By noon she was back on the highway with the roads still shrouded in fog and Anchorage 300 miles or more, at least six hours away. The road out of town went up a steep hill, then leveled off on a plateau and came out of the fog. Once on the straightaway, snow began to appear intermittently on the windshield. She wasn't concerned until the flurries turned into heavy snowflakes, and the road began to go up and down hills and wind around curves.

She drove on roadbeds raised about 4 feet from the surrounding terrain, to about 20 feet where it crossed gullies, to what easily might be hundreds of feet where it hung on rocky mountain walls and snaked down off high ridges. There didn't appear to be guardrails unless they were under the snow, which rendered them useless. Her truck might easily slide right over them.

Jeanne sat hunched forward, straining to see the road, trying to avoid the oncoming traffic hogging the middle of the highway. Big trucks pulling double trailers wore banners across their front grills announcing WIDE LOAD. Jeanne read the sign to mean move over, but she didn't dare move over because she couldn't tell where the road ended. More troubling, she was always fighting the 18-wheelers for the same space when they were winding around a high ledge or rolling across a skinny passage traversing a deep ravine.

Wind gusts, generated by the oncoming trucks as they passed, hit her with a whump and set her pickup wobbling. The blizzard of snow they brought with them reduced visibility to zero, and, although she couldn't see, and had no assurance the road continued straight ahead, she hesitated to use the brake, thinking she might end up sliding out of control.

All she could do was take her foot off the gas, hold tight to the wheel, hold her breath, and try to stay in line, wide load or not, until the big truck passed and the swirling snow settled enough so that the road was visible again. Then she braced herself for the next 18-wheeler to come along, seemingly just when she reached the next curve.

In the dark, fighting sleep, Jeanne finally pulled into Anchorage, and found an RV Park surrounded by stores in the middle of town off a busy main street. She swallowed her disappointment. She could always move to a place with trees after a good night's sleep.

Chapter 35

In the morning, Gulliver threw up his breakfast. At first, Jeanne thought he had bloat again, but he wasn't yelping in pain, and his stomach didn't appear swollen. From the RV park manager she learned the Arctic Animal Hospital was directly across Northern Lights Boulevard, on the other side of the Sears Mall. It was not yet daylight, but the city was awake and busy with morning noise and traffic, so Jeanne drove over to the clinic, hoping it was open. Dr. Sept saw her right away. "You said he had bloat in Whitehorse? When was that?"

"Six days ago. Dr. Kilpatrick gave me his number if you want to call him. He told me to take him to the vet when I got to Fairbanks, which I did, but that vet said Gulliver was fine. He gave him a parvovirus vaccine shot, which he needs to go to Toksook with me, although he said he didn't think I should take him to Toksook. That was yesterday. Now he's throwing up his breakfast."

"When are you going to Toksook?"

"I wasn't planning to go until after his stitches are out. Just a quick visit because I hope to get back to New York for Christmas.

"New York. I thought I detected an accent there." He looked at her with friendly eyes as he sat on a chair beside Gulliver and rubbed his ears, much to the dog's delight. Jeanne thought the young vet looked like he was just out of vet school, but he also seemed experienced and confident. ""Well, he doesn't have bloat, but I see he's a little dehydrated. He could benefit from an IV. I'd like to keep him overnight and give him a good examination to find out what's bothering his stomach." He gave Jeanne an encouraging smile.

When Jeanne returned in the morning, Dr. Sept walked into the waiting room with Gulliver, softly talking to the dog. "Here she is, boy." Jeanne looked into her dog's eyes for signs he was back to his old self. She didn't find any. His extra glint of friskiness wasn't there.

"I'm sorry to tell you this, but your old dog vomited again last night and now he has a temperature. We should x-ray his stomach and see what's going on in there. We'll need your approval to operate if necessary." The vet looked less reassuring than he had yesterday.

"Whatever you think, Doctor. I'll do anything to get him better."

"If I remember correctly, you said you'd be visiting Toksook Bay. Are you planning to be there long?"

"I was planning a week at the most so I can get back to New York for Christmas. Only now, with Gulliver sick, that's all on hold. I don't see how we can go."

"You know, I really don't recommend flying your dog to Toksook. It's way out there, a long trip. You could leave the dog with us and go by yourself?"

"You mean just leave him here while I'm gone?"

"Well, I was thinking of what's best for the dog. If we find something that requires us to operate, we'll want to watch him. And I don't see you managing with him in a camper until he is much improved. This is really the best place for him."

"I can't just go off and leave him."

"But this way, you can get the trip over with and be ready to care for him when it's time to discharge him. In any case, whatever you decide, you shouldn't be thinking of taking him to Toksook."

"Maybe I should just give up the whole idea."

"Well, that's up to you, but you don't have to do that. Just leave him with us."

Jeanne couldn't imagine leaving him behind.

"Tell you what. Think it over and let me know later. Can you call around three? I should have a report for you by then." Dr. Sept was leading him from the waiting room, when Gulliver stopped abruptly at the door to look back at Jeanne. He had questions in his eyes. Dr. Sept encouraged him, speaking his version of puppy talk. "It's okay, Boy. She'll be back."

Jeanne drove back to the parking lot, put up the camper top and pulled her sleeping bag around her. Gulliver's sad eyes preyed on her mind. He trusted her, but there was no way to explain to him. Her small camper cabin felt empty without him.

With hours to wait and nothing to do before she could call, she propped herself up on pillows and wrote a letter to Anna.

You wouldn't believe where I am. Definitely not what anyone envisions of camping in Alaska. I'm parked in a lot in Anchorage in the middle of which is an ugly box of a building with showers and restrooms. Across the street directly from my camper door is Alma's deli where a sign on the window for an ordinary corn beef sandwich says $3.55. A laundromat, cleaners, and a beauty parlor are on one side of the lot and past those stores is a donut shop on the main road. It's called Northern Lights Boulevard. I guess the street name is the most Alaskan thing around here. Across Northern Lights, is the Sears Mall. Through the Mall and out the other side across from Sears is the Arctic Animal Hospital where Gulliver is a patient right now. I'm so worried about him.

A long report on Gulliver followed, from his emergency in Whitehorse, his ride up the highway, and the frigid night in Delta Junction with her walls coated in ice. When she read it over, it only depressed her. She tried writing about the stars but couldn't find the words to make it as spellbinding as she remembered it.

Around 3:00 pm she called the vet on the payphone that hung attached to the outside wall of the motel strip along the RV lot.

"We removed some foreign matter from his stomach, so we made the right call. He'll need a little time to recover, but he should do better now."

She couldn't imagine how he got something in his stomach.

"He'll be okay, then?"

"He's a real trooper for an old dog. Lots of resilience."

"Can I come by and see him?"

"You could, but we have him sedated. He won't know you're here. Did you decide about Toksook? We'll want to keep him for a while, so you don't have to worry about him. He'll be comfortable here and get good care."

Jeanne overcame her reluctance. Dr. Sept's plan made perfect sense. She told him she would make it a quick trip and left the Toksook number in case he had to call.

She headed for the airport early the next morning still worried about leaving Gulliver, even with Dr. Sept's assurances, but she wanted to get the trip finished and not have to think about it anymore.

On her way, she stopped at the supermarket. She had called Barbara to tell her she'd be there the next day, and when she asked Barbara if she could bring anything, Barbara asked for fresh fruit. "Apples, preferably Golden Delicious, oranges, tangerines, grapefruit, pears—big ones. Oh, and avocados."

By the time Barbara finished with her long list, Jeanne guessed it was a good fifteen or twenty pounds of fruit. "Sounds like twenty pounds," Jeanne said, thinking she was making a joke, but Barbara saw nothing strange in that.

"Yeah, that's about right. Just pack it in one of those apple boxes they have."

The need to park at the airport in long-term parking meant a long hike to the check-in carrying all her paraphernalia: her camera case on one shoulder, her pocketbook with the strap over her head and across her chest, her suitcase with the shoulder strap on the other shoulder, and the heavy box of fruit in her free hands. After repeated stops to put the heavy box down, shifting her burdens, getting straps back on her shoulders, and picking the box back up, Jeanne made it to the ticket counter with minutes to spare.

The agent hurried to get her signed in on the flight. "Okay, you're cleared to Toksook. You'll change flights in Bethel. We'll transfer your bags automatically there." She handed Jeanne her ticket. "You can go straight to the plane and board."

At Bethel, Jeanne sat in the airport terminal, waiting for her connecting flight to Toksook Bay, surrounded by people she assumed were fellow passengers. Most wore exquisite fur-trimmed parkas. After what felt like hours, she heard, "Can we have the passenger for Toksook Bay?" *Passenger, like one passenger? Is it only me? Where was ev-*

eryone else going?

Two men stood by the exit in what looked like the coveralls a mechanic would wear. They walked her out to the tarmac where workers were loading a prop plane with packages and boxes, one of which was Jeanne's apple box with the fruit. "That's my box. Are we going in that?" To Jeanne, the plane looked awfully small. The mechanic types shared an expression between them. One of them said, "That's a Twin Otter," in a way to suggest Jeanne should be impressed.

Packages and bags of mail filled the passenger compartment, leaving only enough room around one empty seat for Jeanne. She was settling in her place and buckling her seat belt, when the two men she thought were mechanics climbed into the pilot and co-pilot seats. "You're the pilots?" she asked with the same incredulity as her earlier question about the plane. Once again they shared the same knowing expression.

As soon as they were airborne, the pilot said, "We have a low ceiling today." Jeanne assumed he expected her to conclude something from that, so she just shook her head as though she understood. They were flying through clouds, which Jeanne thought nothing of until she noticed the extra alertness of the pilot and copilot as they peered out their respective side windows. Now and then, the engines revved loudly.

The copilot must have noticed her discomfort because he made a point of telling her they were climbing. More revving, followed by the pilots sharing wide-eyed looks did not inspire confidence. When the copilot yelled, "Take her up! Take her up!" and the plane gave loud voice to a groaning climb, she noted the exit and tried to remember where the pilot said the life jacket was, as if that would matter. He turned to her with an attempt to smile. "We're going to fly around up here for a while until we find a hole."

A hole? Were they lost? *Hail Mary full of grace.*

Eventually, when they found their way out of the clouds, the plane glided along barely above the snow-covered ground for what felt like forever. They landed on a snow-covered strip with no signs of civilization anywhere other than a lone figure standing alongside a small plywood shack. In a hurry to get off the plane, Jeanne got out of her seat.

"Where are you going?" the pilot asked.

His question confused Jeanne. "Shouldn't I get off?"

"Not if you're going to Toksook. We still have three more stops."

Wien Air had never mentioned that the second half of the trip was on the mail plane with the day's deliveries, at least not in a way that she understood.

A full rosary of Hail Marys later, they descended on a snowy landing strip, and as they taxied to a stop, they rolled past a sign that said *Yield to Aircraft*. Who was that for, she wondered. The airstrip looked abandoned.

In minutes, snowmobiles arrived, driving up to the plane along the runway and Jeanne saw the reason for the Yield sign. The riders picked up their mail and packages and left, leaving Jeanne standing with her luggage and her fruit, wondering where Barbara and Paul were until the tall Native man who had been talking to the pilot asked her if someone was meeting her.

"I'm here to visit the Hodgkins. Something must have delayed them. They know I'm coming."

"Paul, ah yes. He told me you might arrive on this flight." He extended his hand to Jeanne as he introduced himself. "I'm Larry, the agent here for Wien. I told Paul I'd give you a lift." He put her bags and the fruit in the toboggan he was pulling, straddled the machine, and told her to get on behind him.

"On the snowmobile?

"Snowmachine. It's called a snowmachine. And yes. Unless you'd rather walk?"

Jeanne got on behind him.

"Hold on," he said.

Hold on to what, Jeanne wondered.

Barbara was at the door when they arrived. She had changed in the year since Jeanne last saw her at Ginger's barbecue. In place of her soft curls, she wore her hair pulled back in a tight ponytail. There was something Jeanne couldn't define. She looked tired.

They greeted each other with big hugs. Paul collected the box of fruit and Jeanne and Barbara followed him into the kitchen, where the enticing aroma of something delicious roasting in the oven filled the room. Barbara opened the fruit box with an audible sigh of delight, took an avocado in each hand and held them out to admire them.

"Oh, thank you, Jeanne, thank you."

Chapter 36

Jeanne woke to the full moon shining in her window and thought it the middle of the night, until noises somewhere in the house and light seeping under the door got her out of bed. She found Barbara in the kitchen preparing grapefruit, delicately cutting around each segment. Barbara stopped to give Jeanne a hug. "Thank you so much for bringing the fruit," she said. "I haven't had a grapefruit in months."

Over breakfast, Jeanne shared Gulliver's problems and why she had left him behind in Anchorage. She talked about meandering around the Maritimes, and her stop at Peggy's college, trying to explain her delay in arriving while avoiding any mention of the current complications with Gary. Barbara was sharing her plans for Thanksgiving dinner, going over all the guests that would join them, until Paul mentioned it was time to get going and invited Jeanne to join them. "We can show you around the school."

"Thanks, Paul, but I thought I'd take my camera and walk around the village."

"Okay. If you need us, you can call on the CB."

Jeanne walked along the main roadway heading for the bay, the feeling of triumph about actually being in Toksook subdued by the absence of Gulliver walking beside her. She passed small homes, low to the ground, lining both sides of the wide snow-covered road. A smattering of newer-looking houses stood out among the rudimentary structures that looked hardly sturdy enough to hold together in a strong wind. Snowmachines sat parked by the front doors in place of the family car.

A carpenter worked on a project in the open air despite the cold; the steady pounding of his hammer echoed in the quiet village.

At the end of the road, Jeanne looked out on a mostly frozen bay. The frigid temperature had quelled her urge to put her feet in the sea, but she intended to gaze upon it, knowing at least she was there, satisfied it met the long-forgotten plan: ocean to ocean, an odyssey complete.

From the bluff where she stood, a smooth icy ramp sloped to the shore where a skiff idled in the water. Two men leaned into it and struggled to lift out something heavy. They placed their cargo on a tarp, then leaned over the side again, repeating the same maneuver.

Jeanne was wondering what required so much effort, when the boat suddenly revved its motor and headed out to sea. At a distance, it slowed and turned, aimed directly at the shore. The outboard motor revved loudly again and the boat made a headlong dash toward land, its bow riding high on the water. Jeanne stood transfixed, certain it would crash.

Just before it reached the shore, the driver whipped the prop out of the water, and the boat slid up the icy ramp on its keel, momentum carrying it to the top of the bluff where it came to rest nicely ensconced, among other skiffs. The other two men followed the boat up the ramp, pulling the heavy tarp behind them. Jeanne saw the seals when the men lifted them into a sled hooked to the back of a snowmachine. They waved to her as they drove off with two riding on the seat while the other stood on the back of the sled.

A clutch of children with a bunch of dogs among them fell in behind her as she headed back up the road. When she turned and said hello, they looked at each other and giggled. Little girls wore parkas in colorful pastel prints that reminded her of old-time prairie dresses. Fur peeked out from under the flouncy bottoms. Care had gone into decorating the outfits with trim along the seams. The boys' parkas lacked the flouncy bottom but had the same sort of embroidered edging over the seams and around the wrists. Fur ruffs trimming the parka hoods of both boys and girls framed the smiling rosy-cheeked faces. Among the children, Jeanne thought the few in plain, store-bought parkas looked somehow deprived.

Still hammering at his task as she walked by, the carpenter waved for her to come his way. "You look like the Pied Piper," he said pointing to the children.

"I guess they're curious."

He shook his head. "Uh-uh, I think they're amused. It's that coat. You look like you're walking around in your sleeping bag. Mind if I ask where you got that?"

Jeanne looked at her Bill Blass coat meant to make her look like a Russian princess. She had to admit it looked long and boxy. "I see what you mean, but it's very stylish back East. I got it in Toronto."

"Toronto. What do they know? Around here, it's too long. It will drag in the snow, and that hood is useless. What good does it do? If you want to keep your head warm, the hood should be snug. At least have a ruff."

Jeanne remembered the hunter in Smooth Rock Falls. She had wondered what he meant when he said, "Get yourself a decent coat."

"I'm Charley by the way. I take it you just arrived."

"Hi. I'm Jeanne. I came to visit Paul and Barbara."

"Oh, right. Barbara said you were coming. She seemed really pleased." He offered to take her for a snowmachine ride. "Give you a tour of the local color."

"I just had some of that down by the bay watching some men land their boat. They rode it right out of the water and up the hill. Amazing. They had seals."

"Yeah, seals are good meat. They've been getting in some good hunting while the bay is open."

"It's amazing to think of them out in that small open boat with no protection."

"Believe me, the clothing they have keeps them plenty warm."

Jeanne was back at the house, when a noisy gang of dogs drew her to the window. Barbara had arrived on a dogsled with Aiden, one of the teachers at the school. Aiden and his wife, Lindsey, had come from Seattle, and with little to do in the tiny village, Aiden had developed a love for dog mushing.

Jeanne was delighted when Aiden offered to take her for a ride. The team of eight husky-type dogs, lined up two by two, pulled on their ganglines as they howled objections to standing still. Aiden helped her get settled in the sled then hopped on the back. When he lifted the hook anchored in the snow, the barking dogs took off in a rush, throwing Jeanne against the back of the sled.

They rode out on the tundra for miles across rolling snow-covered land, under an off-white sky with no building or signpost anywhere in the landscape nor a tree or a bush. In the snow-quieted world, she heard only the steady panting of the dogs and the glide of the sled runners on the snow, and now and then the sound of Aiden's heavy breathing when he ran behind the sled to climb a hill.

They stopped on a high knoll to take in the view. The weak sun, low in the west, bathed the landscape in the subdued light of a sub-arctic afternoon. She imagined the austere beauty of a moonscape, windswept and barren. "I love this spot," Aiden said. "The sea, the sky, the earth—look how they all blend together. I always feel I'm on the edge of the world, at the dawn of time."

He reminded her of Joey, the way pleasure lit up his face. Of all the thoughts she may have had, she returned to the one that troubled her often: the pleasure Joey would never have; the life not lived; the world not seen. Once again she felt she could reach out and touch him and fought the nagging voice in her head arguing it wasn't true.

That evening a steady din of snowmachines prompted Paul to explain that a plane must be due to arrive. They were clearing away the dinner dishes when Charley appeared at the front door to ask Jeanne if she'd like a ride.

The airport was lit in an eerie glow from snowmachines parked side by side along the landing strip, lighting the runway for the plane's arrival. The gathering had a festive air as villagers visited with each other while they listened for the plane. "Looks like everyone in town is here," said Jeanne, "like they're expecting someone important."

"Oh, definitely important. Everyone came for their Thanksgiving turkey." Watching their anticipation, Jeanne thought of Jeff. If she met herself in Toksook, would she know who she was? Surely her coat would be different. But would growing up in such a place make her someone she didn't recognize? Tempered by trying to survive on the edge of the world, fighting the ocean for its bounty in an open skiff in freezing weather, or even relying on a plane to bring Thanksgiving from the outside world, would she have a different heart?

The following day, Barbara walked Jeanne over to Lizzie and Nelson's house, two of the village's many Yup'ik artisans, then left her to visit while she went to the school. "If you want souvenirs," she had told Jeanne, "their work is the best."

In their small two-room home, Nelson sat on the floor by the front window to make use of the light, his worktable a two-foot section of log standing on end. Years of ivory carving had chewed the surface. Pieces of walrus tusk sat on a shelf nearby. Nelson stopped his work to show Jeanne the walrus he was carving, pointing out details that pleased him. Jeanne bought a carved seal figurine as a memento of the seal hunters she had seen by the bay.

In the backroom, Lizzie sat twisting blades of tundra grass into a long yarn-like strand, then put the strand in her mouth and bit along the length of it with her teeth. She reminded Jeanne of her grandmother when she sewed, moistening the thread's tip in her mouth to get it in the needle. A collection of grass baskets stood on a shelf, but Jeanne was more intrigued by the dance fans made with a white fringe of reindeer hair. Tundra grass, woven with bits of red yarn, provided a handle for dancers to hold.

Lizzie had little to say until they sat together drinking tea when her storytelling took over the conversation. With a broad smile lighting up her face, she told the story of how she and Nelson were among the first families that had come from Nightmute to Toksook Bay to help start a new village. She spoke of their struggles in a soft lilting voice, now and then looking at Nelson, who smiled and nodded in agreement. Jeanne could have easily spent hours listening to her talk.

A voice on Lizzie's CB interrupted their conversation. "We had a call for Jeanne from a Dr. Sept in Anchorage."

Jeanne ran to the school to use the phone in Barbara's office.

"Thanks for calling back," said Dr. Sept. "I wanted to let you know your old dog bloated again last night."

She closed her eyes and sighed. "Is he okay?"

"He's fine, now. What we do in these situations is attach the stomach to the abdomen wall. The good news is he came through the procedure nicely. We'll keep him comfortable until you get back. You said after Thanksgiving, right?"

"I can come back right away."

"No need. He's on an IV and I will want to monitor his condition for a few days more. Besides, I think he likes the attention he's getting."

Barbara saw the worry in Jeanne's face when she hung up the phone. "What happened?" she said.

"Barbara, I need to get back to Anchorage. Gulliver got sick again. Is there a flight today?"

Without saying another word, Barbara called the agent for Wien. Larry told her there was a plane scheduled, but it was late. She would be the only passenger. He'd pick her up on his way to the landing strip.

It was late when Jeanne got to Bethel. She spent the night trying to sleep on a bench waiting for the first morning flight to Anchorage. She arrived back in town in a dreary ice fog and drove straight to the Arctic Animal hospital. It was Thanksgiving, but someone who was caring for the animals answered the door. She brought her to the back to see Gulliver. Jeanne looked at her sleeping dog wanting to hold him and pet him, but she worried she'd disturb him. "He looks so fragile. I should probably let him sleep."

Chapter 37

Jeanne climbed into her camper bed exhausted from a sleepless night in the Bethel Airport. When she woke later in the morning, she headed for the donut shop on Northern Lights for coffee. The short walk was a more inviting prospect than brewing a cup in her ice-coated cave. And it saved using the propane she needed for heat. On her way, she noticed a vacancy sign in the window of one of the motel rooms that lined the south end of the camping lot and it occurred to her it might be good to rent a room for Gulliver.

While she waited at the counter, two women came in that Jeanne recognized from the camper lot. They wore matching army surplus, the same big white boots and green parkas with fur ruffs. Jeanne guessed they were mother and daughter.

The older woman said, "Hi, I think we're neighbors. Aren't you the lady in the truck camper?" Jeanne said she was.

"We came in to get warm." Carol was her name, from California she said. She introduced her daughter, Honey, and invited Jeanne to join them at the table squeezed into the corner. Honey had a teenager's sleepy expression, unhappy to be out of bed. "So what brings you to Alaska?" Carol asked.

"I came to visit relatives in Toksook, but my dog got sick, and I had to come back."

"Oh, that's a shame. I hope it's not serious."

"He's having stomach problems. But he's getting good care."

"That must have you worried."

Jeanne nodded and then turned the conversation to her new neighbors.

"So what brings you here?"

"We're here for jobs. Money is good working in Prudhoe Bay."

"That's not why I'm here." Honey finally had something to say. "I want to go to college and tuition is cheap. And don't let my mother fool you. She's here for a husband. She thinks prospects for that are good if she gets a job in the oil industry." Mother and daughter gave each other looks, an unspoken argument between them.

"There's Jimmy," Carol said, waving at him to come join them. Jeanne recognized him from the camper across from hers. He looked past his prime, getting round in the middle, puffy in the face. Jimmy waved back, heading to the door.

Carol told Jeanne everything she knew about Jimmy. He was a teacher from Minnesota, working as a substitute for the Anchorage school district. "Alaska pays better than Minnesota, I gather. He's recently divorced, so I'm steering clear." She had started a story about the young hippy couple living in the van at the end of the lot—"smoking pot to keep warm,"—when Honey interrupted. "Ma, I have to get to work."

After they left, Jeanne went to the payphone to call the animal hospital hoping it wasn't too early. "He's looking much better," the receptionist said. "Hold on. I'll get Dr. Sept." The vet told Jeanne as long as there are no surprises, she could probably pick the dog up the next day.

For the first time in days, Jeanne felt she could stop worrying. When she returned to the RV Park, she noticed the vacancy sign still in the window and went straight to the office to rent the room. It had a bed and a shower, two chairs and a table, and a counter where she could set up a hot plate. And it had heat.

She sat on the bed, thinking the warm room would be cozier for Gulliver and easier on him since he wouldn't have to use the camper steps, but she had to admit it wasn't only for Gulliver. She hated walking in the cold dark across the camper park to the bleak shower room, having to dress in the drafty shower house, then walk through the cold dark back to her camper with her hair still wet. She told herself it was just until Gulliver got better, two weeks at the most. Then she would head down the highway. If all she did was drive and sleep, she still could make it home for Christmas.

Jeanne was at the animal hospital when they opened in the morning. Gulliver didn't have the energy to jump up with a greeting.

He pushed his nose against her, letting out little yelps of excitement, but his tail wagged limply. "You know your old dog has great dignity," said the vet. Then he leaned over and held up the dog's face, looking into his eyes. "You're a fine old gentleman, aren't you, Boy?"

Dr. Sept walked out to the truck with Jeanne to help her lift the dog into the front seat. "I know he looks skinny, but don't give him too much food at once or too much water, only a cup at a time."

The motel room was warm enough for Jeanne to take off her coat. She gently lifted Gulliver up on the bed and sat beside him, petting him gently. His face had deep recesses around his facial bones. She felt his ribs protruding beneath his thin coat. A rounded knobby ridge of vertebrae ran down his back. He looked at Jeanne with tired eyes, lifting his paw to place on her arm and attempting to wag his tail.

Through the week, Gulliver slowly gained strength. When Jeanne took Gulliver to the clinic for a check up, the vet said the dog was recuperating better than he had expected. "Still, I need to tell you, Jeanne, at fourteen, he's old for a collie-shepherd. We can give him time with good care, but not a lot. There's no guarantee his problem won't return."

"When can I take him home to New York?"

"You know, I wouldn't be in a hurry. I should see him in a week. I'll know better then how he is doing.

Jeanne was checking out at the reception desk when Dr. Sept came back. "You know, I should tell you now is not the best time to drive down the Alcan. I hate to think of you getting stuck in a snowbank or something. Can you wait until March or even better, April?"

In the back of Jeanne's mind, she had considered the prospect of snow and thought she could handle it. That they were now five days into December concerned her more. Even if she ignored the road conditions and left in two weeks, she'd have to drive all day every day to make it home for Christmas. She didn't know what toll it would take on the dog. Realistically if she couldn't be there for Christmas, she might as well wait until the roads were better for driving.

And if she stayed around until March or April, she'd need to get a job. If she made enough to cover the room rent, she wouldn't have to bother Gary. That was over. She hated bothering Gary for money. She had to find a way to take care of herself.

In the morning, her fellow vagabonds were in their usual spot in the donut shop. She told them she would be staying for a while to let Gulliver recover and was looking for a job. Jimmy said she should come with him to the school district. "They're desperate for substitute teachers."

Jeanne thanked him but explained, "I need to work at night so Gulliver can sleep while I'm out."

Honey said they were looking for waitresses at Simons, where she worked. Then Ellie, the hippy girl, came out of her fog. "I bet you can get a job at my place." Ellie worked at a 24-hour daycare center. Jeanne asked her if there was part-time.

"Are you kidding? You're an actual teacher. They'll be so happy to get you. I'll bet you can arrange any hours you want."

That night she wrote letters to her mother and the girls explaining why she wouldn't be back for Christmas, telling the girls to go to Florida and spend Christmas with their Dad. She told them about Gulliver's ordeal with multiple problems, how old and fragile he was but also how he had lots of spirit—to give them hope. She wrote an exciting description of her visit to Toksook to leave the impression she was having a wonderful time.

The next day Jeanne drove to the daycare center and got hired on the spot. She would work four hours, every day, from six to ten pm. She could give Gulliver time to get healthy again and wait for better roads.

About two weeks later Jeanne joined the breakfast club meeting in the corner of the donut shop. Jimmy was playing the role of a designated social host as though they all were on a cruise. He had found out about a Christmas Dance at the 35 Plus Singles Club that night at the Carpenters Union Hall and had signed up the motley crew of parking lot inhabitants for the party. "What about you, Jeanne? We need one more to fill a table?"

"Oh, not me, I'm working late, and, anyway, I have nothing to wear to a Christmas Dance."

"You don't have to worry about what you wear. We're not going to some New York yacht club."

"Jimmy, I can't. I have a sick dog. I have to hurry home to take care of him. It could be midnight before I joined you. Exhausted, I might add. Not in a party mood, I can tell you."

"What time do you get off work?" Jimmy wanted to know.

"Ten."

"Just come from work before you go home. Have one drink, just one. I'll wait at the door for you." He got up to leave.

"Jimmy, I can't."

"I'll be waiting at the door." He waved and left.

"Guess you'll have to come," said Carol. "C'mon, one drink won't hurt anything."

After everyone left, Jeanne sat alone with another cup of coffee, watching the car lights faintly glow outside the window. Dawn wouldn't come until midmorning and then with only a whisper of the sun, the weak light fading to dusk by mid-afternoon. She missed its warmth upon her face.

Part Five

Not knowing when the dawn would come,
I opened all the doors...

Emily Dickinson

Chapter 38

Well past her planned 10 pm departure, Jeanne tucked in the last restless toddler finally lullabied to sleep and said goodnight to the young college students in the night crew. She left the daycare center with her mind set on getting home to Gulliver, until the image of Jimmy standing at the dancehall door complicated her intentions. Now she regretted she hadn't convinced him not to do that.

Jimmy was right where he said he would be, and because she was late, he had to have been standing there for some time. He caught Jeanne's eye as she pulled into the parking lot and put a hurry-up in his wave. Her mistake was to park the truck and head his way up the front steps. Had she stopped the truck in front of the stairs and let him come to her, it would have been easier to get away.

Now he held her by the elbow as he ushered her through the doorway while she tried to explain that she only came to tell him she wasn't coming.

"You're here now. It won't hurt to have one drink." He helped her out of her coat and handed it to the coat checker while she protested that she still was wearing blue jeans and hadn't fixed her hair. She probably needed lipstick.

"You look great to me." He smiled, happy with his success. "Listen, you can't hibernate in that room you rented for your dog and spend your days taking care of babies if you hope to get through the winter. You have to spend more time with people. Have a little fun."

She sighed, watching Jimmy beam, his eyebrows lifted, his head nodding. "Okay, one drink, and I'm gone. I mean it, Jimmy."

It took a moment for Jeanne's eyes to adjust from the bright lights in the lobby to the dim lights of the Carpenter's Hall. A first glance brought strong memories of her high school gym—same worn wood flooring, same curtained stage—except the dancers were older, many turning gray. The cigarette smoke and the potent smell of stale beer compounded the dissonance.

In an attempt to make the room more festive, someone had hung tinsel from red and green streamers. A lonely Christmas tree stood in a corner as though hauled in as an afterthought. Round tables lined both sides of the room, with space left empty in the middle of the floor for dancing. Her fellow travelers from the camper lot occupied the table closest to the lobby.

Worn out from tending to unhappy children and eager to get home to her dog, Jeanne wasn't up to the noisy chatter and raucous laughter that filled the room, nor did she want to sit through loud music. Picking up the beer Jimmy had plopped in front of her, she considered how soon she might politely leave.

On the overcrowded dance floor, couples brushed elbows and jostled for space. The jazzy beat of the music had many attempting versions of their old high school lindy, gamely trying to twirl around with their arms pulled in tight. Dancers bumped off one another passing apologies back and forth.

Whenever a gap opened in the crowd, Jeanne got a quick glimpse of the band on stage, or an empty table, until the gap closed as though someone drew the drapes on a window. She was sipping her beer when the curtain of dancers opened again to reveal diagonally across the crowded dance floor a single person sitting at the table closest to the stage. She sat up straight with the sudden thought he was staring directly her way, but before she could confirm that, the curtain of dancers closed. When they parted once again, he was still looking her way.

In the dim light she wasn't sure, but she had the distinct impression that when he caught her looking at him, he smiled. It was too late for her to pretend to have her eyes on something else. Immediately she pictured a sad image of her frazzled hair, her sloppy sweater, her work-a-day blue jeans. Her instinct was to search for an escape, but she couldn't just grab her coat and run. Jimmy had left it with the coat checker. Could she hide in the ladies' room?

When the music ended, she watched him get out of his chair and pause for a moment, as he leaned over to talk to someone. Then he turned her way and walked across the room in long, purposeful strides. She leaned across the table. "Jimmy, I need my coat ticket," but it was too late.

"Is this chair taken?" came the deep, cultured voice.

A warm smile crinkled around his hazel-blue eyes. He loomed over her, tall, brushing back his hair, a lighter strawberry blond than the coppery red in his wiry beard. A strong presence came from his self-assured demeanor. For the moment, she lost her voice.

Jimmy came to the rescue. "Sit, sit, the more the merrier." He reached over to shake hands. I'm Jimmy."

"Ben," he said, returning the handshake. As Jimmy introduced each person at the table, he nodded politely. In his blue button-down shirt and gray button cardigan, Ben didn't blend well with her parking lot comrades. Black-framed glasses gave him an air of the proverbial professor, but Jeanne sensed something else, as though the professor persona was merely a disguise.

"So, are you and Jim together?"

"No, no. We're just neighbors," she said as the band began to play. He invited her to dance.

She mumbled something about having to leave, but the rising clatter of chairs emptying of occupants mixed with the music drowned out her voice. He hadn't heard what she said. She let him take her hand to escort her properly to the dance floor. The warmth and strength of his touch quickened her pulse. She felt the same sensation when he placed his hand on her back. She noticed the deft way he moved her as they danced, his steps executed with skill, speaking of instruction somewhere in his life. They tried small talk, but it was difficult for him to hear her. Her voice had quieted with uncustomary shyness.

When he escorted her back to the table, he proposed they find a quiet corner somewhere. "So we won't have to shout," he said, the engaging expression still filling his eyes, his smile.

While he helped her into her coat and led her out the door, she asked herself, *what are you doing, Jeanne?* She knew she should go home, but he had her completely captivated.

He led her to a bar across the street, and she watched the pleased-with-himself expression disappear as he read the *Closed* sign posted to the door. He looked down the street uncertain about what to do. The momentary hesitation brought Jeanne out of her daze.

"You know, I have to get home. My dog is alone. I didn't get off work until after ten. I only meant to stay a few minutes. I shouldn't even have come." She was talking too much and too fast. He looked down the street again before politely offering to walk her back to her truck.

"So you're here from New York?" He pointed to the license plates.

"Just visiting."

"In the middle of winter?" with a big grin.

"It's a long story."

As he opened the truck door for her, he asked, "May I call you tomorrow? That's a story I'd like to hear."

"I'm sorry, I don't have a phone."

"Wait." He rummaged through his pockets for a piece of paper and a pen. "Here's the number where I'm staying. May I ask you to call me? I'd love to hear your long story." His eyes were searching trying to read something hopeful in her face.

Jeanne watched his back as he walked away, still caught in his long last look, and for a moment, she wished the bar had been open.

She put the truck in gear and drove out of the parking lot, turning the wrong way into a one-way street, then quickly making a right-hand turn when she saw the arrow, only to discover she was going the wrong way on another one-way street. The police siren behind her brought her to the curb. *Pull yourself together; you're acting like a schoolgirl.* In the rearview mirror, she watched the officer coming her way and wondered how to explain.

"License and registration, please, and yes, I understand you're from out of town, so let me advise you up front that's not an excuse." He left her sitting in the truck and returned to his patrol car. When he came back, he said, "Okay, I'm giving you a warning. I don't know what they do in New York, but in Anchorage, you need to follow the signs, okay?"

Gulliver was waiting at the door to go out when she finally got back to the motel. She walked him along the road, gratified by the extra zip in his step as he trotted along before her. At the end of the RV lot, the hippy camper glowed with Christmas lights, and the faint sound of Christmas music came from their van. "Think I'll go shopping tomorrow, Gulliver, and get a tree. And some lights would be nice. What do you think?" He perked up at the sound of his name and gave her his customary quizzical look.

Chapter 39

In the morning, Jeanne hoped to quickly grab her coffee and donut and go back to the motel room, maybe even back to bed, but everyone from the RV lot was waiting for her. While she stood at the counter, she found herself surrounded, grins on all their faces.

"You should see yourselves," she said to them.

"Well?" questioned Carol, and when Jeanne just smiled, she asked, "Are you going to tell us what happened?"

"Nothing happened. The bar was closed, and I told him I had to get home."

"That's it?" It was as though she had suffered a personal affront. "Are you kidding me? A goddamn Viking, and you let him get away. You don't even have to say a word, and he comes strutting across the room and sits down, and that's it. I can't believe this. Did you get a good look at him? Did you see anyone else like him?" Carol suddenly remembered Jimmy. "Oh, and you too, Jimmy." Jimmy closed his eyes and nodded his head, understanding the comment for what it was.

"Well, did he suggest another time?"

"He asked for my number, but I told him I didn't have a phone."

"Oh God, I can't stand it. Why didn't you give him the motel number? Or get his."

"I did, get his number that is, but it was his idea."

"Smart. I knew it." They had retired to their customary corner where they all sat around the table like a mute chorus echoing Carol with nodding heads. For the moment the news of the phone number placated Carol. She sat back and relaxed. In a less agitated tone, she asked, "So when are you going to call him?"

"Carol, I'm not sure that's a good idea. I'm leaving as soon as I can leave. I don't want any complications. Besides, I'm married. Remember? I only took the number to be polite."

"Married? Didn't you say you broke up? You can't use that excuse. I bet he's waiting by the phone. You won't let him sit there, I hope."

Carol's remark made Jeanne realize her new situation. Until that point, she hadn't fully recognized her soon-to-be-single status or the freedom it gave her to see whoever she wished. And Carol was right. She had said she would call. If she didn't plan to get together, he at least deserved an explanation. Unable to escape that long last look, she had him on her mind throughout the day. When she got to work that evening, she went straight to the office and asked to use the phone.

Listening to it ringing, she had second thoughts. She was resisting the urge to hang up when she heard Ben's voice. Her pulse quickened once more and when she spoke, she was conscious of sounding out of breath. When he said, "Why don't I pick you up for dinner?" she was sorry to say she couldn't because she was working late.

"Tomorrow then, are you working tomorrow?"

"Sorry, I work every night."

"After you get off then. I don't mind eating late." Mesmerized by his voice, she couldn't say no.

They went to Clinks, or as the official greeter at the door said, "Clinkerdaggers, Bickerstaff and Pete's Public House." It was as though they had walked into a stage setting for the *Christmas Carol*. Decorated in Christmas greenery, the restaurant was right out of 19th century England with lights resembling candles in sconces on the walls and in the chandeliers. The waiters wore knickerbockers and white socks up to their knees and old-England shirts with puffy sleeves.

Ben ordered a martini, "Gin, dry, and a strawberry daiquiri for my friend."

"Could you make that scotch and water," Jeanne said to the waiter. And then to Ben, "I'm not big on strawberry daiquiris."

"Sorry. Not very polite of me. I should have asked you what you wanted. I'm not big on strawberry daiquiris either." In explanation, he added, "It's their signature drink. Why everyone comes here, or so I'm told."

After a few sips of her whiskey, Jeanne overcame her unusual shyness and found her voice. Although they had barely spoken before, they talked as though they had always known each other. There was something to that. They had a similar East Coast upbringing, similar private schools, she with Dominicans, and he with the Benedictines.

The conversation got to what each of them did for a living and they shared a laugh over she not knowing what a big game guide was and he not knowing what a Montessori teacher was.

And then he said he thought she must be older than he. Who says that? On a first date, no less, because this had all the trappings of a first date. In a way, she found it refreshing, this complete absence of guile.

He must have seen her expression because he laughed and followed with, "Oh, you could easily fool anyone. Besides, you mentioned your children in college. I didn't think you had them at fifteen." A pause, then teasingly, "Did you?"

She smiled with Joey on her mind. She was 19 when he was born.

After a quiet pause, Ben said, "I'm thirty-six, by the way."

"Then you're pretty astute. I just turned forty-two."

As the conversation continued, she referred to Gary in a natural response to a comment, and Ben's entire demeanor changed. "You're married? I didn't know."

"Only technically, I haven't officially dissolved it yet. I need to get back to New York for that." She couldn't read his expression. Was he conflicted with personal mores? Did he want to know the details, but wouldn't pry? She was glad when he changed the subject.

"So tell me that story. What are you doing in Alaska in the middle of winter?"

She made quick work of it. "I came to visit friends in Toksook Bay. Because of one thing or another, it took a while to get here. Then my dog got sick, and now I'm stuck, waiting for him to recuperate."

"That's got to be tough. I imagine you wanted to be home with your family for Christmas."

"Yes, I miss them. It might not be so hard if it weren't so bleak all the time. I hardly ever see the sun. I'd be gone in a minute if my dog was fit to travel."

"Oh, hold on for a while, you'll get plenty of sun. We started gaining daylight a few days ago, you know, Solstice. If you stick around until March, you'll have a full twelve hours of it."

"Solstice? I guess I never gave it much thought."

"You would if you lived in Alaska."

"I could sure do with some light."

They were quiet for a while, Ben seeming to be deep in thought until he said, "So let me see if I have this straight. You came a long way to see Alaska, and instead, you're sitting in Anchorage working at a daycare center, and from what I can gather, spending all your free time in a motel room with your dog. Is that about it?"

"Only because my dog is sick."

"Has anyone told you yet that Anchorage isn't Alaska? You have to get out of town for that. Thirty minutes in any direction will do it."

She told him about the hunter in Smooth Rock Falls who told her much the same thing.

"He's right. If you'd like, I can show you the real Alaska. I have a cabin north of Talkeetna."

"That sounds so tempting, but I can't drop everything and drive off on a trip," even as she thought there wasn't anything she'd rather do.

"You can't drive there. No road. You can fly, but in the winter we snowmachine."

The waiter interrupted with the check, but Jeanne ordered more coffee. In the back of her mind, she worried about Gulliver, but she didn't want the evening to end.

"I was wondering," Ben said, "Christmas Eve is tomorrow. Would you like to go to midnight Mass with me?"

"I'd love that, but I can't. I'm working until 10."

"Okay, so I'll pick you up at 11 then."

Chapter 40

The altar glowed in the golden light of candles with sparkling white lights trimming the fir trees along the periphery. Red poinsettias encircled the crèche. Filled with quiet peace, Jeanne remembered Christmas vigils of the past when the busy day was over, and she allowed herself to breathe.

Standing in the side aisle of the packed church, she felt comfort in the unaccustomed presence of Ben behind her. Christmas carols, sung by the choir, brought her back to another Christmas Eve standing in the aisle in another packed church, weary from the last-minute rush of the day. She had managed enough of a glimpse of the altar that night to see the three of them in the Christmas pageant—little Peggy and Katy with their golden halos and gossamer angel wings, and Joey dressed like a shepherd, the only one with a beard.

With all the fuss to get his beard attached just right, they barely made it to the church on time. She remembered how she prayed Mass would end before his beard became unstuck. Now she thought of all the moments wasted fretting over unimportant things. She pictured her children always together and stifled the tears, wishing they were there by her side.

As she stood with Ben, in this unfamiliar church in this unfamiliar place, her past no longer felt real. It was more like something she had seen in a movie or had read in a book. From the moment her children arrived, she was always running to keep up with every new demand, and it seemed as soon as she learned how to handle it all with ease, they left. The busyness of raising a family that once had her caught in a whirlwind had disappeared. How quickly the life she knew ended. No longer a parent or even a wife, she could hardly remember who Jeanne was, let alone have any clue who Jeanne might be now.

Although it was after one in the morning when they walked out of the Church, Ben suggested they try to find a place for coffee or a drink.

"There's probably nothing open but bars," Jeanne said. "We don't want that, do we? Not on Christmas. We could go to my place. I wouldn't have to be worrying about the dog. I have some Baileys. We could drink a Christmas toast. Or, we could have a cup of hot chocolate with marshmallows, with a slice of fruitcake or a Christmas cookie, unless you'd prefer ice cream. I have that too. Do you like chocolate chip mint?"

"Chocolate chip mint. Sounds good. It just so happens I have a bottle of wine in the car for you. I brought it for a Christmas present. Couldn't think of anything else I could get on the spur of the moment."

Gulliver's loud barks greeted them at the door when they arrived, until Jeanne told him to hush, and he wagged a friendly tail. They sat and sipped the wine: Ben, in the only upholstered chair, Gulliver curled up at his feet, and Jeanne across the room in the straight chair by the table.

Ben admired the small tree on the counter. "Looks like you're in the Christmas mood. Fruitcake. Baileys. Chocolate chip mint?"

"I guess I didn't feel right letting Christmas go without some effort. I had to shop for something."

They reminisced about Christmases past. His family opened presents on Christmas Eve. "While we were out caroling around the block, my father stayed home and got the presents out of the hiding places. When we got back to the house, he'd tell us we just missed Santa. I don't know when I realized the whole routine was a ruse."

Jeanne couldn't imagine it. When did the toys get put together, and the last-minute packages get wrapped? "That used to take us the entire night. Sometimes we didn't even get to sleep before the kids were awake and ready for their presents." They laughed at their different perspectives.

When the wine bottle was empty, she suggested the Irish Cream.

"Thanks, but I think I've had enough to drink considering I have to drive." He stood and picked up his coat. "You're such nice Christmas company, I hate to leave, but I should get going. It's almost morning."

He put on his coat and headed for the door. "Wait," she said, "I didn't wish you a proper Merry Christmas." She stood on tiptoe and kissed him on the cheek. "You know, I was tempted to buy mistletoe. I always hang it over the entry, but I didn't think there was any reason. No big family get-together." She stood on tiptoe and kissed him on the cheek again. "Merry Christmas, Ben. Thanks for a lovely evening."

Once again, she felt his long lingering look, remembering the night they met. She felt his firm hand on her back, pulling her close, her quickening pulse. He kissed her gently at first, then full of passion.

"Why don't you stay Ben? I'd like you to stay."

In the morning, Ben told her he was sorry he had to leave. He had arranged to have a load of freight delivered at his drop-off spot at Aspen Creek, and he had to get back to his cabin to take care of it. "I don't suppose you can come with me?"

Had she any misgivings about their night together, they disappeared with his question. She didn't want to let him go. Apparently, he felt the same way. "That sounds so enticing, but I'd have to make arrangements at work first. And what about the dog? You said you're off the road system. How would we get him there?"

"He can ride in the snowmachine sled. Dogs do that all the time."

They planned a specific time for him to call so she could wait by the motel's payphone. When they stood at the open door saying goodbye, she laid her hand on his arm. He put his hand over hers and said, "You'll come soon, right?"

Chapter 41

On New Year's Eve, she drove to Talkeetna for a long weekend at Ben's cabin. In the railroad parking lot in the small village, Ben stood tall amidst a bunch of individuals dressed in rugged winter gear, looking as though they had just emerged from the woods. He must have referred to her because all heads turned her way as though on the same cue.

The crowd parted as Ben emerged from the pack and came toward the truck, red-bearded and tall, without a hat, his hair askew in the frigid breezy air. The buttoned-down professor had morphed to a modern version of a woodsman: black and white checked wool shirt under an unbuttoned fur-trimmed wind parka and boots covered with tall gaiters up to his knees.

His pleased smile lit up his face, the warm delight in his eyes taking her back to the first time she saw him. He stood by while Jeanne got Gulliver ready for his snowmachine trip, dressing him in Gary's old navy sweater and wrapping him with Joey's North Face jacket. Cooperating in his polite way, the dog lay down without objection on the thick foam mat Ben had put in the bed of the sled.

"You can ride on the back," Ben said. "It's easier than squeezing on the seat with me."

Jeanne stood on the platform on the back of the sled and held on to the crossbar set waist high. "Anything I should know?"

"Hold on tight. I don't want to lose you." He was smiling her way, about to get on the machine, when he said, "I don't think those thin gloves you're wearing will be warm enough. You better take mine. You can put them on over yours."

The mittens were made of beaver fur with knitted strings attached that wrapped around her shoulders. "Won't your hands be cold?" she asked.

"I have other gloves in my pack."

Ben drove the snowmachine out of the parking lot and, in

minutes, traveled across a narrow bridge next to the railroad trestle. At least thirty feet below them, an open lead flowed through the ice on the river. Feeling the immediate reaction in her knees, Jeanne steeled herself against her fear of heights until they cleared the bridge and got on a well-traveled snowmachine trail parallel to the railroad bed.

They traveled north, sometimes crossing small bridges over open creeks, sometimes on a narrow ledge between the tracks and the river with little room for anything to go wrong. Jeanne soon had the hang of it, leaning on the curves or flexing her knees when they went over bumps. Sunshine glistened on the snow and the ice in the river. Now and then, they passed a cabin up on a prominent ridge, the windows reflecting the gleam of the sun.

A few miles up the tracks, they came around a bend to the full majesty of Mt. McKinley rising beyond the nearer hills, pink with alpenglow, massive and awe-inspiring in its wilderness setting. Ben stopped and gestured as though he was sharing a personal treasure. "Denali," he said. "Up here we call it Denali."

They had been riding for a while when they came upon a railroad work crew using a backhoe to scoop slabs of ice out of a trench between the tracks and a steep hill. With the bucket full, the operator wheeled the boom around to the other side of the tracks and dumped the ice into the river. Ben slowed to a stop. "Good time for a cigarette break, he said." He waved to a railroad man standing off to the side who waved back as he came their way.

Ben retrieved a thin Prince Albert tobacco can from the breast pocket of his wool shirt, flipped the top up with his thumb and eased out a square slip of paper. He formed the paper into a trough by putting the index finger on the top of the paper then pushing under the edges with the thumb and the middle finger. Carefully tipping the container, he gently tapped cigarette tobacco into the paper trough. When it was full, he flipped the tobacco can closed, tucked it back into the pocket, and with two hands now available, rolled the paper until the tobacco was tight inside of it, licked the edges, and pressed it closed.

Then he held out his cigarette to admire his handy work. He had it lit with a match and was taking a draw all in a matter of seconds.

From the railroad man's expression when he came up to greet them, it was clear he was pleased to see Ben. He was Alaskan Native, but different somehow from the men she met in Toksook. Ben introduced him as Ned, the section foreman. While Ned rolled a cigarette with much the same skill as Ben, they chatted about the new people moving in six miles south. "Do ya think they'll perish?" asked Ned.

"Not likely. If they can't hack it, they'll just leave."

Ned laughed, then waved. "Better get back to my crew."

A chilly wind picked up as Ben continued north, causing Jeanne to worry if Gulliver was warm enough, but when they left the trail along the river and entered the woods, the wind was calmer and it wasn't as cold. Ben revved the machine to climb a slope, then sped up again on another steeper slope, while Jeanne strained to hold the bar. When they reached flat terrain at the top of the ridge, she found it easier to ride. The trail wound through spruce and birch, ending atop a ridge, looking down into a secluded valley. Ben stopped the machine and pointed. She looked down on a log cabin sitting in a flat clearing beside a rushing stream.

Ben guided the snowmachine down the narrow, hillside trail and parked in front of the cabin. He removed the bolts serving as bear locks for the oversized homemade door and stood aside for Jeanne to enter. The one large room was organized according to its use, one corner for the bedroom, one corner for an office of sorts, a wood stove with an oven in the opposite corner, and in the final corner a kitchen counter.

Except for one upholstered chair by the bed, the furniture was handmade. A frame of peeled spruce supported the bed high from the floor. Empty wooden fuel boxes with rope added for drawer pulls sat on a shelf under the bed to use for drawers.

In the office corner, a piece of plywood attached to the wall served as a desk accompanied by a large chair with a birch frame and moose rawhide for the seat and the back. Another chair had a sturdier birch frame with a moose antler positioned to provide a seat. A pillow in the palm of the antler and a caribou hide arranged over the rest of the paddle made the chair a reasonably comfortable place to sit.

In the few feet between the desk and the stove, a handcrafted table on thick spruce legs stood below a window. Birch tree trunk slabs three inches thick on four legs made of spruce limbs provided stools.

On the far side of the room, Ben opened a door to a second smaller room he used for a workshop, with a shelf at the far end just wide enough for a bed. "I put on fresh sheets, just in case you want to sleep there. I don't want to be presumptuous," he said.

She put her arms around him, "You're not," she said, and they shared a warm kiss.

As Ben built a fire, Jeanne read the titles of books on a shelf above the bed. "*Walden Pond* I get, but *The Complete Works of C. S. Lewis*, *The Complete Works of Jane Austen*, *The Complete Works of Shakespeare*. You do a lot of reading, I see."

"They're mostly from when I taught English at the University of Wyoming."

"So you were a professor. I was right."

"Not quite. Technically I was an Instructor. But not anymore."

"How come?"

He told her how he had come to Alaska on a summer break and there was a huge forest fire, 90,000 acres at Swanson River. "I got a job firefighting and made a ton of money, more money in six weeks than all year teaching, so I stayed and built this cabin. The following season, I did commercial fishing and then started guiding. In the winter I'd do some trapping. Then when the oil companies were clearing the right-of-way for the oil pipeline, they needed tree fallers and since I had experience doing that in Quebec when I was on summer break from college, they hired me. I made even more money."

"But what about the university?"

"I quit. Too many papers to correct. It didn't allow me to live my life."

Ben built a fire in the wood stove and when it crackled quietly, he closed the damper and asked Jeanne if she wanted to go with him to fetch water. Keeping to the packed trail, they walked down the hill to the creek where Ben had built a footbridge on logs. "How on earth did you build this out here in the wilderness?"

"With a lot less difficulty than I built the cabin. Only needed two logs for the bridge."

"But how did you get those long logs suspended across the creek?"

"Actually, it was easier than it looks. I built a temporary snow bridge to snowshoe to the other side of the creek. Then I used a come-a-long to pull the logs across the stream. That was the tedious part. Once the logs were in place, it was easy to nail boards down for the decking."

A shelf of ice covered with snow extended from both shores partway out over the creek, leaving a swift current of open water in the middle. Jeanne shivered, thinking of Gulliver at Smooth Rock Falls. Before she could grab his collar, he trotted out on the ice shelf and quickly broke through into the water. Jeanne screamed his name, as Ben yelled at her to stay back. While Jeanne's heart raced, Gulliver got his front paws on the ledge of ice and Ben grabbed him by the collar. He swung him up onto firm ground where Gulliver shook himself off then stood shivering in the cold until they all headed back to the cabin.

Ben carried back two buckets of water and emptied one bucket into a large, insulated water container on the counter to use for drinking and the other into a large kettle on the stove to heat. They sat at the table drinking Ben's home brew, dark and heavy, and, Jeanne suspected, more potent than ordinary beer. Ben had laid an old sleeping bag on the floor for Gulliver, and as they both watched him make himself comfortable, Jeanne told Ben the story of Gulliver's mishap on the logs in Ontario.

"Not very savvy, is he?" said Ben.

"He may not seem smart for the woods, but he's a herding dog, not a woods dog. He has a strong instinct for herding." She told him the story of Joey's guinea pigs, how Joey had let them out of their cage to play on the back lawn, and Gulliver got anxious watching them run loose. He'd run after one he thought was too far from the cage and put his nose in front of the guinea pig until it turned around and ran back. Then he'd go to the next one and the next one, and then have to start over again when they got away from him. "He'd look at us and bark as though to say, 'Do you see this? Are you going to do something?' We had so much fun watching him corral those little creatures."

"Who's Joey?"

The question startled Jeanne. That's how it always happened. Joey's name just slipped out. Now she'd have to tell the story.

"Joey was my son. He died in a car accident two years ago when he was nineteen. I try to avoid mentioning him because people don't know what to say. It gets awkward."

She felt her throat tightening and worried what would follow. She didn't dare try to speak. She didn't think she could say anything else without losing her composure. Turning away, she barely managed, "I think the dog wants to go out. Come on pup."

Ben came behind her and wrapped her in his arms. "I'm sorry, not that it's much help to say. You must carry a lot of hurt."

Jeanne let him hold her, feeling comfort in his arms. They stood for a while watching the chickadees come to the feeder that hung outside the window.

Chapter 42

*F*resh snow came in the night, coating the woodlands in white, like icing on a cake. Ben and Jeanne sat quietly eating breakfast, not speaking, Jeanne still feeling the awkwardness of last night's revelation about Joey, unsure of what to say.

Ben was first to break the silence. He said he was hoping to take Jeanne ice fishing, but with this fresh snow, he'd need to pack a trail first, and with all the other things he needed to do, it was better to wait a day.

Jeanne nodded, not sure what the other things might be. She couldn't tell if he noticed her discomfort. The awkward quiet resumed while Jeanne considered that if she just focused on the moment, everything would be fine. She mentioned the pancakes Ben had made. "These are delicious. I don't think I ever had sourdough pancakes."

"Probably not. I can't imagine any one with sourdough starter where you come from."

After breakfast, Ben used the sourdough starter to get a leaven going to make bread. When they finished washing the dishes, he checked the leaven and was pleased to see his mixture bubbling away. He added some water, then measured in the flour, working it into the leaven with his fingers, folding the dough over, turning it and folding again until he was satisfied it was the right texture. He covered the bowl with a damp kitchen towel to let it rest and went out to get the fresh snow off the roof. He explained he needed to remove the snow so that it wouldn't slide and take the smokestack with it.

He had made a snow rake with an extra long handle that allowed him to drag the snow off from the ground without having to climb up on the roof. When he finished that chore, he returned to the bread, adding a little salt mixed into some water and working the dough some more after which he covered it with the towel again and placed it on a high shelf over the wood stove to let it rise.

"There. Now while that's rising, I'll shovel the bridge and get the trail packed. Don't want the Élan to get stuck going uphill. Would you like to help?"

"Sure, if I can."

"Think you can handle snowshoes?"

"I can try."

Ben helped Jeanne secure the snowshoe straps and gave her a demonstration. "See, nothing to it. Just walk. Now you try it."

She took a few steps. "I feel like I'm dragging something with my feet."

"That's because you are. Don't think about it. Just walk."

To keep Gulliver out of trouble, Jeanne tied him to a tree before snowshoeing down to the bridge behind Ben. Halfway down the hill she stopped in her tracks. The joyous sweet song of a bird held her entranced. Despite the cold, the songbird sang like the first day of Spring. "What was that?" she called to Ben.

"That's a water ouzel. Some people call it a dipper." He pointed upstream to a small plump gray bird with brownish feathers on his head, perching on a rock, bobbing up and down while bowing this way and that.

Presently he jumped into a shallow pool in the creek, dipping his head in the water to feed on creatures only he could see. He walked along dipping here and there, the water getting deeper until he disappeared entirely with only the tip of his tail popping up when he bent his head to feed. In minutes he emerged on the other side of the creek and hopped on a rock to dance some more, bobbing and bowing, before taking off in a whirr of wings, flying just above the surface of the water following the curve of the creek. He settled on a boulder downstream and with the burbling waters rushing around him, he sang out again, an ebullient medley in whistles and trills.

Jeanne's spirit welled within her, the birdsong touching her soul. The unease of the morning forgotten, she watched and listened until the bird whirred off again and disappeared, following the creek around a bend.

"Oh I hope he'll be back," Jeanne said to Ben.

"No question of that."

Ben turned to shoveling the bridge making quick work of removing the top new layer of snow, leaving just enough for a snow-machine base. Satisfied with his work, he walked back and forth stamping his snowshoes, packing firm what was left. Then he continued up the trail with Jeanne following, until they reached the section that went up a steep hill. "I'll go first. When you follow try to step wherever I missed. You'll see my tracks. Make sure you stamp down good and hard."

Jeanne watched for a while then followed up the steep hill, the snowshoes adding to the challenge. She stamped them down hard in places Ben had missed, evening out the trail base. She stood beside him at the top of the hill surveying the work while she caught her breath.

"Nice," said Ben. "Should be perfect tomorrow."

On the way back to the cabin, Jeanne searched the creek for the water ouzel and listened for his song. "You're sure he'll be back?"

"Positive. See the nest." He pointed out the mossy clump tucked in a crevice of the rocky wall along the creek. "This is a perfect spot for water ouzels. Clean mountain stream with lots of tasty morsels to eat."

Following a hardy lunch of macaroni and cheese with sausage cut up in it, Ben dressed to go back out, telling Jeanne he needed to get dinner. She asked what he had in mind.

"I'll see what I find."

While Ben was off on his mission, Jeanne went through the bookshelf for something to read and found a collection of poetry he had written. She had just read the line *My mistress wore a white lace veil this morning* and thought how perfectly it described Aspen Creek when Gulliver distracted her with a low single woof.

Moments later, he did it again, sharper the second time. Jeanne looked out the window, "Do you hear something, Boy?" She didn't see anything to raise concern.

The next time Gulliver barked, he got up and moved to the door, his nose pointing the way out. Jeanne put on her coat and went out with him. The dog sat gazing intently into gently falling snow, his soft barks continuing, not necessarily filled with alarm, just announcing some presence off in the distance.

Looking for some clue to his behavior, Jeanne was able to make out an image coming forward with a steady gait, gently rocking side to side. She thought of a polar bear moving through its snowy domain. The shadowy figure moved deliberately toward the cabin, slowly emerging more fully into view. In a white anorak, he blended with the snow, difficult to see. Ben, Jeanne thought. Who else could it be?

He carried his rifle slung over his shoulder, and in his right hand, he held an axe. Without losing the rhythmic gait on the snowshoes, he'd raise the axe to whack an errant willow or alder branch, relieving it of its burden of snow, allowing him to pass unassailed.

In his left hand, two white birds hung from their feathered feet. As he neared the cabin, he held them high. "Ptarmigan," he said. "Better than chicken." His beard was white with frost, and icicles hung from the ends of his mustache.

He laid the birds on the counter and stoked up the woodstove to get the oven hot. Then he collected the risen dough from its warming spot on the shelf and put it in the oven. He made quick work of preparing the birds, cleaning them, and cutting them into pieces, which he dredged in flour, then fried in bacon fat. He served the meat with fried potatoes, sourdough bread slathered in butter, and a glass of his malty homebrew.

Jeanne expected the ptarmigan to taste like chicken, but the dark, tender meat cooked medium rare reminded her of the venison she once had when her neighbor Tony hunted deer. "This is delicious," she said.

Ben had been watching for her reaction. "Like I said, better than chicken."

They left for the lake at dawn with Gulliver sharing the sled with two pair of snowshoes, the ice auger, fishing poles and bait and Ben's pack which held peanut butter sandwiches, a thermos of hot tea and even some treats for the dog, along with a flashlight, an extra spark plug for the snowmachine and numerous other odds and ends Ben thought he might need.

The snow-covered lake was drenched in sunlight when they arrived. Ben used the snowmachine to pack a large wide circle around the area he chose to fish, then he shoveled a space wide enough to stand on the ice and augur a hole. Four feet down he finally hit water. He baited Jeanne's hook and started to drill a second hole. Jeanne sat on the snowmachine seat and dropped her line and prepared to wait. Immediately she got a sharp tug. She pulled up a fish wriggling on her line and held it up for Ben to see. He merely nodded and went right back to drilling his hole.

Apparently, it was her job to get the fish off the line, but she didn't want to touch it with her gloves, so without even thinking, off they came. She grabbed the fish, worked it off the hook and dropped it to flop around in the snow. Now her hands were freezing, but she couldn't put her gloves back on with her hands all fishy, so she cleaned them off in the snow and shook them in the air to dry. This only made them colder. In a hurry to warm them in her gloves she forgot to bait the hook. As much as she hated to do it, off came the gloves again. She baited the hook, dropped the line in the hole, propped the pole on its holder. Now her hands were messy from the bait. She rewashed them in the snow, shook them in the cold air to dry and frantically worked them into her gloves.

At this point, Ben was yelling about a fish on the line, but Jeanne's hands were screaming with the cold. She wasn't about to take off her gloves. She jumped up and down to try to get warm then took off jogging around the loop Ben had put in with the snow machine, Gulliver trotting behind her. With all the clothes she had on, it took only one lap for the tingling and burning from the cold to stop.

Back at the hole Ben had pulled in the fish Jeanne had left on the line, baited the hook again and now had another fish. He abandoned the business of drilling another hole. This one worked faster than they could handle.

The sun was low in the sky when they stopped getting keepers. Ben called it quits after throwing back a good half dozen that were too small and they headed home to a delicious dinner of fried land-locked salmon and some more homemade bread.

The last day of her visit they sat eating lunch before she would leave to go back to town. Ben would be taking her to the trailhead to flag down the southbound train. They watched out the window as big flakes of snow built up on the roof, the bridge, the snowmachine, and the antlers attached to the shed. Tree limbs bent under the weight. "It's so peaceful and beautiful here," she said.

"You're welcome to stay, you know."

Jeanne didn't need convincing. She felt completely at home at Aspen Creek. "Are you sure? I don't want to impose."

"I wouldn't have asked if I weren't sure."

"I'll need to go to town and square everything away. Let people know where I'll be."

Ben loaded the sled to leave while Jeanne made one last trip to the creek. The water ouzel wasn't there. "Are you sure he'll be back?"

"Most likely he's already been, and we missed him."

Jeanne took the train to Talkeetna and drove the truck back to Anchorage; her one thought was how soon she could get back to Ben. The next day she gave the daycare center her two-week notice. She sent her mother and Anna quick notes that she'd be waiting out the winter with a friend in the Alaska wilderness and gave them Ben's address. When her two weeks had passed, she gave up her motel room, moved all her belongings back into the truck and drove to Talkeetna to take the train.

Chapter 43

On her first morning back, Jeanne woke to the sound of snow machines in the yard. The light was just coming into the sky. "That'll be Ned and his wife, Molly. They like to stop for coffee when they're checking their trapline," Ben said.

Jeanne hopped out of bed and grabbed her clothes, retreating to the back room to get dressed before their visitors walked in the door. They came in covered in snow in matching fur-trimmed parkas, both wearing oversized moose hide mitts that hung from strings around their shoulders. Jeanne guessed they were in their fifties. Their ruddy weathered complexions spoke of a life lived in outdoor pursuits.

Ned introduced Molly who nodded hello and fixed her smile on Jeanne. They had brought Ben's favorite ice cream, chocolate chip mint, along with his mail from the post office. "There's one here for you," Molly said, handing the letter to Jeanne.

It was from her mother.

Dear Jeanne,
Since I'm not sure if you'll get this, I'm not inspired but I do want to let you know that I miss you. People are always asking about you. Some are impressed, some envious but everyone thinks you're terrific. Everyone wants to know when you're coming home. Especially me. But whatever you do, wherever you go, it's ok with me if it's what you want to do. You have always been the joy of my life.
Love Mom

Jeanne squelched the tears and wished her mother were there in the room so she could hold her close. She was putting the letter back in the envelope when Molly asked Ben, "Should I give them to her?" then not waiting for an answer handed Jeanne a package.

She unwrapped a pair of Athabaskan mitts handmade of canvas with tanned moose hide palms, lined with fur that folded over and trimmed the wrist ends. Sewn into a moose hide strip across the back was a band of colorful beaded flowers.

"They're beautiful," said Jeanne, "Did you make them?"

"Ben asked me to. I'm trading them for one of those tanned beaver pelts he has been hanging onto." Everyone was grinning.

Jeanne didn't know what to say. She wanted to hug Ben, but worried it might embarrass him; she waited to show her appreciation until after they left.

Jeanne's days at the cabin were full of excursions, riding behind Ben meandering through the woods visiting other cabin dwellers up and down the river. Sometimes they went ice fishing or hunted ptarmigan or grouse. Sometimes they took the trail along a high ridge to capture the view of Denali in alpenglow. She practiced driving the Élan on the lake. She learned to use the wood stove to bake chocolate chip cookies.

One magical night the Aurora bloomed. They stretched out on the snow in sleeping bags on foam mats, looking up into the night. Green bands of light flashed and zoomed in a single sweep across the sky, or they spiraled or flared into a spray that seemed to shower down like rain.

She made a point of listening regularly for the water ouzel. More often than not, the beautiful song caught her unaware. It never ceased to fill her with elation.

One morning Ben planned a short snowshoe excursion up the hill on the other side of the creek to an open muskeg to show her the spot were he had once encountered a wolf. He and the wolf had surprised each other, and Ben watched transfixed as the wolf just stood for a moment, intently gazing at Ben before quietly trotting away. Although he sometimes heard them howling in the night, he had never seen one so close to the cabin before or since.

It was early March, the days getting longer and brighter, leaving behind the winter dark. On clear days the sky was a deep violet blue. Ben had packed the trail with the snow-machine so that Gulliver could walk atop the hardened snow without the difficulty of punching through the surface. They had only walked across the bridge and up the first short rise on the other side of the creek when Gulliver stopped. Jeanne called to him to come, but he didn't move. His tail didn't wag, and he hung his head. "I don't think he's up to this, Ben."

Ben suggested they get the toboggan and let him ride. They started back to the cabin, Gulliver following, but only for a few feet before he stopped again. Ben went to his side and crouched down, petting him and talking to him softly. "What's up, Boy?" Then he stood up and said to Jeanne, "I'll go get the toboggan and pull him home. I think he's tired from climbing the hill."

They pulled him back to the cabin, and Jeanne made him comfortable on the old sleeping bag they used for his bed. "Something's wrong with him, Ben. I'm worried. If he gets bloat again, I won't be able to help him. I need to get him to town."

They talked about the options and decided to wait for the train in two days rather than take him by snowmachine. Jeanne was unhappy about it, but she didn't think Gulliver could handle the long bumpy sled ride to Talkeetna.

Back in Anchorage, she took Gulliver to Dr. Sept, hoping he would find a simple problem with an easy solution, but the vet didn't see anything he could treat. "He's just old. You could take him back to New York now, but if I were you, I'd still wait a few weeks. The roads should be better in April."

Jeanne moved to a new RV lot. It had a more comfortable shower room but no coffee shop nearby which didn't concern her. She could make her own coffee and wouldn't have to get dressed to go out. She set up the lower bed in the camper for Gulliver who spent most of his time sleeping, his only exercise when she took him for short walks. She didn't want to think of losing him, but she couldn't deny how old he was.

The empty days alone with nothing to do reminded her of how much she left behind at Aspen Creek. The camper wasn't the satisfying refuge it once was. She missed the night full of stars she never knew where there, the air so clean she could smell its freshness, the creek so pure she could taste its delicious sweetness. She could walk for hours so filled with bliss from the world around her that she knew she would never weary of it. And Ben. He brought her joy. How could she go to New York and leave him behind?

But as the days went by, her other life slowly crept back. Getting Gulliver home wasn't her only concern. She worried about all the loose ends she had been trying to ignore. She had to get her divorce. The thought of it was daunting since she had no idea what it would entail. She had to finish her degree and get her certification, so she could get a regular teaching job that paid enough to support herself. She was sorry now she had put it off.

What plagued her most were thoughts about Joey. She realized she hadn't been thinking about him all the time like she used to. His face was fading. She went through his album looking for his smile. A compelling need to get home took hold, a need to visit him at the cemetery and tell him where she had been.

One morning, the RV camp manager knocked on the camper door to say there was a call from Ben. "I told him he could leave a message, but he said he'd hold on because you wouldn't be able to call back. Something about a railroad section foreman."

His voice had the same effect on her even months after his first hello. "I'm here at the tracks. Ned's letting me use the railroad phone. I just wanted to check to see how the dog is and when you're coming back."

"Gulliver's okay, Ben. The doctor says he's just old. He sleeps all the time. I don't see how I can bring him out there like this. He doesn't have the energy."

Ben was quiet for a moment before he said, "I need to see you."

She asked if he could come to town.

"I could, but the snow in the woods is perfect now for getting into the high country. I wanted to bring you up to my trap line cabin. We could spend the night."

"Ben, I would love that, but it's just not possible. I can't bring the dog."

Two days later, there was another call, this time from his friend Donny's phone. Donny lived close enough to the railroad to tie into the phone wires that paralleled the tracks.

"Donny's friend Nancy is here. She said she'd be happy to watch Gulliver for you if you wanted to come up. She has a kennel in Eagle River. What do you think?"

Jeanne was hesitant, but she missed Ben. She couldn't just ride off to New York without saying goodbye. She went to the kennel to meet Nancy and when Gulliver took to her immediately, Jeanne stopped worrying about him. She dropped him off two days later with the food the vet had recommended and his blanket, telling Nancy, "He likes to sleep with it." Gulliver trotted along without reluctance, stopping just for a second to give Jeanne a perfunctory look. It helped her feel better about leaving him behind. Just for a few days, she told herself, my last chance to be with Ben.

She rode the flag-stop train to Aspen Creek, and the next day they set out on snowshoes for a five-mile trek to his tundra cabin. They walked all morning, working their way up ever-steeper hills. By midday, they crested a treeless slope to an unimpeded view in all directions of a wilderness world with no one in it but them. She looked down on the Susitna River winding through the snow-covered valley between the Alaska Range to the west and the Talkeetna Range to the east.

Ben's one-room cabin sat at the bottom of a long incline, in a patch of trees along a small creek. Made of logs, it was just six by eight feet, with a wood stove made from two rectangular five-gallon gas cans with four Bugler tobacco cans for legs. The window shutter, placed on a bracket, made a counter for the Coleman stove. Opposite the wood stove, a bed was built wall to wall. In the evening they walked to a high place out of the trees where they could see an endless sky. The night was full of stars.

Early the next day, they took a different route back to the cabin the long way around so they could stop at Donny's and let him know the trail was packed for him to hunt spring bear. They arrived late in the day, full of delight, expecting him to be pleased to see them. It took only a moment to realize something wasn't right. Donny looked at Ben for a moment as though he wasn't sure what to do. Then he turned to Jeanne. "I don't know how to tell you this, Jeanne. Nancy called. Gulliver…" he hesitated, "Gulliver passed away."

Ben put his arms around her, but she pushed him away, and stumbled back out the door down to the lake, where she leaned against a tree, and slid down to the ground. Ben came and sat beside her on the snow and tried to hold her, but she shrugged him off. "I shouldn't have left him. I knew it. Why did I do that?"

"Jeanne, what could you have done? He was old."

"I should have been with him. I could have held him." She gave up trying to hide her tears. They sat for some time together with Ben trying to comfort her until she said she had to find out what happened.

Jeanne heard the distress in Nancy's voice on the phone. "I had brought him in from the kennel to spend the night in the warm kitchen, and I knew right away when I saw him in the morning. He didn't move when I went into the room. He didn't meet me with a greeting. I called him, but he didn't move."

Much as she didn't want to know, Jeanne had to ask her, "Was it bloat?"

"No, not that. I would have heard him if he were in pain. He was in the dog bed right where I left him. He just went to sleep and didn't wake up."

Jeanne couldn't talk any longer. "I have to hang up now," she said. "I'll call later."

Ben put his arms around her and this time she let him hold her. "I should go to town Ben. I need to take care of my dog."

"That won't be easy right now. There's not enough snowpack along the tracks to snowmachine and there's no train until Sunday."

They were discussing the possibility of flying out in Donny's plane when Nancy called back. "I know this is so hard, but I realized you probably can't get back to town for a while. If you'd like, I can bury Gulliver in the woods out back with my old dog. I'll take care of him. It's the least I can do."

"Thank you, Nancy. Could you do one thing for me? Could you wrap him in his blanket?"

Back at Ben's cabin, despite her efforts to keep her composure, the tears started again. He reached out and took her hands in his. "I hate to see you so sad, Jeanne, how you hurt."

"You don't understand, Ben. He wasn't just any dog. He kept me going. In my darkest days, he was all I had. He gave me a reason to get out of bed in the morning and go on with my day. He'd follow me around the house from room to room, and when I'd sit, he'd sit by my side with his paw on my knee trying to comfort me. And where was I when he needed me? God, I hope he didn't feel I just abandoned him. I should have been there. I can't stand it."

She got up and went out the door. Ben came behind her. "I wish I could help you, Jeanne. What can I do?"

"I need to go home, Ben."

Ben was quiet for a while, his head down thinking, until he said, "What about us, Jeanne? I thought you liked it here. I was hoping you'd stay."

"I can't think about us, Ben. Not now. Not with Gulliver gone. It hurts too much. I need to go home."

She stood wrapped in his arms until he said, "C'mon, Come inside. You're getting cold."

Ben rode the train with her into Talkeetna. When it was time to go, he stood by the truck to say goodbye. All the light had gone from his eyes. "Just tell me you'll be back."

Chapter 44

Jeanne left in mid-April hoping for clear roads, her devastation over Gulliver's death complicated by her anguish over leaving Ben. She wanted to stay, but she couldn't ignore all the unfinished business of her other life that kept hounding her. She had to put it all to rest.

Canada passed in a blur with Jeanne only stopping for gas or pulling into a rest stop when exhaustion took over and she couldn't keep her eyes open. Most of the time, she fought tears, constantly tormented by the empty seat beside her. She missed Gulliver's warm head on her thigh. She'd fall apart when she'd wake in the morning and realize he wasn't there.

Before she left, she had stopped at Nancy's kennel to see Gulliver's grave and thank her for caring for him. Although she still berated herself for leaving him behind, it helped to think of him wrapped in his blanket in the quiet setting on the edge of the woods.

In her sober moments, she reminded herself how old he was and that if she had been there when he died, nothing would have been different, but she always came back to the deep regret that she hadn't been there. How could she have left him? She couldn't let it go. It brought back the gnawing pangs in her stomach, the ache in her throat. It reminded her of the early days of losing Joey only now she wasn't searching desperately for a way to escape the grief. She knew from experience that was a useless endeavor. All she could do was stumble forward and give it time.

When she wasn't thinking of Gulliver, her mind was on Ben, the sadness in his face when she left. She couldn't imagine a more perfect existence than living with him in his beautiful kingdom in the wilderness. She ached for his strong arms around her, his warmth beside her when she woke in the morning in the joy of new love instead of the dread engendered by grief. "Just tell me you'll be back," he said. It helped to hold on to that.

Just short of two weeks after leaving Anchorage, Jeanne pulled into Peggy's college. She hugged her daughter, holding her for a long time until Peggy pushed her back and searched her face. "I'm sorry about Gulliver, Mom. Are you okay? You look awful."

"I'm just tired, Peggy. It was a long trip."

They drove to *Aunt Janet's* for something to eat, with Jeanne catching Peggy stealing concerned glances. "Peggy. Stop looking at me like that. Really, I'm just tired."

"You look like a basket case, Mom. Is this about Gulliver? Look at you. You keep squeezing your arms like you did after Joey. You're not going there again, I hope. I know you were fond of Gulliver, I was too, but he was old. It shouldn't hit you so hard."

"He wasn't just any dog, Peggy. Why shouldn't it hit me hard? I miss him. It hurts. I'm going to need some time, okay. I'm devastated right now."

"What happened to him, Mom?"

Jeanne told Peggy Gulliver's story, starting in Whitehorse, then Anchorage, and how she flew back early from Toksook when he got sick. When she tried to explain how she left him at the kennel, she felt welling tears. "I don't want to talk about it now."

"Sure, Mom."

Early that evening she parked in her old spot at Round Road and crawled into bed and slept until Peggy came the next day in mid-morning to wake her.

"You're still sleeping? You can't do this, Mom. Stop wallowing."

"I'm not wallowing, I'm exhausted. It was a long trip. I just need to sleep."

Jeanne planned to stay at Round Road for the few remaining weeks of the semester to help Peggy move out of her dorm and drive her home. She spent her time sitting in the sun at Dunkirk Beach or hiking the trails at Lake Erie Park. She hoped by the time Peggy finished school her grief over Gulliver would have subsided, at least enough to protect her from concerned questions.

She was in Peggy's apartment one day when she heard someone knocking. She opened the door to a tall figure back-lit by the light in the hall. It was hard to see his face, but there was no denying it was Ben. Before she could say a word, he reached out and wrapped his strong arms around her. Jeanne leaned her head on his chest and sank into his warmth. "God, I missed you," she said.

"I missed you too."

"But how did you ever find me?"

"Easy. You said you'd be stopping to pick up Peggy, so I called the University and got her address." He explained how his parents lived close by in Jamestown, so it was convenient to visit them and borrow their car to drive over to the school. "I was praying you'd still be here."

"Why didn't you tell me you planned to visit your parents? You could have come with me in the truck."

"Because I wasn't planning it. Actually, I came to see you. You can blame Molly for that. She thought I should be certain you had a formal proposal if I wanted to ensure your return. I thought the understanding between us was enough, but Molly had me thinking perhaps not. Better to have all my bases covered. Right? Anyway, I didn't want to ask you on the phone. I want to see your face when you say yes."

They drove to Lake Erie, where they found a secluded beach to be alone. Later, as they lay in each other's arms, he said, "So should I ask you now?"

"Ben. I want nothing more than to be with you. You must know that. But I have all this debris in my way." She explained about the divorce, not knowing what was involved or how long it would take. Then she told him her need to go back to school. "If I'm going to teach, I need my certification. I won't survive very well on a Montessori teacher's salary."

"You don't have to do that. I can support you."

"No Ben. I need to know I can support myself. I need to finish my degree. I've put it off too long."

The day Ben left to go back to Alaska, he stopped on the way to the airport and woke her in the camper. "This isn't the scenario I had in mind. I was hoping you'd come back with me. At least promise you'll come."

"I'll come. I will. I just can't say when." She watched him drive away resisting the urge to run after him, hoping she wasn't making a terrible mistake.

Chapter 45

Jeanne let Peggy drive the truck back to Northport thankful to have someone else at the wheel. Late in the afternoon they turned onto Timberpoint Drive with Peggy honking the horn to alert the neighbors and Jeanne telling her to stop. She had hoped to arrive unannounced. Beneath the tall oaks, the native rhododendrons on the hillside were in flower.

Katy came rushing down the steps with Mary right behind her to greet them. Jeanne stood by the truck holding her mother in a long embrace. Jeanne's sister, Lisa, and her housemates from across the street soon joined them, followed a few minutes later by Anna and Tony, Anna loudly announcing, "I nearly had a heart attack when I saw the camper." In her exuberant way, she called Jeanne the happy wanderer and fell into song. "Val-deree, val-dera, val-deree, val-dera ha, ha, ha, ha, ha, ha."

Mary ushered everyone inside and while Katy made coffee, Jeanne explained how she got stuck in Alaska because Gulliver wasn't well and couldn't travel, which was true enough, but hardly the complete story. Still feeling the dull pain of Gulliver's loss and dreading the coming of tears, she let Peggy answer questions about the dog. Jeanne made her announcement when Peggy was finished. "If you haven't already guessed, I'm not going to Florida. Gary and I are getting a divorce."

She had intended to ward off awkward questions—someone was sure to ask when she was going south—but when she saw Peggy's shocked reaction, she wished she had waited. Katy merely sighed as though she had expected it. She wasn't sure how to read Mary's face. Anna already knew.

When everyone had left, Jeanne walked Katy and Peggy across the street where they planned to spend the summer with Lisa and her friends. The two girls sat squeezed together in the big wingback chair. As difficult as it was for her, Jeanne told them she and Gary had grown apart and could no longer live together. It was best for both of them to get a divorce. And to be sure they understood there was no fixing the problem, she told them about Rose. Katy showed her unhappiness in her glum expression, while Peggy did all the talking. "But Mommy, you don't have to get a divorce. Daddy wants you to come to Florida. He told me. You need to go down there and throw that woman out of his house." Her voice choked with anger.

"If I wanted to, Peggy, I would. That's not what I want. Not anymore."

She suggested they finish their conversation another time. "I'm tired. We all are. It's been a long day. Let's drive over to the ocean tomorrow. We can sit on the beach and talk, discuss everything on your mind."

She left them sitting in the chair and walked back across the street. Alone in the house, Jeanne and Mary sat drinking coffee, quietly talking about the last few months. Mary tried to comfort Jeanne, telling her to think of Gulliver in heaven, happily romping with Joey. Molly had offered a similar sentiment. It would be so much easier if she could bring herself to believe it.

It was near midnight when Mary got up to go to bed, telling Jeanne not to let her sleep late in the morning. She wanted to make blueberry pancakes to welcome Jeanne back. Jeanne was still sitting at the table when Mary returned. "I almost forgot. I have all these letters for you. There's even one from Germany. Who are all these people?"

Jeanne sorted through the envelopes. "Nice people I met on my travels. This guy from Germany helped me with Gulliver when he got sick."

Along with Bernd's letter was a Christmas card from Rita and Tim and one from Alice and Sean with an aerial view of his farm. They asked about her trip to Alaska.

Did you make it back home? We haven't had a letter from you in a while. Did you get our last notes? Let us know how you are.

Love, Sean and Alice

A second letter from Sean was more recent.

We are fine here, overflowing with lambs and chicks and baby bunnies. We have 18 cattle in the barn now. Seven of them are little Black Angus calves. Really cute. Rosy had thirteen piglets. You should see how proud she is.

Bernd wrote a long travel log of his adventures on the highway, getting to Vancouver to pick up his mail, becoming overcome with homesickness, and going back to Germany to see his girlfriend. He had been working as an assistant prosecutor to get prepared for his law examination and hated it.

But in three weeks I finish. Then life won't be so difficult. Now my traveling heart starts pumping once again. I am planning my next world trip for '82. I'll go to Alaska for the summer and then spend the winter as a youth hostel manager in Banff National Park. Come and visit me there. I insist. Now tell me what happened after Whitehorse. Is Gulliver still alive, this old? Did you go to Florida? Or back to your family? I'm sure you have much to tell, so write, and please let somebody hear from you soon. You know, if you visit Germany, you are welcome any time.

I give you a big hug.

Your Bernd

P.S. Please excuse my horrible English.

The first thing she'd tell him was that his English was perfect. And she'd let him know about Gulliver and how much she appreciated how kind he was to her dog.

There were two letters from Jeff.

Dear Jeanne, I've been sitting here reading my journal of the trip in Nova Scotia and came across our stay in Playland Park campground where we spent a drizzly day in the back of your truck drinking coffee and then later on moved to the camp shelter for supper. Remembering that day, I had to write, see how you are, how Gulliver is, things like that. See if you kept up with your journal. If I remember right, you first told me about it in that coffee shop in Halifax the day you picked me up for the first time. I liked you from the start, Jeanne. And as we drove on, it rained, and we talked, and I liked you more because you were so easy to talk to, and it was raining harder, and I, a hitchhiker, wasn't getting wet.

In his second letter, he wrote: *I've had plenty of time to read John McPhee, Giving Good Weight and Sigurd Olson, Open Horizons. All this reading has got me longing to be traveling again or up north camping and canoeing. McPhee and Olson are both canoe men. And they stoke the fires more. I'd love to do what they do, support the lifestyle I want by writing about it, but how do I ever solve the question of pursuing writing as something practical. I've been working on a plan I think is workable. I've applied to enter anesthesia school. When I'm certified, Gracie and I will move somewhere in northern Minnesota. The job will be such that we should be able to do a lot of traveling, canoeing, camping, cross-country skiing. Maybe, if I'm lucky, I'll find a way to blend in writing an article or two.*

I would so love to hear from you soon. Take Care, Jeff

On the bottom, he wrote *just in case* and left his phone number.

Jeanne had melancholy feelings for her fellow travelers. It was sad to think she may never see them again. She remembered the moment in Belle Cote talking to the old lobsterman when she realized she couldn't just collect people and bring them home with her. She'd answer their letters, but not tonight. The letters needed thoughtful responses, all their respective desires affirmed, not just a breezy happy to hear from you.

The day at the ocean with the girls was just what they needed. They spread their blanket on the sand and settled with their lunch, Jeanne answering questions about her trip, the people she met, Gulliver, and finally Ben. She assured them that she and Gary broke up long before she met Ben. They didn't argue against the divorce. They seemed already resigned. After a while, the conversation turned to Joey.

Jeanne told them how sorry she was that they never had talked, that she never seemed to figure out what she could do to help them. The girls told her they were always afraid that they would say something that would make her feel worse. For a long time they were always trying to protect her. She cried all the time even though she tried to hide it. They hated to see her cry.

She watched them sharing memories of Joey with each other, the pleasure they took in talking about him. It reminded her of how much they enjoyed remembering him when they spent time at the cabin, and she realized how misguided she had been thinking she had to help them learn to live without him, when she should have been looking for ways to keep him in their lives. She should have helped them find the joy in remembering his few short years instead of fearing his memory could only bring pain. She didn't know if this was the talk she always wanted, but she felt at least they had finally talked. Perhaps it only needed time.

Before leaving, they walked together along the shore, Jeanne thinking of Gulliver, all the times he kept her company at the beach in quiet strolls, watching the waves as the sun set. It broke her heart that he was gone.

They drove home from the ocean, everyone with little to say. Jeanne felt an enormous burden lifted. When she told the girls she would meet with Bill O'Keefe about the divorce, they barely nodded.

Later that afternoon, she drove to the cemetery, stopping for flowers on the way. She hadn't asked the girls to go with her. She'd do that on Sunday. This would be the first time she'd see Joey's headstone, and she thought it would be easier to be alone.

The headstone came into view as she drove up the lane. It seemed tilted, leaning slightly forward as though it was reaching out to her. She ran her fingers over the inscription, the remains of her son a message etched in stone.

The next day she went to see Bill O'Keefe. He didn't seem surprised with her long story. He asked where Gary stood, was he agreeable or not, and when she said she wasn't sure, she hadn't talked to him about it yet, Bill told her to wait. He wanted to file the papers first. If Gary didn't contest it, she wouldn't have to do anything but sign the document. He expected to have it done by October. Maybe November at the latest. After all her agonizing about it, she found it hard to believe it would be that easy.

Chapter 46

Jeanne was home less than a week when her mother came in from the mailbox. "Another letter," she said. "This one's from Alaska." Ben wrote he had had a good trip back. He listed phone numbers where she might reach someone if she wanted to talk to him. He missed her. He hoped she would write. The next day her mother came in from the mailbox with another letter from Ben. Every day that week was the same. He filled his letters with the world around him, things he knew she enjoyed.

I watched a chickadee this morning. It sat clamped on the hanging bacon rind with his feet wide apart as if he were a man of action, but he just sat there looking out in the yard for a long time. I thought he must be a chickadee philosopher or a poet from the way he stared off in space. Then I thought he must be in love. I do a lot of staring off in space myself.

He wrote about the hairy woodpecker at the feeder, the gray jays looking for a handout, the water ouzel singing in the creek. *I can't listen to it now without thinking of you.* He told her of a pair of otters he watched in the river floating side by side, their big feet sticking straight up, their heads tilted towards each other: *They reminded me of lovers sharing the same bed.*

The daily letters continued, each one deepening her longing for his arms around her, the sound of his voice. On days there was no letter, there were two the following day. She knew how difficult it had to be for him, the effort it took for him to send them, how he would need to hike the two miles to the railroad every day, hoping to flag down a rail car going by and give his letter to the trainman to mail for him.

She had been back in Northport for three weeks when Ben surprised her with a phone call. He was in Anchorage getting ready to fly to Kodiak. The June salmon season was about to open, and he was the skiff man for a commercial seiner out of Anacortes, Washington. He wanted to let her know not to worry if she didn't get a letter. He still intended to write every day but could only mail letters when the boat was in port. "Just want you to remember if you don't get a letter, I'm still here, waiting."

His letters from Kodiak were sporadic, sometimes a week's worth at one time. When they weren't about running the skiff or long nights on watch, they were about the sea.

We're fishing off a rugged coastline under a gray sky and from my skiff I can see three waterfalls. Thousands of murres are nesting in the cliffs and you'll be happy to hear there are lots of seagulls. I watched a whale jumping like a slow-motion salmon. I'm sorry you aren't here.

Throughout July she would drive to the ocean and hang out at the beach reading his letters over and over. She'd write him back, but never could match his one-a-day. At the end of the day, she'd walk along the shore watching the sunset, and sometimes she'd find a place to park where she could stay the night and listen to the sea.

Ben wrote he had free time in August between fishing and guiding. Could she come for a visit? She flew up when fishing was over and stayed until guiding began. Their two short weeks together were as though she had never left. Ben argued for her to stay, and she wanted to agree, but she had signed up for classes in September. He said he would come for Christmas. She should come back with him then. She didn't see how she could.

True to his word Bill had her divorce finalized in November. It came with none of the trauma she had expected. Just one more item cleared off her desk.

The settlement gave her everything—the house, the truck and camper, the *Quest*, alimony—because Gary never contested it. When he was served notice, he called and tried to talk her out of it, and when he couldn't change her mind, he sent a long angry letter, ranting about it all being her fault. Then he filed his own papers in Florida, ignoring the fact that the judge ruled New York the proper jurisdiction. When his case was dismissed, he flew up to New York to talk. He was the old Gary, the one full of remorse.

She told him he could keep the boat. She didn't want alimony either. When she finished her degree, she'd be moving to Alaska. She'd take care of herself. She watched him walk away, thinking *twenty-three years gone just like that* until she realized they would never be gone completely. They would always have Joey.

Ben flew down for Christmas and pressed her to come back with him. She gave him all the reasons she couldn't. She now had the house to sell. There were repairs to make. And she had to do something about the mountain of things accumulated over the years. It would take time to manage it all.

Back in school for the spring semester, she threw herself into her studies. She had taken a full credit load to get her degree requirements finished as soon as she could, and it took all her energy. Getting the house ready to sell was put on hold until summer break, but Ben convinced her to come to Alaska instead. She flew up after the fishing season closed and stayed longer this time, Ben putting off hunting until September. Again, he implored her to stay. She tried to put an optimistic note on their parting. She only had two more semesters to go.

Ben's letters continued through the fall, the newsy tone giving way to words of yearning. He missed her. The cabin never felt so empty, the bed so cold.

He came again at Christmas. They stayed in the gatehouse of an estate on the Sound that her sister Catherine had arranged. During long walks on the beach, they avoided the topic of living a continent away from each other until the day before Ben had to leave. "I'm living in limbo, Jeanne. I keep hearing about all the reasons you have to stay in New York. Life isn't infinite, you know. Every day you put your life on hold is like throwing that day away. You'll never get it back."

"I'd marry you today if I could," she said, "but I still have the house to sell. And I don't have all my credits yet. I have to do this, Ben. I have to have it done."

The day after Ben left, Jeanne sat alone in the gatehouse apartment and watched the snowfall cover the ground. Across the lane, children rode their sleds down the hill into the road, heedless of any concern for harm. How carefree they are, she thought, blowing all caution to the wind. If only she had their unfettered faith to seize the day.

Back at her mother's house, Jeanne spent her mornings waiting for the mailman. Each day when she gathered the mail, she became more and more distressed with nothing from Ben. She made excuses. He probably had to go straight to the cabin and couldn't get his letter to Ned or Donny to mail. She hoped he hadn't given up on her.

Seeing the disappointment on her face one day when she came in with no letter from Ben, her mother gave her a sympathetic hug. "I hate to see you like this eating your heart out. It makes no sense. What are you even doing here? Anyone can see you should be in Alaska. You should be making plans to leave."

"I want to, Mom, but before I can sell the house, I have to get it ready, and I still haven't finished my courses."

If it's so important, I'm sure you can finish your courses in Alaska. They have a college up there, I presume."

"It's not that easy, Mom. I can't go until everything is done. I want a clean start. I can't have all these unresolved obligations nagging me."

"All I can say is when the good Lord opens a door, you better go through it. That's your life waiting on the other side. You don't want to miss your moment. You don't want to throw it all away." She took Jeanne's hands in hers. "Believe me Jeanne, that piece of paper called a degree won't make you happy."

The drought of letters continued until she couldn't bring herself to go to the mailbox. She tried to pretend it wasn't important.

She was washing dishes when her mother came into the kitchen waving the letter over her head.

Dear Jeanne,

As I lay in bed after a shower, shave, and dinner of sorts, I thought of writing a poem to you, but I can't seem to put my mind to it. For a long time, I was plainly obsessed with the absence of you. It seems to have let up some. Now I'm not so consumed. But although I feel different, my condition is not much better. I used to kill an entire day doing nothing. Now I can't even kill an hour before bed. Even though I don't like being in town, I'm not pining to be back at my cabin. What would I do there without you? I'm not obsessed, but I'm despondent because life seems to have no meaning, no spirit, no direction. From Psalms probably, "You are the light of my life," and my light isn't here. I am flat like a warmed, open Pepsi; if chickens could feel, I'd feel like a hen laying unfertilized eggs. I'm like a plow set too high to turn the earth, a horse in a charge that's lost his rider, a fixed magnet trying to lift a fixed piece of metal, a flower in the dark, fruit in the cellar of a solitary man who has died, shoes on a wooden leg, a garden in a museum, a pail with a hole in the bottom, and anything made for something not doing what it was meant to do. Once I was whole, now I am half. For the sake of hyperbole, you are my world, the water I drink, the fire I am consumed by, but not burned, the earth I stand on, the air I breathe, and I am on the moon without you.

You are a unique person (I don't say to me because your specialness isn't dependent on me, You're especially special to me) with gifts, beauties, and qualities that I am happy and humbled to know. I miss you. I miss you flinging your hair over your head to dry it. I miss you smiling at me. I miss you asleep beside me and me beside you. It is simply not the same without you here.

I was happy to get the letter you didn't send saying you will be here yesterday and stay until tomorrow comes.

Love, Ben

Halfway through the letter Jeanne crumpled in sobs. She read on unable to stop, doing her best to see through the tears, reading Ben's words over and over, yearning to hold him, have him hold her. What was wrong with her? Ben was her life.

She called Molly to get a message to him. "Tell Ben I'm coming. Give me a week, maybe two, but I'm coming."

Six days later, a letter arrived special delivery. Her message had been received.

Dear Jeanne,
As long as we both shall live:
Remember, "I love you," means commitment, oneness, on the one

hand, a forgetting of self, but also that I, and you, are still separate.

She is an individual with her own wants, needs, privacies, selfness.

Don't criticize her personal likes or dislikes.

Don't always be practical, obstinate, frugal, staid, conservative, negative, glum, pessimistic, cynical.

Be joyous, extravagant, lively, open.

Occasionally if you get frustrated, aggravated, bored, disillusioned remember what you feel deeply about her.

Don't ever forget the limbo life is without her.

She likes music, travel, excitement, dancing. You look out for your own daily delights, so don't neglect hers.

Realize she needs meaningful activity to devote her life to.

Realize she is a woman, whatever that means.

Realize she is the mother of two girls and was a mother of two girls and a boy.

Balance being right with being generous.

Realize she is only a person who can be wrong as well as right who can be confused, uncertain, and fickle who may misunderstand you at times as well as understand you better than you can understand yourself.

Be less concerned with expressing how you feel or your attitudes at least part of the time, and honestly try to understand what you don't.

Leave occasional thoughtful notes for her.

Don't forget to express your appreciation.

Don't forget to express your love.

Don't forget you like praise and take criticism to heart, so remember how she may feel.

Remember, you couldn't or wouldn't move to New York, but she came here, and it was a personal struggle for her to leave everything behind.

It is not impossible to lose her love if you don't do your part.

Be less concerned with expressing how you feel or your attitude at least part of the time and instead try to understand the things about her you can't, like feminineness.

At least once a week, make a special effort to get to her so that she glows.

Ask her if you hurt her or said something that made her angry because sometimes you can be blind.

Do things differently occasionally, for she is lively and has a greater capacity for joy.

For every two back rubs, give her one.

Talk to her.

Remember, you love her.

Remember, she loves you.

All my love, Ben

Everything she loved about him was there in his words. Jeanne would be in Anchorage before any response she could write might get to him. She would tell him when she got there that he had missed nothing. Even the two-for-one back rub business was fine with her.

In the end, the obstacles she had put in her way were easily set aside. She went through the house with Peggy and Katy, putting the few things she wanted in boxes to store with her mother, leaving the girls to decide what to do with the rest. Ginger agreed to work with the realtor to sell the house. Lisa offered to take care of the truck until Jeanne could return to get it in the spring. She switched her classes to correspondence. She packed some things to take with her, among them her last photo with Gulliver walking beside her on the bridge at Aspen Creek, and the picture she had framed of Joey and Gulliver together when Joey was eight and Gulliver a pup.

Then she went to the cemetery for one last visit. She told Joey she was leaving, but she didn't come to say goodbye. *I don't think it matters to you if I don't come here to see you anymore because we both know you're not actually here. I don't know where you are, but I've always felt wherever I was, even miles away from here, you were close. I'm going to Alaska and hope you will come with me. I want you beside me when the water ouzel sings to the morning sun, and on clear nights when the moon throws shadows across the snow and when the aurora dances in the sky and when the sun peaks over the tundra hills to break the day. I'll think of you then and every beautiful moment. You'll always be with me in my heart.*

A week later, Jeanne flew to Alaska. A week after that she married Ben.

Chapter 47

They walked in the sun on a golden carpet with the fruity scent of high bush cranberries filling the woods from the morning frost. September had come to Aspen Creek, the early Fall prompting the birch and alder to shed their autumn leaves. The fireweed along the trail had gone to seed, the silky white fluff of their capsules still holding tight to the stems. The ferns were browning and if the bears hadn't found them yet, the blueberries were ready to pick.

The day before, Ben walked with the scythe to cut the brush. In rhythmic sweeps, he cleared one side of the trail from the cabin to the tracks and the other side on his return. Now Jeanne moved with ease in the widened pathway, no longer concerned about tripping in the tangle of tall grass and ferns or stalks of cow parsnip and false hellebore.

Along the way there were places to rest. Ben had set off on the trail one morning to provide places for her to sit. He worried she might get tired walking the two miles to catch the train. He carried his handsaw and some boards with hammer and nails in his pack. In a small spruce grove beside the trail, he anchored wooden planks between two trees. Further on, he nailed boards to the top of a fallen birch to make a seat and made another bench near the tracks with a wood slab resting on two logs.

It was his way to do things to make life easier for her. He had seen her carrying water from the creek one day struggling up the trail with a heavy pail, water slopping out because she had filled it too full. The next day he climbed the hill behind the cabin and used old boards to dam a spring that seeped from the ground. He plugged a hose through the board into the small pool, and the water flowed through the hose to the small brook right outside the cabin's back door. She'd have fresh spring water in just a few steps.

They left early for the train that day, so she wouldn't have to rush. He carried her pack tied to his own to lighten her burden as she made her way up the steep hill out of their valley. Dr. Calder wanted her in town sooner, but she had felt confident delaying until now. She still had two weeks to go, time enough to gather the things she would need.

In town, they settled into the guest room at the hostel, happy to find it available, so they wouldn't need to stay with friends. Tonight Jeanne wanted to be alone with Ben.

Something woke her at two in the morning. She first wondered if it could be a contraction, but it was only a flutter, unlike the sudden cramp she remembered. Flu-like aches and an unusual chill gave her more concern. The soreness in her throat that she had first noticed when she went to bed seemed worse.

When she woke again, her throat hurt more, and now she shivered despite her quilt. In the morning, on waking, she knew at once she was sick. Or was there a problem with the baby? Ben woke with a start when she called his name. "Is it time?"

"No, at least I don't think so, but I think I have a fever, and Dr. Calder won't be in today. It's probably only a virus, but I'm worried. I think I should go to the hospital clinic to check it out."

The admitting nurse showed more interest in her condition than her fever. She insisted on putting the baby monitor on her, and when later she came to check, she said to Jeanne, "Did you know you're in labor?"

"Oh, it's nothing. It's only starting. I'm more concerned with why I'm sick. I'm worried about the baby."

"No need to worry about the baby. He has a good strong heartbeat. You probably just picked up a virus. We'll do some labs as soon as the doctor sends over an order. He said to give you Tylenol in the meantime."

"If I only need Tylenol, I can take that at home."

"Oh, no, my dear, you need to stay. Dr. Calder wants us to admit you."

Convinced real contractions were a long way off, Jeanne was

sorry now she had come. She could be comfortable at the hostel instead of spending a long day in the maternity ward. She looked at Ben sitting restlessly in the chair, watching her with high interest. "This is going to be awhile," Jeanne said. "Why don't you go get some breakfast? And take your time. There's no hurry."

It wasn't long after Ben went out the door that her contractions began in earnest.

She must have fallen asleep at some point because now she didn't recognize her surroundings. Garish lights in the ceiling flooded the room with a glare. She heard Dr. Calder's voice coming from somewhere in the room and wondered how long he had been there. He seemed to be arguing with the nurse.

"I told you to wait on that," he said.

"But she's dealing with chills and fever. It has her worn out. I thought it would help to relieve some stress."

Jeanne assumed their conversation was about the medication the nurse gave her. She had told Jeanne it would help the baby. Jeanne wanted to explain that to the doctor, but she spoke only to herself as though she were outside the room looking in the window, and no one knew she was there. It frustrated her not to get their attention. She must have dozed off because she woke to the doctor and nurse in a new position in front of the bed. She wondered how long she had slept. She thought she had asked them that, but no one responded.

Ben's voice brought her awake again. He stood to her left saying he needed a cigarette. Jeanne heard the stress in his voice.

She saw the nurse and doctor turn to each other as though on cue, eyes wide with concern. What's wrong? She wondered. They were discussing something she couldn't grasp until the nurse asked if she should prepare for a Caesarean?"

"No." Dr. Calder's response relieved Jeanne's momentary alarm until he said, "We don't have time for that." Looking at someone behind her, he gave directions. "Give her oxygen." Then to Jeanne, he said, "Just a little oxygen, Jeanne. It will be good for the baby."

She wanted to ask why, but the nurse was at her side helping her up. "Okay, time to get this baby born."

Out of the hum of voices, Ben's voice was sharp and clear.

"Why is he blue?"

She waited for someone to answer but no one did.

Dr. Calder was now at her side, leaning close. She was unclear how he got there. Wasn't he just in front of the bed? His all-business look of concern was gone, his features softened with a smile, a tired look in his eyes. "You have a healthy baby boy. A big guy like his father, 10 pounds, 5 ounces." Self-satisfaction filled his voice. "Now we gave him a little help with the forceps, but don't let it concern you. He was getting tired, and I didn't want to waste any more time."

The lusty cry of a newborn filled the room. "There, what did I tell you?" Dr. Calder's face opened to a beaming smile. "That's a healthy pair of lungs."

Jeanne tried to rise on her elbows to see where he was. She wanted to hold him. The nurse brought a bundle wrapped in a blue blanket. Jeanne felt as though she had just awoken from a dream. A warm sensation surged through her body when she felt the weight of him in her arms. She gazed at his plump pink cheeks, his rosy lips, his tiny, sculpted fingers. "How perfect he is," she said to Ben.

That night, Jeanne repeatedly woke with a start in momentary panic. She kept recalling Ben's voice, sharp, not demanding, but insistent. "Why is he blue?" In her half-conscious state, Jeanne waited for an answer that never came. Now the question haunted her sleep. She needed to quiet her troubled mind. Then she remembered his rosy cheeks, the weight of him heavy in her arms and felt the warmth in her body again.

When finally she settled in quiet sleep, she didn't wake until the long night ended. Ben stood by her bed, gazing down into the bassinet. In the brief seconds, before he knew she had woken, she saw the wonder in his eyes. When he turned her way, his face filled with his smile.

She looked at the bundle sleeping in the bassinet beside her, wrapped in blue, the tiny cap on his head, his plump pink face in sweet repose. With Ben's help, she lifted him into her arms and relished the full weight of him once more. She touched her fingers to her lips and laid them on his rosy cheek. "Good morning, little William, welcome to the world."

Outside her window, morning had come. The day glowed in the light of the sun.

Epilogue

Lo, when the sun streams through the wood,
Upon a winter's morn,
Where'er his silent beams intrude
The murky night is gone.

Henry David Thoreau

Epilogue

In the early morning dark, the glow of a still-brilliant moon streamed through the cabin window and splashed against the dark logs of the cabin wall. The bright patch of light called Jeanne from her sleep, stirring her in her bed. In her half-awake state, she realized the empty sheets beside her were cold. Ben must have left early to snowshoe his trap line. He would take advantage of the full moon to light his way. She had a dreamlike memory of him pulling the bed quilt up around her shoulders, saying he would be back before dark.

Jack was onto her wakefulness now, in his usual spot beside the bed, his paw pulling at the blankets while his busy tail drummed on the bedside table. She turned to give him a pet. He pushed his muzzle beneath her chin, urging her up with his cold wet nose. "OK, boy, I'm coming." Unfolding her achy joints, she dangled her legs over the side of the bed and lowered her feet into her waiting boots sitting ready to save her from the cold floor. Embers still burning red in the wood stove told her that Ben must have stoked the fire before he left. He would want to keep the cabin warm. She added a piece of dry birch to catch on the smoldering coals and turned the damper down.

At the front door, Jack patiently waited, his nose pointing the way out. Jeanne pulled her anorak over her pajamas and when she opened the door the cold on her face reminded her to get her hat. Outside, the setting moon threw long shadows and lacy patterns across the snow. Moon glow bathed the yard in white light bright enough for her to see her way to the outhouse.

Jack stood by the door on her return, happy to cut short his morning romp. He followed her inside looking for a treat. Jeanne lit the lanterns, made coffee and toast, then curled up next to Jack on the couch with her quilt and her book.

Jeanne could easily read the winter away with so many good books lining the shelves over the bed, sitting in piles on the table next to the chair, on the floor next to the table. They filled more shelves up in the loft. But Jeanne was wary. In the midst of January, winter was always lurking, and Jeanne was on watch, lest winter grab hold. Wise to its ways, she knew how it could fill the cabin with the dark and the cold, lure her into her bed, wrap her in down, and when it had her sufficiently seduced, seep slowly into her soul; how it could render her dormant, like a bear asleep in her den.

So she did what she needed to do to keep the winter dark in its place. She fed the fire with dry spruce and birch. She burned the lanterns to cancel the gloom. She baked. Bread and cookies often filled the cabin with delicious aromas of good things to eat. Whenever it got too quiet, the radio filled the room with music.

Her fears disappeared when Will came home and lit up the cabin with his warmth. He had come on the first day of solstice when the college where he taught closed for the holidays. Jeanne had climbed the hill behind the cabin, not once but twice, hoping for a glimpse of the snow-machine light flickering through the trees, hoping to hear the far-off hum of the engine. She had brought Jack with her because he would hear Will coming before she did, but he had sat quietly beside her unperturbed. When Will had finally arrived, all her frets of moose in the trail, of the open lead in the river, a freight train on the tracks, weak ice on the small streams he would need to cross—all the imagined perils to shorten his life—went away.

They had gone on their snowshoes in search of a spruce tree, Ben leading the way up the hill carrying the saw, Will behind him pulling the old black toboggan, and Jeanne following with Jack tagging along. They hauled the tree home and trimmed it with a garland of popped corn interspersed with some of the raw red cranberries Will had brought with him for their Christmas dinner. They cut folded aluminum foil four layers thick in strips and twisted the strips into icicles. The icicles would turn in the natural current of air and twinkle in the reflected light of the kerosene lanterns. Fresh foil covered the old cardboard star for the top of the tree.

The night before Christmas the aurora bloomed and they rolled foam mats out on the snow and climbed into their sleeping bags in their wool, fleece and down to lie on their backs and peer into the sky. Legends of aurora music had them straining their ears, but in all the years of listening, she had never heard it, even in the silence surrounding them. They saw only the dance, a celebration of the night, green waves bouncing off each other then breaking out to zoom in a joyful sweep across the sky.

When the holiday ended and Will had gone back to his students, winter once again skulked in the corners and rattled at the door. Whenever Jeanne sensed winter creeping in, she left the books behind and went to feast her eyes on the sun. It had been weeks since the sun stopped coming to Jeanne's cabin, stopped rising high enough in the sky to show its face above the southern ridge. Since then, her valley sat in a dim light, a subdued world of neutral shades in a background of white. But when alpenglow warmed the far-off tundra hills and the frosty treetops above the cabin began to glint and sparkle, when she could see hints of blue in the winter white sky, Jeanne knew the sun was there.

Today, she would ski out of the valley and head for the north ridge. She knew of a high bench where she would have a clear view all the way to the river. If she could get there in the short window of daylight before the sun set, she would look to the west and see the sun in all its glory when it came out from behind the hill and hung over the river, getting ready to go down.

Jeanne wore her wide backcountry skis with strap bindings that would accommodate her winter boots. Her feet would be warm. In her daypack, she carried a thermos of hot tea and some trail bars. She had dog biscuits for Jack. She grabbed some hand warmers to put in her mittens.

Yesterday's light snow covered the debris of twigs and spruce cones and birch seeds the wind had gathered in the trail. The fresh cover provided the best conditions for a perfect glide, not too slick and icy, not too deep, and cold enough not to pack up under her heels.

Jeanne fell into the pleasant rhythm of kicking and gliding across the snow, a new spring in her stride. Jack frolicked along before her, pointing out every weasel track and dainty vole trail and a scattering of tracks she thought might be ptarmigan. He poked his nose in all the holes he discovered, then lifted his head to scan the countryside for what his nose would find.

Up ahead, amid a grove of trees just off the trail, Ben had built a bench for summer trail breaks, when the way into the cabin was on foot with all the gear and supplies on his back. It was the perfect spot to take a break and have some tea. Jack sat on the snow in front of her, watching her open her pack, knowing a treat was on the way. Jeanne didn't take long to get back on the trail. She needed to keep moving to stay warm and the sun wasn't going to wait.

Soon she and Jack came to the spot where she needed to veer off toward her lookout spot. Off the trail in deeper snow, her progress slowed somewhat. Jack soon tired of taking the lead and followed behind, her ski tracks providing him a path.

Deep in the woods, Jeanne skied in the stillness that comes with new snow. Nothing stirred. Pressing on, she soon found herself near the edge of the ridge looking down on the valley and knew she was getting close. At the top of the hill, her destination just ahead, she followed a curve around a knoll, and came upon a golden light drenching the snow and gleaming on every frosted twig. Shafts of light streaming through gaps in the trees were full of sparkles, frozen crystals glinting in the sunlight and floating gently down to settle on the snow. A dusting of diamonds.

She looked west, and there it was: the sun's full face shining through the trees. It hung framed in the canyon where the south ridge gave way to the river before rising back up on the other side. She moved a few feet for an unobstructed view, and gazed at the fullness of it, a quiet version of its summer brilliance. Warm shades of pink and yellow painted the sky. With Jack sitting quietly, she drank it all in and let it fill her up with the sweet taste of triumph. Joey stood beside her. He always came for the sunset. She felt if she reached far out she could touch him.

As she watched the sun angle low toward the horizon, she knew it was time to head back. There was no way to know what the woods had in store for her, and there was always the chance she could run out of light. She had found what she had come for; she had conquered one more day of dark. She let Joey go. There will be other sunsets. She'll see him again.

Jeanne took a different route back to the cabin, sticking to the trail following the edge of the ridge above her valley. Nearing home in the gathering twilight, she looked down from the ridge to a welcoming yellow glow shining warm in the cabin windows. Ben had arrived. He'd have the fire crackling, something smelling good on the stove. He'd have good stories to tell of his day in the woods. She would have some stories of her own.

She hurried to get home.

Acknowledgments

Out of the Dark would not have found fruition without the generous supporters who came to its rescue whenever they were needed.

Before there was a book, there was a choir of true believers lighting the candle: my daughters Mary and Margie, my daughter-in-law Sarah Sjostedt, my sisters Virginia Swartz, Catherine Green, Donna Tewksbury, Jody Synan-Williams, Margaret Mary Synan-Russel, longtime friends and just-met acquaintances. All sang the same song encouraging me to tell my story.

Their exhortations kept the story simmering as I wrote it over and over in my mind until long-time friends Pat Tyree and Margie O'Malley Richmond introduced a sense of urgency reminding me that they couldn't read it until it was printed. I came away from our conversation with a determined commitment to stop putting it off.

Sarah Birdsall, author, and extraordinary writing teacher gently guided me past the hurdles that kept me from putting the words on paper. Her encouragement convinced me that not only was my story worthy of telling, I was worthy of the task of telling it.

Genevieve Gagne-Hayes generously read my overly long first draft and shared her literary insights on how to rein it in and strengthen it in terms of its inclusivity to the reader.

For a long time, my finished manuscript sat on my desktop unsure of where to go until Shannon Cartwright prevailed on me not to leave it there and sent me down the road to find a publisher.

Along that challenging path, Lanning Russell enlightened me on the process of finding a publisher and gave me an extra shove offering to help me navigate the challenges.

Sandra Klevin and Michael Burwell rescued my book from oblivion when they gave it a home at Cirque Press. Michael's sharp editorial eye found the holes in my narrative and showed me how to fill them to strengthen the story.

All through the years-long process, my husband Dan and my

son Will, were my two pillars of perseverance, generous with their time, never tiring of reading draft after draft and providing much needed cheerleading. Their critical guidance brought clarity to what I wrote and helped keep my writing true to the story I wanted to tell.

Because I had the good fortune to be blessed with so many generous supporters who picked me up and carried me forward, *Out of the Dark* found its way between two covers and is no longer a story untold. I am forever grateful to them all.

ABOUT THE AUTHOR

Marian Elliott was born in New York City and grew up in Brooklyn, NY and the Long Island suburbs before moving to Alaska when she was 42. When she retired from 35 years of teaching young children, she turned her time and energy to creative writing. Her short story, "In Its Place," won first place for fiction in the Open to the Public category of the creative writing contest sponsored by the University of Alaska, Anchorage and the *Anchorage Daily News*. It was published in the May 2017 issue of *We Alaskans* and the November/December issue of *Event Horizon* literary magazine.

The cover art for *Out of the Dark* is a pastel painting by Marian Elliott's daughter, Mary Salvante, the gallery and exhibitions program director at the Rowan University Art Gallery in New Jersey. Mary is an artist with dozens of paintings related to trees, her predominate theme.

About Cirque Press

Cirque Press grew out of *Cirque*, a literary journal that publishes the works of writers and artists from the North Pacific Rim, a region that reaches north from Oregon to the Yukon Territory, south through Alaska to Hawaii, and west to the Russian Far East. Cirque Press is a partnership of Sandra Kleven, publisher, and Michael Burwell, editor. Ten years ago, we recognized that works of talented writers in the region were going unpublished, and the Press was launched to bring those works to fruition. We publish fiction, nonfiction, and poetry, and we seek to produce art that provides a deeper understanding about the region and its cultures. The writing of our authors is significant, personal, and strong.

Sandra Kleven – Michael Burwell, publishers and editors
www.cirquejournal.com

Books From Cirque Press

Apportioning the Light by Karen Tschannen (2018)

The Lure of Impermanence by Carey Taylor (2018)

Echolocation by Kristin Berger (2018)

Like Painted Kites & Collected Works by Clifton Bates (2019)

Athabaskan Fractal: Poems of the Far North by Karla Linn Merrifield (2019)

Holy Ghost Town by Tim Sherry (2019)

Drunk on Love: Twelve Stories to Savor Responsibly by Kerry Dean Feldman (2019)

Wide Open Eyes: Surfacing from Vietnam by Paul Kirk Haeder (2020)

Silty Water People by Vivian Faith Prescott (2020)

Life Revised by Leah Stenson (2020)

Oasis Earth: Planet in Peril by Rick Steiner (2020)

The Way to Gaamaak Cove by Doug Pope (2020)

Loggers Don't Make Love by Dave Rowan (2020)

The Dream That Is Childhood by Sandra Wassilie (2020)

Seward Soundboard by Sean Ulman (2020)

The Fox Boy by Gretchen Brinck (2021)

Lily Is Leaving: Poems by Leslie Ann Fried (2021)

One Headlight by Matt Caprioli (2021)

November Reconsidered by Marc Janssen (2021)

Callie Comes of Age by Dale Champlin (2021)

Someday I'll Miss This Place Too by Dan Branch (2021)

Out There In The Out There by Jerry McDonnell (2021)

Fish the Dead Water Hard by Eric Heyne (2021)

Salt & Roses by Buffy McKay (2022)

Growing Older In This Place: A Life in Alaska's Rainforest by Margo Wasserman Waring (2022)

Kettle Dance: A Big Sky Murder by Kerry Dean Feldman (2022)

Nothing Got Broke by Larry F. Slonaker (2022)

On the Beach: Poems 2016-2021 by Alan Weltzien (2022)

Sky Changes on the Kuskokwim by Clifton Bates (2022)

Transplanted by Birgit Lennertz Sarrimanolis (2022)

Between Promise and Sadness by Joanne Townsend (2022)

Yosemite Dawning by Shauna Potocky (2022)

The Woman Within by Tami Phelps and Kerry Dean Feldman (2023)

In the Winter of the Orange Snow by Diane S. Carpenter (2023)

Mail Order Nurse by Sue Lium (2023)

All in Due Time by Kate Troll (2023)

Infinite Meditations For Inspiration and Daily Practice by Scott Hanson (2023)

Getting Home from Here by Anne Ward-Masterson (2023)

Crossing the Burnside Bridge & Other Poems by Janice D. Rubin (2023)

A Variable Sense of Things by Ron McFarland (2023)

Tiny's Stories: An Athabascan Family on the Yukon River by Theresa "Tiny" Demientieff Devlin with Sam Demientieff (2024)

If Singing Went On by Gerald Cable (2024)

May the Owl Call Again: A Return to Poet John Meade Haines, 1924 – 2011 by Rachel Epstein (2024)

Out of the Dark: A Memoir by Marian Elliott (2024)

CIRCLES

Illustrated books from Cirque Press

Baby Abe: A Lullaby for Lincoln by Ann Chandonnet (2021)

Miss Tami, Is Today Tomorrow? by Tami Phelps (2021)

Miss Bebe Goes to America by Lynda Humphrey (2022)

More Praise For *Out of the Dark*

Elliott's memoir is one of grief and recovery. The relationship between the author and her dog as they make their way across Canada is subtly developed until it becomes powerful and keenly felt. Elliott's healing is evident to the reader as she meets new people and begins to engage with the life happening all around her. It is through this lens that the reader sees the healing power of the natural world. This book will be appreciated by anyone interested in travel memoirs or books about characters overcoming profound emotional pain.

 —Mark Heisey, *US Review of Books*

In the end, *Out of the Dark* is a story of trust, self-knowledge, and healing. The journey with Jeanne/Elliott satisfies not only as a road trip marked by the kindnesses of strangers; readers will delight in the company of a woman traveler who grows into the self she's in fact happy to recognize.

 —Nancy Lord, *Anchorage Daily News*

Marian Elliot writes so movingly and piercingly about grief and loss. Her unforgettable writing reminds me of the best nomads of the open highway from the 1970s. Her work evokes the spirit of classic road novels and memoirs from that era, such as *A Walk Across America* by Peter Jenkins and *Zen and the Art of Motorcycle Maintenance* by Robert Pirsig. She is a welcome new voice in fiction and non-fiction. I'll read anything she writes.

 —Independent Book Publishers Association

Elliott's memoir *Out of the Dark* is both absorbingly rich and quiet, trembling with feeling but unafraid of looking at and into life and death in all their power and beauty and heartbreak and harrowing effect. Read it with your soul.

> —Guy Kettlehack author of 25 books and volumes of poetry including award-winning works *Alter Ego* and *Weather OK Report*

Marian Elliott's third person memoir, *Out of the Dark*, touchingly, and deftly, addresses the query: How did we get to this place and time in our lives? For the heroine, Jeanne, the road is sometimes pitted with obstacles but more often blessed with kindness; marred by delays yet propelled by good fortune, tormented by loss but buoyed by love. Encompassing the entire narrative, from east to west to north, is the persuasive power of nature to restore and humble. Elliott's story is a beautifully written journey from sorrow to new beginnings.

> —Eric Wade, author of *Squirrelland: Imagination and the Alaska Red Squirrel*

Marian Elliott's book, *Out of the Dark*, is a guide. It is a calm clear voice to accompany a survivor—for anyone who has been close to the stupefying loss of a child. The story is mostly a memoir but also a travelogue. There is wreckage. There is confrontation with meaninglessness. There is no promise of redemption. But finally, life among the living must be navigated in some way. Elliott journeys from New York through Canada and finally to Alaska. It is a narrative about living and a suggestion for the path to acceptance.

> —Lanning Russell, editor of *Event Horizon* and author of the blog *Bumper Sticker Wisdom*

www.ingramcontent.com/pod-product-compliance
Lightning Source LLC
LaVergne TN
LVHW061606070526
838199LV00078B/7198